The postmodern Marx

Terrell Carver

Manchester University Press

The right of Terrell Carver to be identified as the author of this work has been asserted by him in accordance with the Copyright, Designs and Patents Act 1988.

Published by Manchester University Press
Oxford Road, Manchester M13 9NR, UK

British Library Cataloguing-in-Publication Data
A catalogue record for this book is available from the British Library

ISBN 0 7190 4918 0   *hardback*
      0 7190 4919 9   *paperback*

First published 1998

05 04 03 02 01 00 99 98   10 9 8 7 6 5 4 3 2 1

Typeset by Helen Skelton, London
Printed in Great Britain by Biddles Ltd, Guildford and King's Lynn

The postmodern Marx

Contents

For Judy

Acknowledgements

I wish to express my deep appreciation to numerous readers, reviewers and audiences over many years for their generous help in enabling me to get my thoughts and prose together for this book.

I am also grateful for kind permission from copyright holders to draw on my previously published material for certain chapters as follows: chapter one, 'Making capital out of vampyres', *THES*, 15 June 1984, p. 13; review of Jacques Derrida, *Specters of Marx*, trans. Peggy Kamuf (London, Routledge, 1994), in *History of Political Thought*, vol. 28, no. 2 (1997), pp. 345–8. Chapters two and three, 'Putting your money where your mouth is: the social construction of individuality in Marx's *Capital*', *Studies in Political Thought*, vol. 1, no. 1 (1992), pp. 19–41. Chapter four, 'Marx's commodity fetishism', *Inquiry*, vol. 18 (1975), pp. 39–63; 'Marx's two-fold character of labour', *Inquiry*, vol. 23 (1980), pp. 349–56. Chapter five, 'Communism for critical critics: a new look at *The German Ideology*', *History of Political Thought*, vol. 9, no. 1 (1988), pp. 129–36; 'Communism', in *Ideas that Shape Politics*, ed. Michael Foley (Manchester, Manchester University Press, 1994), pp. 24–38. Chapter six, 'Marx, Engels and democracy: 1848/1989', *Political Theory Newsletter*, vol. 4, no. 2 (1992), pp. 130–7; 'Market socialism: peace in our time?', reprinted from *Journal of the History of European Ideas*, vol. 19, nos 1–3, pp. 279–84 © 1994, with permission from Elsevier Science. Chapter seven, 'Translating Marx', *Alternatives*, vol. 22, no. 2 (1997), pp. 191–204 © 1997 by Lynne Rienner Publisher, Inc. Used with permission of the publisher. Chapter nine, 'Marx – and Hegel's *Logic*', *Political Studies*, vol. 24, no. 1 (1976), pp. 57–68. Chapter

Acknowledgements

ten, *Gender is not a Synonym for Women*. Copyright © 1996 by Lynne Rienner Publishers, Inc. Used with the permission of the publisher; 'A political theory of gender: perspectives on the "universal subject"', in *Gender, Politics and the State*, ed. Vicky Randall and Georgina Waylen (London, Routledge, 1998).

Re-assessing Marx

If Marxism is to be reformulated as a protocol of interpretation having practical implications, it will have to come to terms with problems of 'reading' in their modern forms. It will have to recognise texts – including the texts of Marx – as significant historical events worthy of careful study and related to other events in ways we are still attempting to fathom. It is not a sign of elitist prejudice to assert that certain texts have a special status: they are special not because they are the sacred pillars of a canon or the preserves of a mandarin class but because the processes they engage are among the highest and the best in our culture and still have broadly educational value. This value may become most evident and accessible when texts of the canon are reopened through more or less non-canonical, contestatory readings – readings that explicitly explore their own relations to larger historical processes and possibilities.[1]

Readings of political theorists change with changing political contexts. They also change as political theory itself alters its methodology. Marx has an established position in the canon of 'classic' thinkers, and in the body of ideas to which politicians and 'the people' have recourse for policies and ideologies. Marx will always be there, whether as a positive or a negative point of reference. The collapse of the Soviet empire and of the East/West bifurcation of European political and intellectual life have already had profound consequences in the world of ideas and in global politics. Marx is no longer of necessity the theorist of proletarian revolution, inevitably burdened with the ideas and deeds of those who came after. Rather he can now come into his own as the premier critical theorist of commercial society. The 'triumph of capitalism' may be somewhat hollow, because it is grist to his mill. There is a growing consensus that it is time for Marx to enter the canon in a new way.

This book is intended as a contribution to this process of re-assessment. In the course of thematic chapters, I address certain ways in which Marx is changing. These include:

- A shift in what Marx is read. The traditional organisation of Marx-texts, from which the traditional 'Marxist' reading arose, is not the only possible one. New texts have been discovered and published, and the doctrinal and biographical defences for selecting and ordering Marx's texts in the familiar manner have collapsed. In my account, Marx's critical work on contemporary democratic and authoritarian movements takes centre stage, along with his critique of the categories of contemporary economic life, read in a 'postmodern' way.

- A shift in how Marx is read. The hermeneutics of Gadamer and Ricoeur, Derridean deconstruction, and the Cambridge 'contextualists' have profoundly altered the way that reading is conceived, as well as views on authorial intention, the status and import of language itself, and the role of the writer. Interpretative work on Marx needs to catch up with the postmodern intellectual age.

- A shift in why Marx is read. Marx has been read as a revolutionary, a scientist, a philosopher, an economist, and no doubt as other *personae*. I read him as something of a politician. Marx's interventions into left-liberal and left-socialist politics are precisely relevant to the free market/mixed economy debates that are crucial to the future everywhere. I look for a context of political action and political audience that can be reconstructed around each text as a way of drawing contemporary politics into focus.

In the ten chapters which follow I have used techniques of textual and narrative analysis within what I would call a mild form of postmodernism. I use the word 'mild' in order to distance myself from any grand confrontations with modernity, the Enlightenment, postmodernity or hyperreality, and to warn readers that I am merely handling language in a way that the hermeutically or 'interpretatively' inclined will find commonplace. My ambition is to look carefully at Marx's language, and at the language around Marx, to see what emerges. These are exploratory chapters, and my aim is to open dialogue about the issues that are raised as the book unfolds.

Chapter one begins with a methodological discussion concerning the 'linguistic turn', and it foregrounds *Capital*, vol. 1, as a textual surface. Getting the wonders of Marx's *Capital* to the reader is one of the principal objectives of this book; seeing *Capital* as wonderful in these particular ways can only be done with the methodology employed. This methodology involves noticing how metaphor is used to create meaning, being self-conscious about the tropes Marx deploys, and confronting the writer–audience nexus. Derrida is a useful foil to get this process underway, and I pursue the activity of reading *Capital* afresh through three further chapters.

Chapter two explores the relationship between language and life by reading Marx in a way that aligns him, surprisingly, with the philosophical idealism that he once praised for developing abstractly 'the active side'.[2] General questions of individuality and agency in society are then pursued in chapter three via a re-analysis of Marx on the concept of money. My views are developed in contrast to those of analytical and rational-choice Marxists, producing a Marx considerably different from theirs.

Chapter four sets *Capital* against Marx's own background experience in a politics of satire and parody, examining his dependence on, and critique of, the political economy of his day. It also sets me in opposition to Marx in a particular respect, in that I argue against certain propositions in his text on terms that I believe would have been available to him.

Chapter five takes the reader from the wealthy prolixity of *Capital* to the relative poverty of text devoted to communism, his avowed political goal. After developing a history of communist theory in order to situate the constituents of Marx's communism, I resolve an important apparent inconsistency in these fragmentary texts by focusing on a textual fragment within *The German Ideology*. This fragment is only available for re-interpretation thanks to recent scholarship originating in Japan.

In chapter six I re-examine Marx's political theory and strategy as a political animal of his own times by exploring his relationship with the liberalism and socialism of his contemporaries. Marx is not well known as a proponent of democracy, as it has suited commentators and partisans to situate him as a theorist and practitioner of revolutionary communism. These may have been his conclusions and goals, but his practice and argument can be located in a struggle to make economic issues political within the democratic terms, subjecting them to regulation and control as a matter of public good. Much of this battle has been won, such that the original issue has disappeared, and Marx appears to have been nothing to do with the struggle. Sometimes questions become so settled that they are re-opened as if the original debates had not happened. This seems to me somewhat the position today, and my reason for revisiting Marx in this regard.

Chapter seven opens up the question, 'Who is Marx?' by examining the process through which Marx is translated for English-speaking readers. Translators are of course readers and interpreters, but I also view the process of interpretation as one of translation, in that meanings are constructed by a reader/translator and conveyed to other readers. To illustrate this I discuss my own strategies as a translator in producing new English versions of the *Communist Manifesto* and *The Eighteenth Brumaire of Louis Bonaparte*.

In chapter eight I explore the authorial voice, with which readers are in dialogue in their own minds, in conjunction with circumstances that are peculiar to Marx – the joint works he wrote with Engels, and the construction of the canonical Marx using posthumous writings. I use concepts of 'voicing' and 're-voicing' to do this, and argue that current controversy surrounding the scholarly edition of *Capital*, vol. 3, may have an important impact on the whole framework through which Marx has most commonly been interpreted. This is an orthodoxy depending crucially on Engels' characterisation of Marx's life and work.

Chapter nine deploys a rather similar strategy in considering Marx's relationship in all the classic commentaries to Hegel, or rather to 'Hegel'. This signifier means so much in so many commentaries, and so little in Marx, that I argue for an interpretative move to 'minimise Hegel' in looking at Marx. In support of this I give an extensive commentary on one of the few texts that link very specific passages in Marx to very specific passages in Hegel, and suggest that only in detailed analysis of this kind can anything very useful be said linking the two.

In chapter ten I push my luck as a commentator by putting questions to Marx that he would certainly have not understood in terms that are like those which – I hope – my readers and I can share. These questions concern women and gender, and concerning the latter term, I offer my own definition: 'ways that sex and sexuality become political.'[3] In pursuing these contemporary issues in a contemporary way, I draw out from Marx's fragmentary texts and allusions a narrative dealing with women and gender. Rather than proving Marx deficient, my object is to explore the argumentative character of the quasi-naturalistic and quasi-historical narratives that are often deployed in contemporary sexual politics.

Finally, in an Epilogue, I outline the relationship between the reading strategies that I have pursued through the ten substantial chapters in order to explain and defend the multiple Marxes that this volume has constructed. I contrast this kind of commentary with another narrative strategy commonly employed in writing about Marx, but hardly exclusive to that enterprise. An authoritative commentator producing a single Marx (even a single 'schizophrenic' one) has long been the norm. This seems to me to confront the reader with an attempted closure in terms of 'what to think about Marx'. More crucially it seems to discourage any further engagement between the reader and Marx, and to leave the issues that he raised firmly in the past. At the end I detail exactly what I think these issues have been, though I am also hopeful that readers will have discovered many others as well.

The continued recovery of 'classic' thinkers is an important element in the way that politics is actually done. Re-assessments are periodically in order, and the new interpretative methodologies of postmodernism provide an intellectual reason for doing this. The new political situation globally provides another more pressing political one. Re-reading Marx is itself an important way of moving on intellectually and politically. There is more Marx 'out there' than can ever be discovered, and I offer this book as the barest hint of what can be done.

Notes

1 Dominick La Capra, *Rethinking Intellectual History: Texts, Contexts, Language* (Ithaca NY and London, Cornell University Press, 1983), p. 345.
2 Karl Marx, *Theses on Feuerbach*, in Karl Marx and Frederick Engels, *The German Ideology, Part One*, ed. C. J. Arthur (London, Lawrence & Wishart, 1970), p. 121.
3 Terrell Carver, *Gender is not a Synonym for Women* (Boulder CO, Lynne Rienner Publishers, Inc, 1996), pp. 5–8.

CHAPTER ONE

Spectres and vampires: Marx's metaphors

The 'linguistic turn'

The 'linguistic turn' in intellectual life has prioritised the textual surface.[1] The 'turn' was away from the reality (whether concretely material or phenomenologically ideal) that language purportedly described, and towards the subjects (writers and audiences) and objects (meaningful activities or 'discursive practices') that language was said to construct or constitute. As Michael J. Shapiro has argued, this has made subjects and objects (that is, who writes or speaks, and what is being talked about) increasingly fragile. This means that the 'uninvolved, objective analyst', and the presumed regularities in a world which is simply 'observed' as what it is, independent of the analyst, have both dissolved into politicised 'communities' of writers and audiences. Such communities do not merely know and learn but rather construct and rationalise a world in and through communication. For this communication, language is not a neutral or transparent medium but is rather the constitutive material from which identity and knowledge are formed.[2] This is not to say that the same world is constructed for everyone in the circle of communication; rather that if we understand at all, we understand differently.[3]

Shapiro summarises what it is to 'textualise' and draws two interesting corollaries from this rejection of 'the old referential theory of meaning'. Once we '"textualise" and thus foreground ... writing practices', then we recognise that 'the language of analysis itself, far from being transparent, is an opaque medium'. Given that language is not a window on the world (hence transparent), what exactly happens when we find that it is a surface, and moreover an opaque one? Shapiro's answer is that analysis – textual analysis – penetrates this opacity and reveals 'grammatical, rhetorical, and narrative structures' that 'create value' and 'bestow meaning'. Having rejected the presumptions of empiricism (that the material world is mirrored in human sensation and language), Shapiro – like others – finesses the idealism (the view that the only reality is consciousness and ideas) from which the hermeneutic and phenomenological traditions derived. He does this when he comments that linguistic structures 'constitute (in the sense of imposing form upon) the subjects and objects that emerge in the process of inquiry'.[4]

Thus the existence of a world, usually termed 'material', is not denied, but rather the claim is that it cannot be known in itself and cannot therefore be used to validate the language that we use. 'Material' is itself a contested concept in physics, or at least the ways that scientists understand it are now so varied, and so out of tune with commonsensical presumptions, that gesturing at something 'material' or kicking it (as when Johnson tried to refute Berkeley), are absurdly contextless and confused, even in terms of philosophical strategies.[5] Scientific subjects (knowers) and objects (what is known) are by no means apart or immune from the corroding character of textual analysis. Thomas Kuhn, perhaps inadvertently, undermined the hallowed unitary method and supposedly cumulative practice that were generally invoked as epistemic and political validations within communities of scientists. Donna Haraway has advanced this process considerably, if very controversially, by applying to the natural sciences just the kind of analysis that Shapiro employs on the social sciences.[6]

This brings me to Shapiro's two corollaries that follow from this critique of referentialism (the view that 'the locus of meaning lies in the relationship between statements and the "things" that they are about'). The first corollary is that the 'radical distinction between literal and figurative language' no longer holds: there is no neutral or transparent or objective language which merely 'describes' but does not 'interpret'. The second corollary is that 'good science', whether natural, social or philosophical, is good because and when it avoids language that is seemingly non-literal, i.e. 'figural' or rhetorical.[7] Rather, it is argued, and not just by Shapiro and those he cites, that the tropes and codes, the narrative and genre, within which meaning is generated, all function to construct and validate authority within a writing practice, and also play a discernible role in selecting and structuring the content of the information actually conveyed.[8]

Amongst those analysts concerned with textual surface, and with analysing figural language, Jacques Derrida is certainly in the front rank. And amongst those works thought to be boringly literal in their scientificity, it would be hard to find one more widely derided than Marx's *Capital*.[9] My purpose here is to argue that Derrida is right to 'textualise' Marx, but does it badly, in ways that I detail in my critique. I argue that Marx is not only an exceptionally rich and fruitful writer when 'textualised', but that his texts can be read as constructions consistent with the views that the 'linguistic turn' comprehends. To do this I shall review – in a highly critical way – Derrida's recent *Specters of Marx*, which treats the *Communist Manifesto* – a text that is obviously rhetorical in style and rich in metaphor – as central.[10] I shall then turn, however, to *Capital*, a supposedly unpromising text which Derrida cites only secondarily, in order to demonstrate that Marx's imagery plays an important role in constructing a political argument. Without that political argument, his critique of an economic category ('the commodity') makes little sense. While 'spectre' has a role in Marx, Derrida overplays it. For more interesting results, we will interview the vampire.

Spectres of Marx

Derrida's book is certainly an instance in which *parole* is prior to *langue*. The work arises from two plenary addresses to a California conference 'Whither Marxism? Global Crises in International Perspective', and the printed text is said (by Derrida) to be 'augmented, clarified'.[11] Strikingly, Derrida presumes a critical divergence between Marx and the Marxian, on the one hand, and Marxism and the Marxist tradition, on the other. It is to the former that he suggests we turn ('we are placing our trust, in fact, in this form of critical analysis we have inherited from Marxism'),[12] and indeed he specifically jettisons the defining categories of Marxism in order to do this:

> We would be tempted to distinguish this *spirit* of the Marxist critique, which seems to be more indispensable than ever today, at once from Marxism as ontology, philosophical or metaphysical system, as 'dialectical materialism', from Marxism as historical materialism or method, and from Marxism incorporated in the apparatuses of party, State, or workers' International.[13]

While Derrida is hardly the first to take up this position (the suspicions of divergence between Marx and Marxism with respect to 'materialism' began to arise in public shortly after the death of Engels in 1895), his lapidary statements will be welcomed (by some) in the continuing debate, recently sharpened by both the post-1989 collapse of European Marxist regimes and by the post-1995 retrospectives on Engels. Derrida's view of Marxism remade is that it is 'a procedure ready to undertake its self-critique', 'explicitly open to its own transformation, re-evaluation, self-reinterpretation'. This 'spirit', he says, 'is heir to a spirit of the Enlightenment which must not be renounced'. He distinguishes this spirit of deconstructive Marxism from 'Marxist doctrine', notably 'dialectical method' or 'dialectical materialism', and from 'fundamental concepts of labour, mode of production, social class, and consequently the whole history of its apparatuses (projected or real)'.[14] This line between the Marxian and the Marxist tradition opens the way for an 'anti-foundational' reading of Marx; whereas reading Marx through the categories of Engelsian dialectics, which are paradigmatically foundational, universalising, and literal, would turn deconstruction into derision.

Derrida's new Marxism also contains 'a certain emancipatory and *messianic* affirmation', so it is not merely 'spiritual' or 'abstract', but rather aims 'to produce events, new effective forms of action, practice, organisation, and so forth'.[15] Indeed Derrida announces a 'new Enlightenment' that maintains 'an ideal of democracy and emancipation' and tries 'to think it and to put it to work'.[16] He aims to consider 'all the questions concerning democracy, the universal discourse on human rights, the future of humanity, and so forth', bearing in mind 'the interest of capital in general' and 'the world–wide market [which] holds a mass of humanity under its yoke'.[17] However, that is not the kind of discussion he actually produces.

Derrida is preoccupied instead with what are sometimes called surface features of Marx's texts, indicating that this kind of reading gets to grips with what is by no means superficial. Indeed, I wish he had argued more strongly that this is the only way to grasp certain sorts of arguments, something which I aim to substantiate below. Specifically he is interested in metaphors or figurations to do with spectrality: ghosts, spirits, spectres, and spooks, taking substantial texts from the *Manifesto*, *The Eighteenth Brumaire of Louis Bonaparte*, *The German Ideology*, and occasionally *Capital*. While he does not favour his readers with any very direct summaries of what his argument is and how it works, I would venture to suggest that he is demonstrating that Marx's critiques of philosophical idealism, of religion and other forms of ideology, and of the classical political economists and their 'economic categories', are all tightly related, and that the key to this inter-relationship lies in the tropes employed.

Derrida's analysis of Marx's spectral tropes is, on the one hand, diffuse and wayward in terms of his communication with readers (me, at least), and on the other hand, philosophical and narrow in terms of the conclusions that he draws (in my view). He spends considerable time on *Hamlet* (ghosts and 'time out of joint'), on the rather feeble grounds that Marx liked Shakespeare and quoted *Timon of Athens* at length (on money, as it happens). The ghost in *Hamlet* is not particularly employed by Marx, nor is it any more relevant than the allusions and images that he actually uses. Nor is ghostliness, as in *Hamlet*, nearly as pertinent to the arguments being made, for instance, as Marx's striking invocation of 'inverted Schlemihl's'. These are shadows which have lost their men, a figure Marx uses when he writes about the revolution of 1848 – to take an instance from *The Eighteenth Brumaire* which Derrida cites in passing. Marx's argument there seems to me to say that the revolutionary factions of 1848 paralysed themselves by viewing each one to the left as a 'red spectre', thus making it easier for the 'party of order' to emerge and take power – ironically in the *red* breeches of the soldiery.[18] This seems a useful lesson to draw – a contemporary 'Discourse on the History of the French Republic' in a Machiavellian mode – but Derrida's discussion wanders off disappointingly to 'the specter of the specter' and 'simulacra of simulacra'.[19]

The conclusion that Derrida stresses is a strongly philosophical one: actuality is never adequate to its concept, and this failure to fulfil 'haunts' any project in advance. One summons 'the very thing that will never present itself in the form of full presence',[20] he writes; 'to haunt does not mean to be present, and it is necessary to introduce haunting into the very construction of a concept'.[21] The extent to which Marx's concepts of communism and a non-monetary economy, for instance, would necessarily be inadequate to their conceptual promise is an issue that he merely notices but unfortunately does not dwell on. Derrida's argument seems to me to say little other than that things are never quite what they are cracked up to be, and nothing is ever quite as it seems. Revealingly, he calls for further research on the 'egoist' Max Stirner (roundly criticised by Marx in *The German Ideology*), whose 'exemplary fault … would be the vice of modern speculation'.[22]

Derrida's *segue* from spectres to fetishes is via madness, which seems a little tenuous:

> Let us not forget that everything we have just read [in *Capital*] was Marx's point of view on a *finite delirium*. It was his discourse on a madness destined, according to him, to come to an end, on a general incorporation of abstract human labour that is still translated, but for a finite time, into the language of madness, into a delirium … We *will see* … the end of this delirium and of these ghosts, Marx obviously thinks.
>
> This madness here? Those ghosts there? Or spectrality in general? This is more or less our whole question … These questions posed, or rather suspended, we can perhaps return to what *Capital* seems to want to say about the fetish …[23]

Derrida then drops the question of fetishisation,[24] but goes on to announce a research programme and produce a page or two of notes. There are three areas of current interest:

1. Fetishist phantomaticity in general and its place in *Capital*.
2. The place of this theoretical moment in Marx's corpus.
3. Everything which *today* links Religion and Technics in a singular configuration.[25]

Overall, Derrida's reading of Marx leaps about from trope to trope, text to text, in a way that is bereft of political contextualisation in any very extensive sense, much as one would expect in plenary lectures, I suppose. Nonetheless for me his discussions of what may or may not be important distinctions in Marx's choice of, and use of, various related metaphors (*Geist, Gespenst, Spuk*, etc.) are largely empty in terms of argumentative context. Instead he relates this language to presumed distinctions that are not discussed at any length. It is no surprise to find that in Derrida's view one trope turns easily into the other.

This explains to me why for most of the book Derrida seems to read the opening of the *Manifesto* so perversely, believing that Marx portrays communism as a spectre ('of a communism then to *come*'[26]) in order to announce that one day it will *return* to haunt Europe and its reactionary powers. By contrast I read this passage as a fairly straightforward claim that the 'spectre of communism' is an apparition created by right-wing hysteria, and as such bears a merely fantastic relationship to the real doctrines and views which Marx and Engels were at pains in the *Manifesto* to announce openly to the world. Eventually I think that Derrida comes to something like this understanding, but it is hard work for the reader, given Derrida's propensity to focus on 'just the word' and then to give a rather all-purpose account of what the image is supposed to mean, and how it is in the abstract similar to and different from some of the other images that Marx employs.

Early on in Derrida's discussion his method leads him paradoxically to view the spectre of communism as something created by right-wing powers 'so as to reassure themselves' as if to say, 'it's merely a ghost',[27] whereas the *Manifesto* says (to me, anyway) that the red-scare version of communism (i.e. the spectre) was created by reactionary powers precisely to terrify themselves and others into a witchhunt, hence the slanted and inaccurate image of communism that the spectre portends.[28] Later in *Specters of Marx* Derrida, wandering even further from what I take Marx's argument to be, writes that 'communism has always been and will remain spectral: it is always still to come'.[29] Confusing ghosts with spectres, Derrida wonders why Marx uses the term 'spectre' in 1848 in a sense opposite to the one which Derrida intends in the 1990s:

> Where I was tempted to name thereby ... the return of the dead
> which the worldwide work of mourning cannot get rid of ... Marx,
> for his part, announces and calls for a presence to come.[30]

Shortly after this, Derrida argues that reactionaries fear the communist 'ghost' 'through the spectre', without quite getting the point that the spectre is one that they themselves have created to frighten themselves still further.[31] For me there is too much 'mourning' in Derrida's analysis (subtitled 'The State of the Debt, the Work of Mourning, and the New International'), and not enough (for my taste, anyway) about the anger wrapped up in horrific imagery and political smears.

Moving to 'the whole totalitarian inheritance of Marx's thought', Derrida suggests that *both* camps – Nazis and fascists, and Leninists and Stalinists – are 'equally' terrorised by 'the ghost', and that this is 'a reaction of panic-ridden fear before the ghost in general'.[32] Having reflected on the imagery of the apparition in Marx, Derrida ventures that this 'perhaps gives one to think that the figure of the ghost is not just one figure among others. It is perhaps the hidden figure of all figures'.[33] However, my view is that something which 'perhaps' tells us everything, actually says very little about anything.

Marx's vampires

Rather than constructing an all-purpose trope and reading it into a selection of texts, *Capital* amongst them, I propose to examine in detail a metaphor that is actually deployed in *Capital*, namely capital as vampire. While the vividness of this image has hitherto attracted some comment, I have been intrigued to trace the deployment of similar imagery throughout the text, noting the ways that Marx links the occult with religion generally and with Christianity in particular.[34] By using this imagery Marx is able to recapitulate an intellectually profound and politically important argument, derived from his early days as a Young Hegelian. He did this within *Capital*, a work executed for a different audience under different political circumstances.

'Capital is dead labour which vampire-like, lives the more, the more labour it sucks'. Surprisingly Marx, a lifelong rationalist and scourge of all that is claimed to be supernatural, used the vampire motif three times in *Capital*. The opening sections of that work have established its reputation as a dry volume of economic theory, an 'economics' supposedly unintelligible to all but committed Marxists who can penetrate the hermetic system. The uninitiated are generally directed to the empirical and historical chapters on 'Machinery and Large-scale Industry' and 'Primitive Accumulation', where industrial sociology and social history provide modern readers with an easier intellectual point of entry. The more zealous tackle the now famous chapter on 'The Fetishism of Commodities', examining the reification – 'material relations between persons and social relations between things' – that is said to characterise politics and culture in capitalist society.[35] Perhaps the vampire is merely the kind of extravagant metaphor we might expect from Marx, whose stock-in-trade, the polemic, demanded exaggeration. The theory of exploitation in *Capital* – that surplus value arises exclusively from labour power expended by workers beyond the time needed to produce a value equal to their wage – certainly lent itself to Marx's graphic if *recherché* imagery.

Vampires are well known as creatures of the night, an attribute Marx exploited when he wrote that the 'prolongation of the working day beyond the limits of the natural day, into the night, only acts as a palliative'. 'It only slightly quenches the vampire thirst for the living blood of labour'. Capitalist production, he concluded, has an inherent drive 'towards the appropriation of labour throughout the whole of the 24 hours in the day'. The vampire will not let go 'while there remains a single muscle, sinew or drop of blood to be exploited'.[36]

Why should a self-professed social scientist like Marx titillate us with images of vampirism? Moreover, why should he also have included references to an amazing array of supernatural, paranormal, sacramental and occult phenomena to explain what he termed the 'natural laws of capitalist production'?[37] The famous 'fetishism', introduced at the end of the first chapter of *Capital*, is not of course anything to do with psycho-sexuality, but rather follows from Charles de Brosses's definition of 1760: an inanimate object thought to have magical powers or to animated by a spirit – idol-worship, in other words.[38] There are also allusions throughout the volume to witchcraft, animism, tribal religions, spiritualism, magic, monsters, ghosts, wizardry and the Cabala, mysterious hieroglyphics, werewolves, the soul, alchemists and alchemy, deism, unnatural metamorphoses, raising of the dead, metempsychosis and transmigration of souls, creation *ex nihilo*, miracles, conjuring tricks, levitation and perpetual motion machines. Marx refers to religion generally and in particular to these aspects of Christianity: God the Father, God the Son, the Lamb of God, the garden of Eden, the Holy Grail, the beast of the apocalypse, the whore of Babylon, the incarnation, baptism, transubstantiation, Protestants, Catholics and popes. Religious or quasi-religious rituals are also mentioned, including (male) circumcision, cannibalism, human sacrifice and orgies. *Capital* also contains the more general metaphor of phenomena that are invisible, concealed or veiled, that are symbols, secrets, fantasies, enigmas, illusions or riddles, that are mysterious and in need of deciphering, or phenomena that are simply imaginary or absurd but are believed none the less. Marx's vision of capitalism is a kind of unholy Chartres Cathedral where Christian iconography mingles with the nightmarish creatures and pagan practices that Christianity itself professed to abhor (though often incorporated). Curiously I have not yet found a reference in *Capital* to the devil.

While *Capital* is not an occult work, the occult (very broadly defined) plays a distinctive and unappreciated role in the argument. Marx was doing more than merely portraying capitalists as nocturnal bloodsuckers with a 'werewolf-like hunger for surplus labour'.[39] Moreover his approach was every bit as rationalist as one would expect, having its roots in the works of the *philosophes* themselves. Tracing this argument opens out the text to illuminate many more social phenomena than are usually considered to be Marx's brief, and it helps us to understand the analysis of the commodity, value and money that occurs in the first sections of the work.

These concepts – commodity, value and money – should feature prominently in social and political theory today, but generally do not. Instead they are dumped with relief on to economists who employ them for their own purposes, but do not offer the wide-ranging conceptual exploration that Marx had in mind. In addition to a novel view of social phenomena that transcends our usual presuppositions about economics and the occult, Marx was also telling us something, so I think, that is interesting about the very concept of metaphor itself.

In his exploration of the concept 'commodity', Marx argued that in capitalist society we commonly regard useful objects as of so-much 'value', measured by a common standard. By means of this standard, quantities of bread, books, nails, etc., can be of equal value, and he proposes to analyse how exactly this important social practice arose and works. Value-in-exchange, he argued, is not itself a physical property of any object, nor is it explicable simply by referring the reader to the obvious role played by money in representing this common exchange-ability in precisely quantifiable terms.

While there are many difficulties with Marx's version of the labour theory of value (see chapter four below), his objects of study – value-in-exchange, money, price, capital – represent an important area of conceptual inquiry. This is because they define the way that we regard most of the resources that there are, or might be, in the world. His argument that exchange-value as a social institution has a historical origin in certain cultures and is itself conventional is well supported, quite apart from whatever factor or factors we might consider to be the correct explanation for the particular standards of value that have arisen.

Marx's thesis in *Capital* is that exchange-value exists in the same realm as other social institutions such as the law, the state, the church and other complicated entities that are composed of shared assumptions, definitions, expectations, norms, standards of adjudication and accepted social sanctions, otherwise known – following the 'linguistic turn' and post-Foucauldian theory – as discursive and disciplinary practices. Indeed, from Marx's point of view, commodity production and exchange is not merely one institution among others but the one that 'conditions the general process of social, political and intellectual life'.[40] Whether or not we take this claim to be true in some sense is again a separate question from the further points about the institution of commodity exchange and other social institutions that Marx was concerned to make. 'The existence of one commodity as value is manifested in its equality with another, just as the sheep-like nature of the Christian is shown in his resemblance to the Lamb of God.'[41] Or in plainer language, an individual exhibits certain qualities of meekness, but these qualities are only Christian by analogy with the supposed qualities of the Christian God.

Marx went on to assert that, metaphorically, commodities speak a language that only they really understand. When one commodity 'tells us' that it is worth so much of another, that is, my commodity has a value-in-exchange of so much of yours, it has uttered something that is – or rather should be – mystifying to us. Commodities, he said, are citizens of their world. On that basis, laws are drafted, interpreted and enforced, and institutions are formed and function. That world, though intangible as a world of commodity-values (rather than as mere useful objects), is not imaginary or just symbolic. Rather it has social validity, since that world and its languages are generally accepted as given features of our society, indeed of an aggressive global society. It is in terms of these features that claims are made – and decisions taken.

Marx has pushed economic concepts into what was for him much the same contentious and socially constructed realm as religion. He was the theorist of practical concepts – the ones in common use in society and its institutions. Products of labour become commodities, 'sensuous things which are at the same time suprasensible or social'. He made this specifically analogous to 'the misty realm of religion [where] the products of the human brain appear as autonomous figures endowed with a life of their own ... So it is in the world of commodities with the products of men's hands'.[42]

This argument was not, however, confined to conventional forms of religion. Marx invoked similar phenomena that exist socially, because people believe in them, but he took it that those phenomena had no rational basis. They were, of course, the phenomena listed above as 'occult', including werewolves and vampires. But for Marx, as I read the text, those phenomena were not simply fantasies or collective delusions. They were constituent concepts within oppressive institutions which opened the possibility – and usually the actuality – of fraud, manipulation, and keeping people in ignorance and fear so that they are easily cowed and intimidated. Here Marx was alluding to the arguments of the *philosophes*, Rousseau and Voltaire among others, that the true significance of miracles, vampires and other popular superstitions was to bolster the sacred and secular authorities in society, 'the sombre and nefarious tyranny of opinion exercised by priests over the minds of men'.[43]

If we are liberal and rational and do not believe in these occult entities and rites, we are none the less normally encouraged to see them as merely laughable – silly errors and delusions – and thus we miss what I take to be Marx's point, that they are the sort of social phenomena that assist some in getting the better of others. Whether or not we agree with Marx's analysis of how these economic concepts arise from the private ownership of the means of production, or with his conclusions about the necessity for a revolutionary reorganisation of production itself, we can admire the scope and sophistication of his theoretical exploration of capitalist society. In that exploration he deployed a powerful concept of metaphor.

For Marx a metaphor may sometimes work in both directions between the object and the thing or idea likened to it. The commodity as fetish, for instance, tells us something important about fetishism (it is oppressive and exploitative), as well as something very striking about the commodity (it is mysterious and conventional). The capitalist as vampire reveals the exploitative character of vampirism as a real social institution, as well as the contrived and sinister nature of the social role of 'capitalist'.

Marx warned his readers that the capitalist would not be presented 'in rosy colours', and the vampire imagery bears this out.[44] It highlights Marx's use of the terms living and dead labour in his theory of surplus value, his argument that the class struggle has a deadly character, and his overall contention that economic deprivation results from human institutions, rather than natural limitations (such as scarcity of resources) or metaphysical predicaments (such as original sin or 'the human condition'). But in *Capital* Marx also explored the way that structures of oppression interact with exploitative institutions, though he did not pursue this to the point of distracting the reader from his critical analysis of capitalist society. In Marx's hands the Young Hegelians' criticism of heaven had come down to the earthly realm of commodity production, and a critique of the supernatural persists in *Capital* as a consequence of his theory of exploitation. Economics for Marx was not itself an exorcism, and his text is not mere interpretation; action is required outside the text, and his imagery compounds the political message.[45]

Conclusions

Marx did not accept a commonplace distinction between literal and figurative language, and he did not attempt to avoid the latter in what is taken to be his most scientific work. Rather his use of figurative language to make a political argument aligns him with the 'textualising' approach delineated by Shapiro at the opening of my argument. Marx's critique takes political economy as a textual surface, and by means of a thorough, and thoroughly linguistic analysis he refigures, in a parodic text, a supposedly familiar and uncontentious world[46] as strange (requiring explanation) and problematic (requiring political action). Thus a 'textualising' reading of Marx need not be 'against the grain'. Given the idealist origins of both Marx's thought and methods, and of subsequent hermeneutics and the contemporary 'linguistic turn', it should not be surprising that this kind of reading can be undertaken and that Marx begins eerily to track postmodernism. My quarrel with Derrida in this chapter is that he flies off the textual surface too readily into a discursive space that I find puzzling or meaningless; in the next chapter I explore in much greater depth the relationship between Marx's work in *Capital* and the conceptual methodology – and substantive claims – of philosophical idealism.

Notes

1 For an introduction to the philosophy and issues of the 'linguistic turn', albeit with a personal slant, see Quentin Skinner, 'Reply to my critics', introduction to James Tully (ed.), *Meaning and Context* (Cambridge, Polity Press, 1988).
2 Michael J. Shapiro, 'Metaphor in the philosophy of the social sciences', *Culture and Critique*, 2 (1985–86), 191.
3 For an explication of this view of language and communication, see Paul Ricoeur, 'Metaphor and the main problem of hermeneutics', in Mario J. Valdés (ed.), *A Ricoeur Reader: Reflection and Imagination* (London, Harvester/Wheatsheaf, 1991), pp. 303–19.
4 Shapiro, 'Metaphor', p. 192; for another short statement of this view, see David Campbell, *Writing Security* (Manchester, Manchester University Press, 1992), pp. 5-7.

5 Ludwig Wittgenstein, *On Certainty* (Oxford, Basil Blackwell, 1969) explores these issues.

6 Thomas S. Kuhn, *The Structure of Scientific Revolutions*, 2nd edn (Chicago IL, University of Chicago Press, 1970); Donna Haraway, *Simians, Cyborgs and Women: The Reinvention of Nature* (London, Free Association Books, 1991).

7 Shapiro, 'Metaphor', pp. 192–3.

8 Hayden White, *The Content of the Form: Narrative Discourse and Historical Representation* (Baltimore MD, Johns Hopkins University Press, 1987).

9 I am concerned here with vol. 1 (of three), the only one Marx saw through the press. Even where the metaphors in the work have come under scrutiny, my impression is that the authors involved are working to highlight, by contrast, the presumed literalness of the language – typically commodity, money, capital, exploitation etc. – that they take to be the theoretical reflection of 'the real world' of capitalism. See, for example, Stanford M. Lyman, *The Seven Deadly Sins: Society and Evil* (New York, St. Martin's Press, 1978), p. 311, n. 26; George E. Panichas, 'Vampires, werewolves, and economic exploitation', *Social Theory and Practice*, 7:2 (1981), 223–42; Mark Matcott, 'Vampires and socialism', *Monash and Latrobe Revolutionary Communist Clubs* (March 1974), cyclostyled.

10 Along with most commentators I take this joint work to be wholly Marx's for present purposes, as he had it last (so far as is known) before it went to press, and it certainly had his imprimatur when it was subsequently reproduced (though his views on its subsequent status are interesting in themselves; see his Preface to the German edition of 1872, and chapter seven below). For a discussion concerning 'who did what' in the joint composition of the text, see Terrell Carver, *Marx and Engels: The Intellectual Relationship* (Brighton, Harvester/Wheatsheaf, 1983), pp. 78–94. For a consideration of the Manifesto as 'wholly Engels' in the light of his subsequent writings, see Terrell Carver, *Friedrich Engels: His Life and Thought* (London, Macmillan, 1989), pp. 232–52.

11 Jacques Derrida, *Specters of Marx*, trans. Peggy Kamuf (New York and London, Routledge, 1994), pp. ix–x.

12 Derrida, *Specters*, p. 55.

13 Derrida, *Specters*, p. 68.

14 On the distinction between Marx and the 'Marxian', on the one hand, and Marxism and the Marxist tradition, on the other, see Carver, *Marx and Engels* passim.; for post-1995 re-assessments of Engels, see Christopher J. Arthur (ed.), *Engels Today: A Centenary Appreciation* (London, Macmillan; New York, St. Martin's Press, 1996), and Manfred Steger and Terrell Carver (eds), *Engels after Marx* (University Park PA, Pennsylvania State University Press, forthcoming 1999); Derrida, *Specters*, pp. 88–9.

15 Derrida, *Specters*, p. 89.

16 Derrida, *Specters*, p. 90.

17 Derrida, *Specters*, pp. 93–4

18 Quoted in Derrida, *Specters*, pp. 117–18.

19 Derrida, *Specters*, pp. 117-18.

20 Derrida, *Specters*, p. 65.

21 Derrida, *Specters*, p. 161.

22 Derrida, *Specters*, p. 146.

23 Derrida, *Specters*, pp. 163–5.

24 Derrida, *Specters*, p. 167.

25 Derrida, *Specters*, p. 167.

26 Derrida, *Specters*, p. 37.

27 Derrida, *Specters*, p. 38.

28 Note that the traditional English translation (of 1888 – by Sam Moore) seems to support Derrida by using the verb 'to haunt'. 'A spectre is haunting Europe'. While no doubt an improvement on Helen MacFarlane's version (of 1850) – 'A frightful hobgoblin stalks throughout Europe' – it does render the German *geht um* as 'haunts', which suggests 'ghosts' to me, ghosts being apparitions of the dead. *Umgehen* itself is nothing much to do with ghosts or haunting (as the otherwise awful MacFarlane translation reveals). In my recent re-translation of this text I render the sentence as 'A spectre stalks the land of Europe' in order to expunge the suggestion that Marx is talking about something dead but come back to life, and instead to picture something that is at the same time fantastical and actually at large in the political realm. See Karl Marx, *Later Political Writings*, ed. and trans. Terrell Carver (Cambridge, Cambridge University Press, 1996), p. 1.

29 Derrida, *Specters*, p. 99.

30 Derrida, *Specters*, p. 101.

31 Derrida, *Specters*, p. 103.

32 Derrida, *Specters*, pp. 104–5.

33 Derrida, *Specters*, pp. 119–20.

34 See note 9 above.

35 Karl Marx, *Capital*, vol. 1, trans. Ben Fowkes (Harmondsworth, Penguin, 1976, repr. 1986), pp. 342, 367, 416. See also pp. 353, 382 for similar metaphors to do with blood-sucking. For 'reification', see p. 166. Note also that one of Marx's pithiest comments on religion ('The religious world is but the reflex of the real world') is unaccountably omitted from p. 172 of the Penguin translation; the history of this passage, which derives from Marx's hand in the French translation of 1872–75, is traced in Christopher J. Arthur, 'Engels as interpreter of Marx's economics', in Arthur, *Engels Today*, p. 178.

36 Marx, *Capital*, vol. 1, p. 416; Marx is quoting from an article by Engels on the 'Ten Hours Bill', cited in Marx's n. 66.

37 Marx, *Capital*, vol. 1, pp. 180, 394. Given that Marx regarded commodity production as a thoroughly artificial and historically created social form, his use of 'natural' here is highly and deliberately ironic (see p. 36 below).

38 See the discussion in Terrell Carver, 'Marx's commodity fetishism', *Inquiry*, 18:1 (1975), 49–54.

39 Marx, *Capital*, vol. 1, p. 353.

40 See Michel Foucault, *The Foucault Reader*, ed. Paul Rabinow (Harmondsworth, Penguin, 1986); Karl Marx, Preface to *A Contribution to the Critique of Political Economy*, in *Later Political Writings*, p. 160; quoted in *Capital*, vol. 1, p. 175 n. 35.

41 Marx, *Capital*, vol. 1, p. 143.

42 Marx, *Capital*, vol. 1, p. 165.

43 Christopher Frayling and Robert Wokler, 'From the orang-utan to the vampire', in R. A. Leigh (ed.), *Rousseau after Two Hundred Years*, (Cambridge, Cambridge University Press, 1982), pp. 117–18.

44 Marx, *Capital*, vol. 1, p. 92.

45 For a discussion that uses irony as a way of examining Marx's texts, and his evident expectations of political action from his readers, see John Evan Seery, 'Deviations: on the difference between Marx and Marxist theorists', *History of Political Thought*, 9:2 (1988), 303–25, esp. 319–20.

46 Paul Mattick, Jr., makes a similar point, arguing that Marx takes a view of capitalist society that somewhat resembles an anthropologist's approach to a society that is thoroughly unfamiliar, asking questions about everyday social practices which seem laughably naive to those already initiated, e.g. 'How is it that you can exchange one thing for another?' See his *Social Knowledge: An Essay on the Nature and Limits of Social Science* (Armonk NY and London, M. E. Sharpe and Hutchinson, 1986), ch. 1.

CHAPTER TWO

Minds and meaning: Marx's concepts

Reading *Capital*

What kind of book is *Capital*? What is it actually about? Or rather, is there more than one way of answering these questions? And in particular, is there a reading alternative to the one handed down through tradition? If so, what makes it plausible? My aim in this chapter is to explore the textual 'surface' in Marx in a way that leads beyond metaphor. Initially I examine how presuppositions about genre and narrative frame the understandings of method and content that readers construct as they work through 'the words on the page'. As this discussion develops, I arrive at rather surprising conclusions as to what Marx's text might be saying and then consider the political implications.

Capital is commonly taken to be a 'positive' work, in one sense or another. This could be positive in the sense of consistent with, and following on from, a positive foundation in 'dialectics', as outlined by Engels in published form in *Anti-Dühring* and *Socialism Utopian and Scientific*, and in manuscript form, in notes that were posthumously published as *The Dialectics of Nature*.[1] While dialectical materialism was explored and expounded by Georgii Plekhanov and numerous later 'orthodox' philosophers, the relationship of dialectics to *Capital* was always more of a claim than a well-defended argument.[2] Besides the difficulties raised by Engels' ambitions for a theory of 'nature, history and thought' based on 'matter in motion', there was in any case a good deal of nervousness within the Marxist community about the 'Hegelian' passages in *Capital*, particularly those in the crucial Chapter 1. Louis Althusser's concern to establish an 'epistemological break' by which Marx 'freed' himself from Hegelian influences was a notable instance in which this anxiety was explicitly aired, whereas the alternative strategy was more usual – ignoring these passages or skating over their obvious difficulties, in order to get back to a presumed factuality and literalism in the remainder of Marx's discussion.[3] While Engels' famous mixed metaphor – inverting Hegel and setting him on his feet – might seem to reconcile scientific materialism with Hegelian dialectics, as orthodox theorists claimed, it was actually rather difficult to read extended passages of *Capital*, and to regard Marx's fulsome praise in mid-career for Hegel's *Logic*, in a way that made the conceptual analysis of *Capital* consistent with a 'positive' view of theory. A 'positive' approach to theory says that it is the job of theory to reflect the structure and motion of the world – whether a world of physical objects, historical events, or logical relations – rather than to construct this as reality and refigure it as politics.[4]

As a variant reading, *Capital* has been taken as a 'positive' work in another sense, that of 'positive economics'. From Eugen von Böhm-Bawerk onwards economists constructed a Marxist economics alternative to the equilibrium theorists and to their presumed neutrality towards, or enthusiasm for, the 'free' market.[5] Marx, of course, famously comments in *Capital* that the realm of economic activity, in those societies where 'the capitalist mode of production prevails', is not 'a very Eden of the rights of man' nor a realm of freedom and equality, except in an illusory sense – over which he expends several chapters in explanation.[6] Unfortunately these explanations do not seem to establish 'foundations' from which a theory of justice can be extrapolated, hence the moral position, from which many passages of political criticism proceed, remains unclear and fraught with the contradictions of Marx's own condemnations of moralising and of morality. Paradoxically these passages are often referred to as 'descriptive' in an otherwise theoretical work.[7]

However, a Marxist economics that was both positive and critical did arise and form a counterpoint to an orthodoxy – conventional economics – that generally prided itself on not communicating with its severest critics. As with conventional economics, Marxist economics presumes that economic theory is a realm that is 'positive', in the sense that it generates testable predictions and verifiable (or at least falsifiable) explanations for what can be observed in the relevant realms of human activity. Rather than observing, or postulating, self-interested individuals interacting in the labour, commodity and capital markets, Marxist economists tend to see class struggle, heritable hierarchies of power and differential life chances, and a special role for labour in modelling market economies. They also take a suspicious view of claims that capitalism is an efficient way to develop technology, and that progress is simply a consumer society that is 'growing'.

Rational-choice Marxists, most notably John Roemer in this context, parted company with both traditions within 'orthodoxy' – 'materialist dialectics' and 'positive economics' – in two crucial respects.[8] On the one hand Roemer has no time for any 'dialectics', whether material in some substantively physical way or Hegelian even in some inverted way, and on the other hand, he accepts, rather than rejects, the assumptions and methodology of conventional economics, which takes the market to be uncontroversially foundational rather than politically debatable. The twist is that Roemer aims to deduce a theory of exploitation (and hence class advantage) from the very principles which, according to conventional economics, make exploitation a nonsense. However, his theories are still positive in the sense that they are models, based on game-theoretic presuppositions, from which explanations are said to be deduced. For Roemer, the language of the models (often sieved into algebraic relations) is extrinsic to the phenomena being modelled (rather than observed), and the object of the exercise is 'explanation' in some rather narrow social scientific sense, rather than 'understanding' in some wider sense of political engagement.

What links all these rather different Marxisms together – dialectical materialist, Marxist economics, rational-choice Marxists – is a view that theory reflects or models reality, and that reality exists independently of this theoretical reflection. None of these views is particularly concerned with the language from which theory is constructed, and none sees any defining relationship between human behaviour and language as such. Indeed the ordinary language employed by individuals is really of no interest to any 'positive' view, except in so far as it provides 'traces' or records of the behaviour from which 'economic phenomena' are subsequently defined in technical or scientific terms.

My view of *Capital* is rather different, founded as it is on a supposition that Marx, as I read him in *Capital*, was primarily interested in the language employed ordinarily within capitalist and commodity-producing societies. In my view *Capital* is an analytical work proceeding from that ordinary language, through a critique of the 'science' of political economy which purported to explain it, ascending ultimately to a realm in which conceptual relationships, deemed 'logical' or 'conceptual', can be traced out. That realm relates to meaning, rather than to 'matter' or anything 'material', in so far as 'the material' is conceived as something apart from and indifferent to language. This leads me to see Marx's analysis as profoundly alterior to common sense, something which he regarded as in any case pretty commonly misleading. More startlingly it also leads to a Marx who is highly 'idealist' in the philosophical sense, that is, holding a view that concepts construct or determine reality, and even give rise to it.

This need not, however, generate a Hegelian Marx, in the sense that concepts need not literally (or even figuratively) generate and control the reality that 'the philosopher' comes to know. Rather, in introducing this re-reading of *Capital*, I refer to Marx's condemnation of traditional materialism and to his fulsome praise for philosophical idealism in his *Theses on Feuerbach*.[9] Idealists, he wrote, developed the 'active side' in analysis, and I suggest in the present chapter below that Marx bridged the gulf between traditional idealism as a metaphorical theology of creation, and his own 'new materialism' as an analytical and political approach to social and economic relationships. My view is that he did this by taking as his datum the language of real life, portraying capitalism as something very like a Foucauldian 'regime of truth', and attempting to generate a type of politics that is both constrained and empowered by the conceptual relations of capitalism.[10]

Individuals and commodities

'Beginnings are always difficult in all sciences', Marx rightly warned.[11] The complexities of Chapter 1 on the commodity are so notoriously daunting and the misconceptions surrounding his 'new' materialist outlook so pervasive, that the point (for me) of his discussion, only revealed at the opening of Chapter 2, has been somewhat obscured.[12] His work is thus not about commodities as such but about human behaviour in markets and the capitalist economy that results:

> Commodities cannot themselves go to market and perform exchanges in their own right. We must, therefore, have recourse to their guardians, who are the possessors of commodities.[13]

Capital is not a work about material things or concepts of material things so much as about *individuals*, who are amongst other things the bearers or occupiers of social roles. These individuals use 'economic' concepts in certain kinds of practice which Marx attempts to explicate in theoretical terms.

Marx would have done well to call himself an individualist as well as a materialist, though he hardly ever did that anyway. As a 'material-ist' Marx carefully distinguished 'materialist method' from 'the abstract materialism of natural science ... which excludes the historical process'.[14] He could have made good use of this bold statement from *The German Ideology* (unpublished in his lifetime) by incorporating it into *Capital*, vol. 1, which he saw through the press himself:

> The premises from which we begin are not arbitrary ones, not dog-mas, but real premises from which abstraction can only be made in the imagination. They are the *real individuals*, their activity and the mat-erial conditions under which they live, both those which they find already existing and those produced by their activity.[15]

These remarks on *individuals* and their economic circumstances (their material environment and productive activities) could well have *pre-ceded* Marx's discourse on the commodity – the 'elementary form' of 'wealth' in 'societies in which the capitalist mode of production pre-vails' – in order to clarify the terms of the discussion.[16] In any case we could do with some better arguments than are found anywhere in his work on why the production of objects is necessarily the critical activity in social development. Instead all we have is the sketchy remarks on 'social production' and its 'modes' delivered in his 1859 Preface to *A Contribution to the Critique of Political Economy* and off-handedly reproduced in a footnote in *Capital*, vol. 1:

> My view is that each particular mode of production, and the relations of production corresponding to it at each given moment, in short 'the economic structure of society', is 'the real foundation, on which arises a legal and political superstructure and to which correspond definite forms of social consciousness', and that 'the mode of production of material life conditions the general process of social, political and intellectual life'.[17]

Almost uniquely, feminist arguments begin to press Marx and others on just this point. For example Irene Diamond and Nancy Hartsock write:

> Attention to the sexual division of labour also calls into question the appropriateness of the language of interests for understanding political life ... We should remember that the language of interests emerged along with the changes in the division of labour in production and reflected society's understanding of itself as dominated by rational economic men seeking to maximise their satisfactions.[18]

Steven Lukes also comments from a somewhat similar perspective:

> there is an individualist mode of thought, distinctive of modern Western cultures, which ... indelibly marks every interpretation we give of other modes of thought and every attempt we make to revise our own.
>
> Central to this mode of thought is a distinctive picture of the individual in relation to his roles and to his aims or purposes ... For, as Mary Midgley has well said, the 'whole idea of a free, independent, enquiring, choosing individual, an idea central to European thought, has always been essentially the idea of a male ... taking for granted the love and service of non-autonomous females (and indeed often of the less enlightened males as well).' It is a picture that has many well-known variants, from Hobbes through Bentham and the Utilitarians to modern existentialism ... [and] for many liberals and neo-classical

> economists he [the individual] becomes no more than a calculating
> machine interacting with others in the marketplace on the basis of
> revealed preferences.[19]

In using the economic concepts of everyday life, individuals enter,
as Marx says, 'independent of their will', into social 'relations' or roles
– but it is from those relations, economic ones such as 'capitalist' as
well as others not specifically considered by Marx, that their individuality is constructed.[20] For every individual, the whole constructed
individuality may very well be unique. In part this is because individual agency may play a role in such constructions, and we know
incontrovertibly that Marx accepted such a concept of agency from his
voluminous 'political' writings. In all those works, individual agency
and indeterminacy are all too manifest.[21]

However, the social construction of individuality is not the problem
set by Marx in *Capital*. Rather it is the theoretical specification of *capitalism* such that we can see the 'capitalist' in some individuals, how it
is possible for some individuals to be 'capitalists', and what has to be
true in order for 'capitalist' to be a way in which individuality can be
constructed by some individuals. It is of course a kind of individuality that is of crucial importance to them and to others.

Marx's discussion of this problem oscillates between presenting his
theory from the point of view of objects, specifically commodities (as
if they had a point of view), and from the point of view of their
'guardians' who are individual persons, owners of commodities, 'wills'.
It also oscillates between a conception of the individual as agent, who
might or might not perform the actions and use the concepts from
which social relations, over time, are constructed and maintained, and
a conception of the individual as 'bearer' or 'personification' of such
roles and relations entered in some fashion and performed in some
way that is independent of the will. Perhaps it would be better to say
that Marx's work *includes* these antinomies familiar to us all from
everyday life, and I shall be defending this reading of Marx below.

Concepts and activities

In pursuing his overall plan to present 'capital' through a critique of political economy, Marx works his way down an agenda of concepts, ones that were commonplace in that body of theory: commodity, value, money, capital, etc. But these are also in his view the elements in conscious individual behaviour – the roles, relations and concepts – through which 'things', 'products of labour' attain a life of their own. These 'things', human creations, come to control their makers' lives in crucial ways, and this is summarised in his theory of commodity fetishism.

The fetishism of commodities, according to Marx, consists in thinking and acting (because of the peculiar way in which production is organised) as if ordinary labour-products contained an inherent property (value), representing the socially necessary labour-time contained in that sort of commodity. Labour and its products, in that system, are related to one another by people as equalisable exchange-values. Hence labour-products appear (in a capitalist, commodity-producing society) to have 'inherent magical powers' or to be 'animated by a spirit', since their relationships to one another and to people (and some of the relationships between people) are determined less by conscious, collective human decision than by an uncontrolled process of equalisation in terms of value, by means of money.[22]

Marx presents economic concepts as denoting a world of things to which human individuals are then made relevant – with appropriate irony. This reinforces his critique of capitalist society as a pervasive, calculated and calculating fetishism. The historical origin of these concepts in human activity is more crucial for Marx than it is for the political economists (never mind conventional modern economists), because he argued that radically different concepts, roles and relations had existed in the past, still existed in the present and could exist in yet further forms in future. Therein lay a problem. If capitalist relations, roles and concepts did not exist beyond a certain time in the past, and if they had somehow to be invented by individual 'wills' or agents, who were in fact the 'bearers' or 'personifications' of already existing concepts, roles and relations, how precisely did the invention of capitalism come about?

Adam Smith's primeval hunters and fishermen were rightly ridiculed by Marx,[23] and Rousseau threw the difficulties in all our faces.[24] Marx had rather a plausible go at it in terms of the 'primitive community of natural origin', on the one hand, and a 'relationship of reciprocal isolation and foreignness', on the other. This 'relationship' did not, for Marx, arise out of anything, nor solve any problems. In that way he avoided developmental teleology and imputed rationalism. His account is impressive precisely because he located this new way of conceptualising human relations (with humans and to things) in historical circumstances, and then fought shy of producing a meta-theory about *why*. Something happened – something new – and, analytically speaking, that is enough:

> Things are in themselves external to man, and therefore alienable. In order that this alienation may be reciprocal, it is only necessary for men to agree tacitly to treat each other as the private owners of those alienable things, and, precisely for that reason, as persons who are independent of each other. But this relationship of reciprocal isolation and foreignness does not exist for the members of a primitive community of natural origin, whether it takes the form of a patriarchal family, an ancient Indian commune or an Inca state. The exchange of commodities begins where communities have their boundaries, at their points of contact with other communities, or with members of the latter. However, as soon as products have become commodities in the external relations of a community, they also, by reaction, become commodities in the internal life of the community ... They become exchangeable through the mutual desire of their owners to alienate them. In the meantime, the need for others' objects of utility gradually establishes itself. The constant repetition of exchange makes it a normal social process. In the course of time, therefore, at least some part of the products must be produced intentionally for the purpose of exchange.[25]

The difficulties concerning what might count as evidence for this kind of account, and the difficulties concerning how to gather it once what counts as evidence is determined, are very well known. I doubt that anthropologists and paleo-anthropologists are much further forward on this hypothesis, or something like it, simply because Marx's horror of anachronism has triumphed in principle, even if in practice it sometimes creeps back in.[26]

Consciousness and paradox

What then are the basic forms of consciousness from which capitalism emerged and which, in formal terms, characterise it? In Marx's historical anthropology, these are relationships of reciprocal isolation and foreignness, mutual desire for exchange, need for others' objects and intentional production for exchange.[27] In his *formal* explication of what it is to be the guardian of a commodity, the same terms occur:

> In order that these objects may enter into relation with each other as commodities, their guardians must place themselves in relation to one another as persons whose will resides in those objects, and must behave in such a way that each does not appropriate the commodity of the other, and alienate his own, except through an act to which both parties consent. The guardians must therefore recognise each other as owners of private property. This juridical relation, whose form is the contract, whether as part of a developed legal system or not, is a relation between two wills ...[28]

Somewhat surprisingly Marx goes on to argue that the 'content of this juridical relation (or relation of two wills) is itself determined by the economic relation'.[29] Here his account departs from the naturalism and nominalism of everyday 'commonsense'. Very crudely his argument is that economic concepts as they arise in the consciousness of social individuals are not best understood as mere effects of deeper 'desires' or feelings, or as neutral forms through which behaviour patterns or 'interests' are manifested and described. The concepts 'commodity', 'value' and 'capitalist' are not mere labels. While they were derived (somehow) from deeper elements of conscious behaviour (unspecified), they have a further, distinctly formative effect on human behaviour and individuality. They have a conceptual structure quite independent of the 'desires' or 'interests' of agents. They almost have agency themselves:

> The historical broadening and deepening of the phenomenon of exchange develops the opposition between use-value and value which is latent in the nature of the commodity. The need to give an external expression to this opposition for the purposes of commercial intercourse produces the drive towards an independent form of value,

which finds neither rest nor peace until an independent form has been achieved by the differentiation of commodities into commodities and money.[30]

Marx's claims on this account are very strong, so strong that they explain why and how commodity fetishism – control of persons' lives by their own products – is possible, and why he is happy commencing *Capital*, the *critique* of political economy, as if it were a work of political economy itself, i.e. with an apparently straightforward review of the *concepts* commodity, value, money and capital (see also chapters three and four below, which investigate the character and implications of Marx's critique). In Chapter 1 of *Capital* Marx presents the commodity as an abstraction that can be explicated in considerable detail, quite apart from any account of the feelings and desires of the individuals who must obviously be present in order for the concepts to have any meaning, and the things denoted to have any significance. The political economists had read the commodity back into individual consciousness and behaviour in a way that was anthropologically, historically, sociologically and politically outrageous, because they made commodity production seem primeval, invariable, unchangeable and authoritative. Marx suffered none of these faults, and he set down his own view in one quite breathtaking, doubly paradoxical sentence: 'The natural laws of the commodity have manifested themselves in the natural instinct of the owners of commodities.'[31]

I take this to mean that whatever 'instincts' or 'drives' or other biological imperatives one cares to assign to human beings as they became distinct (somehow, somewhere) from other primates, these 'instincts' have long been overlaid with socially constructed patterns of behaviour which have varied amongst different groups throughout history so far. There is not only no obvious way of checking any presumptions about human instincts against their original form, there is no presumed continuity of a biological character which is so significant with respect to complex contemporary behaviour patterns that these patterns are explained or determined by any such characteristics. 'Desire and aversion', 'propensity to truck and barter', 'rational self-interested utility maximisation' etc., all fail on this view as trans-historical categories.

Commonplace categories like the 'commodity' have a useful, though limited function, however, if we confine our view to commodity-producing societies (which are historically specific and not universal) and within those societies to commodity producers. We must also note that in Marx's view labour (hence the labourer, from which it is inseparable) becomes a commodity, even though it is not strictly covered by his own original definition: 'an external object, a thing which through its qualities satisfies human needs of whatever kind.'[32] Thus, as commodity production extends across more and more activities in society, and eventually becomes the predominant framework within which the activities pursued by individuals are located, so the individuals themselves are socially constructed as commodity producers to the point where their very instincts, which seem so 'natural' to them, derive from the 'laws' or conceptual structure of commodity production.

The first apparent paradox in Marx's statement is that natural instincts in individuals are not generally conceived as the manifestation of some historically peculiar, socially created *object*. Rather, the individual human is usually taken as a datum and given trans-historical 'instincts' that exist independently of external things. Indeed the external objects are usually relevant only because the instincts are supposed to require them, and certainly not the reverse. In my reading, Marx has done rather more here than gently reprove Smith and Ricardo for their assumptions concerning supposed trans-historical characteristics of human nature; and he has done rather more than gently pat their successors on the back for admitting that their economics relates exclusively to commodity-producing societies, so leaving anthropologists and historians to make what they can of social activity in other circumstances.

Commodity-producing societies, as I read Marx, are distinct from other types of society in history and in the contemporary world. In commodity-producing societies there are socially constructed cat--egories of commodity production and socially constructed individuals, down to their 'natural instincts'. These categories are not a mere manifestation of instinct, whether primeval, invariable and unchangeable in character, or historically or culturally developed in some superficial way. Rather they are constitutive of individuals and of society. About the ultimate origins (causal or otherwise) of commodity production itself, Marx has nothing very substantial to say. As noted above, he provides no explanation why some individuals begin to see themselves as 'isolated' or 'foreign' with respect to others, and why they see the exchange of material things to satisfy individual 'desire' as a possible activity. Enigmatically he says: 'They have therefore already acted before thinking.' Whatever the historical circumstances (now inaccessible), we have the results before us in societies 'in which the capitalist mode of production prevails'.[33]

So far this is none too surprising for the contemporary social theorist who has the anthropological and historical awareness that Marx's work so successfully stimulated. What might truly surprise is his second apparent paradox. On Marx's account the commodity is said to have 'natural laws', yet it is pre-eminently a human creation, and therefore presumably 'artificial' rather than 'natural' in some extra-human way. Moreover it is something created by humans in a specific form of society, a form that is historically peculiar. For Marx this form is far removed from any preceding 'natural' condition of humanity that might have existed before the development of whatever technological advances made surplus production a reality and commodity production a possibility.

It seems to me that Marx is arguing that a relatively recent social construction such as the commodity has in it 'natural laws', or a specifiable conceptual structure, such that individuals are socially constructed in predictable ways and that the development and downfall of a society in which these laws prevail can be predicted as well. Yet he permits no ultimate sacrifice of individual agency, as individuals may well attain a consciousness of this conceptual structure. Moreover, if that structure is to be replaced, they must act to overthrow it. He envisions a conceptual structure alternative to the 'natural laws' of the commodity such that society – and socially constructed individuals – could be built anew (see chapter five below). He discusses this possibility in terms of a revolutionary politics that depends on conscious, individual agents (see chapter six below), not on some holistic agency that is metaphysical or teleological. Marx's language concerning 'class' and 'history' has traditionally been read in a way that is contradictory to any very strong doctrine of individualism; whereas it makes more sense, it seems to me, to read it as presupposing the individualism I have outlined, by which individuals are socially constituted, yet capable of individual innovation and collective change.[34]

Money and production

What are the 'natural laws' of the commodity? What predictions about society can be derived from them? And what is their relation to individual agency?

Marx's explication of the concept money, a special instance of the commodity, traces the conceptual structure he sees in that concept very clearly and allows him to generalise about society (as an entity with an inherent pattern of laws) and about individuals (as socially constructed). On my reading, Marx's specification of the conceptual structure inherent in the concept money is the centrepiece of his critique of political economy, and his critical model of the capitalist economy. This is because he sees money as a conceptual and practical development of the exchange of surplus goods and a conceptual and practical prerequisite for capital. Money is said to be a measure of equivalence in exchange-value, and to entail a quantitative expansion to infinity by its very definition. From these conceptual properties Marx derives the possibilities for human behaviour that characterise the socially constructed individuals of capitalist society, pre-eminently capitalists, who have the best chance to display the greed and selfishness that appear at the *conclusion* of his discussion in the opening chapters of *Capital* (I trace this conceptual derivation in chapter three). Most social theorists, pre-eminently those in the rational-choice and game-theoretic schools, produce precisely the opposite kind of argument, moving from 'need' or 'desire', 'interests' and selfishness.[35] For Marx workers are by no means excepted from this greedy and selfish behaviour, though he is not at pains for political reasons to stress this fact. In the *Communist Manifesto* he writes: 'The organisation of the proletarians into a class ... is disrupted time and again by competition amongst the workers themselves.'[36]

Because of the way that Marx relates the structure inherent in socially constructed concepts to the possibility for individual agents to act on their own volition in certain ways, his explication sometimes gives the impression of an oddly dissociated anthropomorphism, as in this passage where the locus of the mentioned 'need' and 'drive' is not specifically established:

> The hoarding drive is boundless in its nature. Qualitatively or formally considered, money is independent of all limits, that is, it is the universal representative of material wealth because it is directly convertible into any other commodity. But at the same time every actual sum of money is limited in amount, and therefore has only a limited efficacy as a means of purchase. This contradiction between the quantitative limitation and the qualitative lack of limitation of money keeps driving the hoarder back to his Sisyphean task: accumulation.[37]

This sometimes seems to commit Marx, rather in contrast to the indeterminacy he assigns to actual human agents, to a determinism in social development:

> Money necessarily crystallises out of the process of exchange, in which different products of labour are in fact equated with each other, and thus converted into commodities.[38]

And to teleological accounts of social phenomena:

> There is a contradiction immanent in the function of money as the means of payment ... This contradiction bursts forth in that aspect of an industrial and commercial crisis which is known as a monetary crisis ... As the hart pants after fresh water, so pants his [the soul of the bourgeois] after money, the only wealth.[39]

And even to an anti-individualistic holism:

> In truth, however, value is here the subject of a process in which, while constantly assuming the form in turn of money and commodities, it changes its own magnitude, throws off surplus-value from itself considered as original value, and thus valorises itself independently.[40]

And ultimately to a crypto-idealism: 'Its [money's] mode of existence becomes adequate to its concept.'[41]

A reconstruction of Marx's explication of the concept money can account for these comments in a way that is consistent with his general view of social concepts and individual agency, as I have presented it, thus undercutting conventional accounts which either present one side or the other, or present Marx as offering contradictory theses, unawares. On my reading, Marx is committed to a view that a commodity-producing society is by definition one in which useful goods are valued for exchange in accordance with some measure – money, a standard of price. This is a definition with which few, least of all economists, would disagree. More controversially he takes money to be, or to represent, one kind of commodity, e.g. gold, which measures value because it becomes a universal equivalent. A certain weight of gold becomes fixed as a unit of measurement, and the amount of the universal equivalent, e.g. gold, that measures the value of a commodity, is then itself reckoned in terms of standard units which are familiar to us in prices.[42]

That commodities are valued for exchange in money terms is uncontentious; what is contentious in Marx's account is his view that it is not money that establishes the commensurability of commodities commonly seen in prices, but that their commensurability is already established within the commodities themselves in terms of objectified labour (this difficulty is explored in chapter four below). Because of this pre-existing commensurability[43] certain relations can be traced, and certain conclusions drawn, about social behaviour that 'must' eventually appear or must be 'necessary' in some sense. Note that in Marx's account the very first exchanges do not presuppose a commensurability based on labour, so in those exchanges quantitative relations are 'determined purely by chance'. Only after 'constant repetition of exchange' does 'the quantitative proportion' between things exchanged become dependent on 'their production itself'.

For Marx, concept anticipates action, indeed creates the possibility for actions of certain types that simply could not exist other than as an instance of the concept he claims to discern. This conceptual structure is said to have been initiated in the rudimentary exchanges of social groups he could not observe, and because they were presumably pre-literate, it seems unlikely that evidence of the earliest kinds of exchanges could ever be found against which his view might be tested. The upshot of this is that Marx's social theory is crucially dependent on a structure alleged to inhere in concepts, particularly money, and the way those concepts provide possibilities for individual and social development along certain lines, as and when agents undertake it.

Thus in Marx's work there is, in my reading, an explanatory and predictive consistency between his concepts and the observable behaviour of individuals in capitalist society, but this consistency is no simple reflection of the observable behaviour, nor is the observable behaviour a definitive test of the validity of his analysis as social science. Marx observes of his own society that the owners of commodities bring them 'into relation as values ... by bringing them into an opposing relation with some one other commodity, which serves as universal equivalent'. But he mentions that kind of observation only to remind the reader: 'We have *already* reached that result by our analysis of the commodity.'[44]

In the next chapter I shall be pursuing this discussion further by focusing on Marx's treatment of money, the crucial concept in his work in *Capital*, as it is only when money is established that capitalism becomes possible in practice, and conversely, it is from the logic inherent in money as a concept that the practical possibility of capitalism arises. By doing this I shall be linking his explication of that particular economic concept with much wider issues about individuality and agency, and also addressing the relationship between Marx's theoretical work and contemporary rational-choice theory.

Notes

1 For discussions of Engels' 'dialectics', see Terrell Carver, *Engels* (Oxford, Oxford University Press, 1981); Terrell Carver, *Marx and Engels: The Intellectual Relationship* (Brighton, Harvester/Wheatsheaf, 1983); Terrell Carver, *Friedrich Engels: His Life and Thought* (London, Macmillan, 1989).

2 See George V. Plekhanov, *Fundamental Problems of Marxism*, trans. Julius Katzer (London, Lawrence & Wishart, 1969); Z. A. Jordan, *The Evolution of Dialectical Materialism* (London, Macmillan, 1967).

3 Louis Althusser, *For Marx*, trans. Ben Brewster (London, Allen Lane, 1969). For diverse essays on the relevance of Hegel (in various guises) to an understanding of Marx's method, see Fred Moseley (ed.), *Marx's Method in Capital: A Reexamination* (Atlantic Highlands NJ, Humanities Press, 1993).

4 Carver, *Engels*, p. 49; Carver, *Marx and Engels*, pp. 105–6; Terrell Carver, 'Marx – and Hegel's *Logic*', *Political Studies*, 24:1 (1976), 57–68; Richard Rorty, *Contingency, Irony and Solidarity* (Cambridge, Cambridge University Press, 1989), ch. 1.

5 Eugen von Böhm-Bawerk, *The Positive Theory of Capital*, trans. William Smart (New York, Stechert, 1930; first published 1891); John Eatwell, Murray Milgate, Peter Newman (eds), *Marxian Economics* (London, Macmillan, 1990).

6 Karl Marx, *Capital*, vol. 1, trans. Ben Fowkes (Harmondsworth, Penguin, 1976, repr. 1986), pp. 125, 280.

7 See Steven Lukes, *Marxism and Morality* (Oxford, Oxford University Press, 1987), and R. G. Peffer, *Marxism, Morality and Social Justice* (Princeton NJ, Princeton University Press, 1990).

8 See Terrell Carver and Paul Thomas (eds), *Rational Choice Marxism* (London, Macmillan, 1995).

9 Karl Marx, *Theses on Feuerbach*, in Karl Marx and Frederick Engels, *The German Ideology*, ed. C. J. Arthur (London, Lawrence & Wishart, 1970), pp. 121–3.

10 For 'regime of truth', see Michel Foucault, *The Foucault Reader*, ed. Paul Rabinow (Harmondsworth, Penguin, 1986).

11 Marx, *Capital*, vol. 1, p. 89.

12 On this theme, see Carver, *Marx and Engels*, pp. 96–158.

13 Marx, *Capital*, vol. 1, p. 178.

14 Possibly the term 'individualist' was too closely associated in Marx's mind with the arch-egoist Max Stirner, who was ruthlessly pilloried as 'Saint Max' in *The German Ideology*, Part Two; Marx, *Capital*, vol. 1, pp. 494–5 n.

15 Marx, *German Ideology*, p. 18, my emphasis.

16 Marx, *Capital*, vol. 1, p. 125.

17 Marx, *Capital*, vol. 1, p. 175 n.

18 Irene Diamond and Nancy Hartsock, 'Beyond interests in politics: a comment on Virginia Sapiro's "When are interests interesting? the problem of political representation of women"', *American Political Science Review*, 75:3 (1981), 719.

19 Michael Carrithers, Steven Collins, Steven Lukes (eds), *The Category of the Person* (Cambridge, Cambridge University Press, 1985), pp. 298–9; see also Jeff Hearn, *The Gender of Oppression: Men, Masculinity, and the Critique of Marxism* (Brighton, Wheatsheaf Books, 1987), pp. 98, 100.

20 Marx, Preface to *A Contribution to the Critique of Political Economy*, in Karl Marx, *Later Political Writings*, ed. and trans. Terrell Carver (Cambridge, Cambridge University Press, 1996), pp. 159–60.

21 See, *inter alia*, *The Eighteenth Brumaire of Louis Bonaparte*, in Marx, *Later Political Writings*, pp. 31–127. Very few commentators have attempted to read Marx's brief methodological comments in the light of his voluminous writings on history as 'men' made it in his own time, rather than the reverse procedure, which has been standard since Engels; Richard W. Miller in *Analyzing Marx* (Princeton NJ, Princeton University Press, 1984) is an important exception, and I have employed the former strategy myself in *Marx's Social Theory*

(Oxford, Oxford University Press, 1982).

22 Marx, *Capital*, vol. 1, pp. 167–8. See the exposition in Terrell Carver, 'Marx's commodity fetishism', *Inquiry*, 18:1 (1975), 39–63.

23 See the 'Introduction' in Karl Marx, *Grundrisse: Foundations of the Critique of Political Economy (Rough Draft)*, trans. Martin Nicolaus (Harmondsworth, Penguin/New Left Review, 1974), pp. 83–5, and commentary in Terrell Carver (ed. and trans.), *Karl Marx: Texts on Method* (Oxford, Basil Blackwell, 1975), pp. 88–101.

24 Introduction to the *Discourse on the Origin of Inequality*: 'Let us begin then by laying all facts aside, as they do not affect the question. The investigations we may enter into, in treating this subject, must not be considered as historical truths, but only as mere conditional and hypothetical reasonings, rather calculated to explain the nature of things, than to ascertain their actual origin; just like the hypotheses which our physicists daily form respecting the formation of the world'. Jean-Jacques Rousseau, *The Social Contract and Discourses* (London, Dent, 1973), p. 45.

25 Marx, *Capital*, vol. 1, p. 182.

26 For a discussion and defence of Rousseau's anthropology, see Robert Wokler, *Rousseau* (Oxford, Oxford University Press, 1995), ch. 3; for a critical discussion of the way that pre-history has been conceptualised and written, see Michael Shanks and Christopher Tilley, *Social Theory and Archaeology* (Cambridge, Polity Press, 1987).

27 Marx, *Capital*, vol. 1, p. 182.

28 Marx, *Capital*, vol. 1, p. 178.

29 Marx, *Capital*, vol. 1, p. 178.

30 Marx, *Capital*, vol. 1, p. 181.

31 Marx, *Capital*, vol. 1, p. 180.

32 Marx, *Capital*, vol. 1, p. 125.

33 Marx, *Capital*, vol. 1, pp. 125, 180–2.

34 This view owes a good deal to Anthony Giddens' theory of structuration; see, for example, *The Constitution of Society* (Cambridge, Polity Press, 1984).

35 Marx, *Capital*, vol. 1, p. 280.

36 Marx, *Later Political Writings*, p. 10.

37 Marx, *Capital*, vol. 1, pp. 230–1.

38 Marx, *Capital*, vol. 1, p. 181.

39 Marx, *Capital*, vol. 1, pp. 235–6.

40 Marx, *Capital*, vol. 1, p. 255.

41 Marx, *Capital*, vol. 1, p. 241.

42 Marx, *Capital*, vol. 1, p. 192.

43 Marx, *Capital*, vol. 1, p. 182.

44 Marx, *Capital*, vol. 1, p. 180, my emphasis.

CHAPTER THREE

Individuals and agency: Marx's vision

Commodities and money

Suppose we accept, for the moment, Marx's contentious claims that money is a commodity whose commensurability with other commodities is established 'in themselves' by means of their common property 'being the products of labour', just for the sake of noting the analytical principles he employs and the kind of conceptual structure he establishes for his concept of money.[1] Having explicated those principles it is of course open to us to consider, as a quite separate exercise, whether some similar conceptual structure can be found with respect to the more commonplace and less contentious claim that the commensurability of useful objects as commodities is established in terms of monetary value alone, which *itself* establishes equivalence, i.e. the conventional view in modern economics. For the moment I am asking readers to focus on the general character of Marx's analysis on the assumption that it does not stand or fall on an acceptance or rejection of a 'labour theory of value', generally regarded as the chief difference between Marx's work and most economics developed since his time (I address that issue in chapter four below).

Marx begins his analysis of money in conceptual terms as follows:

Everyone knows, if nothing else, that commodities have a common value-form which contrasts in the most striking manner with the motley natural forms of their use-values. I refer to the money-form. Now, however, we have to perform a task never even attempted by bourgeois economics. That is, we have to show the origin of this money-form, we have to trace the development of the expression of value contained in the value-relation of commodities from its simplest, almost imperceptible outline to the dazzling money-form. When this has been done, the mystery of money will immediately disappear.[2]

From the 'simple, isolated or accidental form of value' Marx deduces the 'whole mystery': 'x commodity A = y commodity B'. In this simple equation itself, the conceptual relation most central to Marx's analysis of exchange-value, and hence of money, he notes that the value of A is represented in B, or is 'relative to B'; the first commodity plays an 'active role'; B fulfils the function of an 'equivalent', a 'passive role'. To further this conceptual analysis he uses other principles:

> The relative form of value and the equivalent form are two inseparable moments, which belong to and mutually condition each other; but, at the same time, they are mutually exclusive or opposed extremes, i.e. poles of the expression of value ... The same commodity cannot, therefore, simultaneously appear in both forms in the same expression of value. These forms rather exclude each other as polar opposites.

The simple or isolated form 'automatically passes over into a more complete form' in his conceptual analysis, because it 'only expresses the value of a commodity A in one commodity of another kind', exactly which being 'a matter of complete indifference'. This leads to an infinitely expandable series z commodity A = either u commodity B or v commodity C, etc., etc., limited only by the number of commodities distinct from A.[3]

As I read the text, Marx's simple or isolated expression of value was never derived straightforwardly from the 'desires' or 'interests' of two real or hypothetical commodity owners. The value-form is supposed to be a conceptual development of the relations inherent in the concept 'commodity'; historical exchanges merely manifest the consequences of this conceptual structure without necessarily tracing the exact stages of it fully developed forms. This point is rather well caught in C. J. Arthur's discussion of Marx's methodology, as he contrasts it with Engels' attempted distinction between 'logical' and 'historical' methods. *Capital* presents a fully developed inter-relationship of money and commodities as capital, and analyses this in a formal and abstract way, attributing it to 'societies in which the capitalist mode of production prevails', though leaving aside both contingent deviations between contemporary societies and the model. As Arthur says, Marx was quite clear that the historical development of capital as money and commodities, linked together eventually to produce 'surplus value', did not reproduce the stages of his abstract analysis exactly. While Chapter 1 of Marx's work begins with 'The Commodity', Part 1 of the book is entitled 'Commodities and Money', and the title *Capital* frames the discussion of both. Arthur writes:

> What is distinctly different about capitalism is that the actualisation of value [in the exchange relations of commodities] as a totality of form[al] determinations imposes a requirement for these separate functions to be integrated through the evolution of a single money commodity. Given a single, though complex, concept of money, then the exposition of the totality can develop its functions in the most appropriate systematic order, without any historical implications. Thus money has a key role now as an internal moment of capital; this gives it quite different determinations than any 'money' that performs some particular function (e.g. as circulating medium) in pre-capitalist formations.[4]

At a rarefied level of discourse, then, Marx identifies 'defects' in the relative side of each equation, taking the chain equation by equation in Chapter 1 of *Capital*:

> Firstly, the relative expression of value of the commodity is incomplete, because the series of its representations never comes to an end. The chain, of which each equation of value is a link, is liable at any moment to be lengthened by a newly created commodity, which will provide the material for a fresh expression of value. Secondly, it is a motley mosaic of disparate and unconnected expressions of value. And lastly, if, as must be the case, the relative value of each commodity is expressed in this expanded form, it follows that the relative form of value of each commodity is an endless series of expressions of value which are all different from the relative form of value of every other commodity.[5]

And similarly he finds defects in the equivalents:

Since the natural form of each particular kind of commodity is one particular equivalent form amongst innumerable other equivalent forms, the only equivalent forms which exist are limited ones, and each of them excludes all the others.[6]

Altering the series to separate equations yields:

z commodity A $=$ u commodity B
z commodity A $=$ v commodity C, etc.

Reversing the equations yields:

u commodity B $=$ z commodity A
v commodity C $=$ z commodity A etc.

And simplifying to a general form yields a list of different commodities in varying amounts all equal to z commodity A as a common equivalent.[7] 'By this form', Marx comments, 'commodities are, for the first time, really brought into relation with each other as values, or permitted to appear to each other as exchange-values'.[8]

Overall Marx recounts this conceptual development as one of 'polar antagonism'. In the first form, it is contained but not yet fixed, depending on whether the equation is read forwards or backwards. In the second form, the relative and equivalent poles can no longer be reversed. And in the last form, relative value has become general for all commodities except one, which is uniquely excluded from the relative pole because it is a universal equivalent.[9]

When this exclusion becomes restricted to one commodity, such as gold, it 'confronts' other commodities 'as money only because it previously confronted them as a commodity'.[10] Gold as coin has a 'price form', and the universal equivalent has become money. Its conceptual relation to commodity exchange can be retraced, as the stages in that relation are entailments of the commodity itself, and ultimately of the relationship entered into by the 'isolated' and 'foreign' wills when they initiated the exchanges from which commodity exchange and commodity production eventually proceeded. In that way the inherent opposition between use-value and value which is latent in the concept of the commodity is developed historically by agents who discover in that conceptual relation the 'need to give an external expression' to an opposition – the 'drive towards an independent form of value' – for the 'purposes of commercial intercourse'.[11]

Forms and contradictions

For Marx the physical existence of commodities distinct from money is the eventual external expression in social life of an inherent opposition between use-value and value that the concept 'commodity' necessarily contains, but does not abolish. Rather it provides, conceptually speaking, the form within which this contradiction has 'room to move', and that 'room to move' in conceptual terms is what allows humans to develop the physical reality of commodities and money in society. That 'room to move' is analysed as an opposition within the commodity; but both sides of the opposition between use-value and value appear in social reality as commodities (commodities and the money-commodity). In Marx's analysis we have a 'unity of differences' (commodities as the unity of the 'opposition' use-value and value) expressed at 'two opposite poles' (commodities and money) and 'at each pole in an opposite way':

> This is the alternating relation between the poles: the commodity is in reality a use-value; its existence as a value appears only ideally, in its price, through which it is related to the real embodiment of its value, the gold which confronts it as its opposite. Inversely, the material of gold ranks only as the materialisation of value, as money. It is therefore in reality exchange-value. Its use-value appears only ideally in the series of expressions of relative value within which it confronts all the other commodities as the totality of real embodiments of its utility. These antagonistic forms of the commodities are the real forms of motion of the process of exchange.[12]

Marx traces these oppositions through the process of simple circulation of commodities and money, and he concludes:

> Circulation bursts through all the temporal, spatial and personal barriers imposed by the direct exchange of products, and it does this by splitting up the direct identity present in this case between the exchange of one's own product and the acquisition of someone else's into the two antithetical segments of sale and purchase.[13]

He explains this process in conceptual terms:

> To say that these mutually independent and antithetical processes form an internal unity is to say also that their internal unity moves forward through external antitheses. These two processes lack internal independence because they complement each other. Hence, if the assertion of their external independence proceeds to a certain point, their unity violently makes itself felt ...[14]

Marx's conclusion, as I draw it, is 'the possibility of crises'. Crises are a possibility because of the 'room to move' that there is in the conceptual structure of the commodity. This 'room to move' opens the possibility for human agents to produce physical and temporal disruptions in the circulation of commodities and money that takes place between sellers and buyers. Practical relations between persons as buyers and sellers are created as they 'act out' or instantiate the concepts that are constitutive of economic behaviour, including the 'tensions' inherent in the way that these concepts are related to each other. The conceptual structure of the commodity specifies behavioural 'tensions' that are possible between persons. This is because it is the relations amongst the concepts that define the commodity itself, particularly contradictions or oppositions, that make these 'tensions' a possibility in human practice. Thus economic behaviour proceeds only more or less smoothly – giving rise to the possibility of crises that disrupt the production and exchange of goods – because the particular conceptual structure of the commodity is what it is.[15] Eventually in 'world money', the currency of world trade (which Marx took to be bullion), commodities develop their value universally. This marks the full extent of development in actuality of the money-commodity, and Marx then makes the startling claim: 'Its mode of existence becomes adequate to its concept.'[16]

This is an almost unearthly pronouncement in which the full extent of Marx's method is made plain. He argues that the structure and development of society is prefigured in the very categories which agents use, and that analysis of these categories yields non-trivial results. Moreover these are the categories which allow human beings to be *individuals* of a certain kind and *agents* of a certain type. Thus Marx argues that the sphere of exchange has created the possibility for the liberal 'Eden of the innate rights of man', the 'exclusive realm of Freedom, Equality, Property and Bentham'. This is the realm of free wills, free persons, equality before the law, equality in the exchange of equivalent value, and calculation of advantage: 'the selfishness, the gain and the private interest of each.'[17]

These are precisely the presumptions of liberal individualism, especially in its economic mode, and in my reading, they are the *conclusion* of Marx's analysis, not his starting point. His starting point is not biological or behavioural in any important degree, but conceptual, in that the important transformations in behaviour that have produced a world where there is 'Benthamite behaviour' are only possible because of the concepts through which individuals are constructed, as they learn to use them. On this theme Lukes writes: 'We may ... reject individualistic ways of conceiving the person ... But these are the ways by which we are culturally formed and they inevitably colour our every attempt to interpret the worlds of others or to seek to change our own.'[18] We are enmeshed in this conceptual structure, and we are to some considerable degree a self-created image of it, as are the social institutions that we construct on that basis. What, then, are the intellectual and political consequences of taking this view of history, agency and society?

Individualism and holism

Individualists and holists alike have discovered some affinity with Marx, but have also taken him to task for inconsistency. This is not surprising, as Marx put himself squarely in their line of fire. On three now famous occasions he raised the crucial issue: What is the relationship between individuals as autonomous agents and individuals as socially determined or constructed? In doing so he made comments that now bear on these classic debates: Can any concept of autonomous agency be assigned to individuals? To what extent must explanations in social science be constructed exclusively from 'properties' that are said to be those of individuals? Does social science support or undermine ethical systems or moral doctrines that presuppose individual autonomy in making choices and bearing responsibility? Marx wrote on these themes in varying contexts; here are three well-known passages:

> As individuals express their life, so they are. What they are, therefore, coincides with their production, both with what they produce and with how they produce. The nature of individuals thus depends on the material conditions determining their production.[19]

> The mode of production of material life conditions the general process of social, political and intellectual life. It is not the consciousness of men that determines their existence but their social existence that determines their consciousness.[20]

> My standpoint, from which the development of the economic formation of society is viewed as a process of natural history, can less than any other make the individual responsible for relations whose creature he remains, socially speaking, however much he may subjectively raise himself above them.[21]

D. F. B. Tucker has argued a case for Marx as a methodological and ethical individualist – a case that spells out in what senses Marx is identified as such and is not associated with holistic alternatives. Tucker regards Marx as an 'ethical individualist' because 'he places great value on the achievement of autonomy', so much so that 'his critique of liberalism arises out of his claim that the prevailing conditions in liberal society actually serve to frustrate our efforts to be self-directing'. Tucker also characterises Marx's methodology as individualist, saying that this is so 'because the motor mechanisms … are the choices which rational individuals would make if they were intent on protecting and enhancing their individual interests'.[22] In Mark Warren's terms, Marx adheres to a methodological individualism of events, and a methodological individualism of actions as objects of explanation, eschewing a methodological individualism of subjects, which entails a reductionist view that only properties of individuals are explanatory.[23]

However, Tucker's work falls short of a full account, because Marx's individualism has peculiarities that he does not suspect. These lie in the way that the individual is socially constructed, and in tracing these arguments it becomes evident how Marx was sometimes identified, quite incorrectly, as a holist.[24] In my view, Marx's individualism is conceptually rather than biologically or psychologically based, so it is unusually general in its presuppositions. This means that it is consistent with respect to individuals who do not always behave in an 'individualistic' manner presupposing self-interest and modern self-consciousness. In that way he also escapes anachronism and cultural imperialism. He attacked other theorists, chiefly political economists, for these faults.

This had two further results. One was that his criticisms of simplistic individualism based on 'drives', 'sentiments', 'interests' and so on, have been very largely accepted, and few outside the domain of strictly conventional economics now wish to defend the political economists from his charges that their view of 'human nature' was unhistorical, ideological and viciously circular. Rom Harré comments:

> In recent years the study of human psychology has been undergoing profound changes ... Behind the more superficial changes to be seen in every branch of psychology there lies a deeper revolution ... This deep-lying revolt appears in the rise of cognitive science, through which human action can be related to the reality of processes of thinking. It also appears in the shift towards research programmes which pay attention to the languages of mankind, their diversity, and the very distinctive practices within which they play a major role. This change of focus in research has been accompanied by a sudden realisation that much of what passed for scientific psychology in the era of simplistic empiricism may be no more than a projection of local custom and practices, even local political philosophies.[25]

And Claire Armon-Jones writes:

> The principle of the 'sociocultural constitution of emotion' is one aspect of a general theory concerning the sociocultural constitution of individual experience ... One outcome of these analyses is a model of general experience as constituted by what it is conceptualised as, and of conceptualisations as essentially deriving from the language, beliefs and social rules ... of the agent's cultural community.[26]

The other result was that in making these criticisms Marx was taken to be rejecting – though possibly in an inconsistent way – any individualism at all. This, as Tucker argues, is far from being the case.

Marx's individualism

What kind of individualist was Marx? Can his views on the social construction of individuals generate a plausible individualism? What concepts and methods does he use to reconcile the social construction of individuals with individual agency?

I have argued that Marx's best work on the social construction of individuals lies in *Capital*, vol. 1, where he considers the category 'capitalist' as defining a social role played out by real individuals, some of whom turn up, for example, in the *Reports of the Inspectors of Factories* which he cites. 'Capitalist' for Marx was not purely an ideal type. However, his famous comment in the Preface to the first edition of *Capital* (1867), like all his other attempts to explain himself, has hardly dissipated misunderstanding as he intended:

> To prevent possible misunderstandings, let me say this. I do not by any means depict the capitalist and the landowner in rosy colours. But individuals are dealt with here only in so far as they are the personifications of economic categories, the bearers of particular class-relations and interests.[27]

This passage indicates that for Marx there are real capitalists and landowners who are real individuals, though in his book aspects of their real existence *other than* their performance of certain social roles are ignored. From standpoints *other than the one from which his book is written*, aspects of an individual landowner's or capitalist's real existence as an individual might be noteworthy, even the object of the moral judgements which *Capital* itself does not take up, and which Marx eschewed as a *political* strategy for communists. 'Socially speaking', the individual is not responsible for the existence of social roles and for the one s/he occupies, but from other points of view responsibility may very well be relevant. When an individual avoids or condemns certain social roles, which Marx fully admits is a possible action for individuals to take, the roles remain in existence. These are the roles he intends to analyse in his book, but commitment to this project does not necessarily entail any radical claims that individuals have no real existence, that there is no such thing as agency, that morality and ethics are meaningless. As I see it, Marx's position is carefully agnostic, and he neither claimed to explore all these areas nor offered comprehensive albeit implicit theories.

The battle over rational-choice Marxism has been raging for some time,[28] and there is no doubt that this 'paradigm' is rooted in individualism, though understandably different practitioners define it in various ways.[29] Still, this individualism can invariably be traced to the presumptions of neo-classical economics,[30] and there are many social scientists (or simply students of society) who are unhappy with that approach for a host of different reasons. Marxists have no monopoly on criticisms of individualist premises. What has happened recently is that theorists inspired by economic individualism have begun to overlap the Marxist agenda in their interests, and an almighty explosion has been the result.[31]

Just to make matters even more complicated and less tediously binary, I propose to explore in detail where rational-choice Marxism and Marx's own work overlap, a project that rational-choice Marxists have not themselves addressed in any notably productive way. Either they have simply adopted what they take to be problems associated with the Marxist tradition, such as class conflict and exploitation, without being overly concerned with Marx's own views, or they have critically reconstructed views that they ascribe to Marx, with great emphasis on the criticism, typically arguing that his work would have been better had he adhered rigorously to the assumptions of economic individualism and game theory.[32] Contrary to both those strategies, I have argued above in this chapter that Marx explored, to great effect, the very nature of individualism, and that the strengths and weaknesses of rational-choice and game-theoretic presumptions, however applied, can be more accurately assessed once Marx's own position has been explicated.

Rational-choice Marxism

At this point the relevance of rational-choice Marxism to Marx's work can be freshly established. In particular the application of certain analytical methods — strategic analysis, equilibrium theory, collective action and decision-making theory — looks like an obvious way to develop the theory of the 'commodity owner' (which includes, of course, the wage labourer) already produced by Marx, provided the work is confined to commodity-producing societies. Indeed, Roemer attempts to distinguish 'analytical Marxism' from 'conventional Marxism' by pointing to 'an unabashed commitment to abstraction' not found among Marxists. Yet this is the very method that Marx himself recommended in *Capital*, vol. 1, p. 90. Roemer very convincingly sketches in a rational-choice view of class formation by 'agents in the working-class' that is, unbeknownst to him, fully consistent with Marx's view of agency in general, commodity owners in particular and market relations overall.[33]

Roemer also alludes to a more basic problem, that of the way that individual preferences are formed, commenting that little work has been done on this within the rational-choice framework. This was for the simple reason that many theorists preferred to take the rational self-interested utility-maximiser as 'given' and 'timeless' for one reason or other, none of them very good. George Ainslie writes:

> Quantitative description of the value of concrete objects became the science of economics. By restricting its attention to goods that trade in a cash market, this discipline has been able to describe striking regularities in how we value these goods. It has created a nucleus of well-articulated rules for understanding value. However, this restriction of attention has had a distorting effect. The territory of monetary transactions has sometimes become disconnected from the broad realm of human choice. Money has often been spoken about as 'behaving' in various ways, almost as if it had a life outside the minds of its owners. For all the usefulness that this analytic fiction may have had, it has tended to create a self-contained body of procedures without reference to the human motivational processes that actually determine value.[34]

And Shaun Hargreaves-Heap and Martin Hollis comment:

> How people think of themselves affects the way they make their own history and economists are powerful guides. If orthodoxy were to succeed in getting us to see ourselves as maximising individuals, bound only by a cash nexus or other instrumental relationships, and if it can get governments to treat us so, then, perversely, its predictions might fare better. That would be a terrible price for progress in economics.[35]

To Marxists, Roemer attributes a vague view that the individual is formed by society, and possibly the *reductio* that only the evolutionary development of modes of production really matters in historical change, so 'the preferences of agents play only a passive role'. By way of compromise between rational-choice theorists and this Marxist view, he suggests that 'culture chooses a person's preferences for him [*sic*]' *and* that there might be rational foundations behind an individual who 'chooses' amongst 'meta-preferences' or 'preference profiles'.[36] These rational foundations are only vaguely sketched:

> A theory of ideology formation is needed. Perhaps ideology is an institution which cuts transaction costs of various kinds; or perhaps ideology should be conceived of as a set of satisficing rules which an agent adopts to limit his own feasible set.[37]

Marx's work in *Capital*, vol. 1, is much closer, on my reading, to the research programme Roemer outlines for 'rational-choice Marxism' than he seems to realise. This is because he relies on a version of 'conventional Marxism' and admits a 'lack of Marxian exegesis' in his work and in the work of his associates.[38] Re-reading *Capital* reveals that the 'teleology' Roemer wants to jettison is no part of the methodology Marx employs, and what Roemer calls 'micro-foundations' and 'mechanisms at the level of preference formation' are precisely what Marx is working on. Marx's novel account of preference formation is worth considering for its particular methodology – the structure of concepts inherent in a specified relationship between 'two wills' – even apart from the exact way that he fills this in.[39]

This brings us to the question of the provenance of the principles Marx uses to fill out the conceptual structure of this relationship. The principles that he employs receive no special justification or defence. In fact they are an eclectic mix of concepts from traditional school-logic and sharp insights from their 'Hegelian' critique. Whilst some stages in his analysis depend on a notion of contradiction from which new relations follow,[40] there is no general 'dialectical' or 'Hegelian' model for all stages in the progressions that he traces. Crucial steps in his analyses do not depend on a principle of contradiction – for example, equality between two things presupposes a quantitatively measurable substance common to both.[41] Also, the ultimate deductions he makes concerning the ability of the capitalist system to sustain itself are basically algebraic relationships involving surplus value and the ratio of constant to variable capital, hedged about with numerous 'counter-vailing tendencies'.[42] Whilst the analytical principles Marx employs and the conceptual structure he traces in concepts like the commodity are both, as I read him, human creations, he offers no view on their metaphysical status with respect to any reality separate from human consciousness, no complete account of his repertoire of analytical principles, and no persuasive argument that the commodity, and concepts like it, contain one and only one inherent structure, namely the one he traces.

Individuals and agency

Whilst Marx's account shows the utility-maximiser presupposed by rational-choice theory to be a social construction, some further concept of agency still lurks within his conception of the individual. This is not the trans-historical rationality sketched by G. A. Cohen and about which Roemer is wisely silent. Cohen's view of rationality is far too close to the ruminations of Smith, Ricardo and numerous other economists whom Marx despised and whom Roemer considers to be discredited in such naiveté. Cohen writes:

> Rational beings who know how to satisfy compelling wants they have will be disposed to seize and employ the means of satisfaction of those wants. Men are certainly rational to some extent ... Here is what we understand by scarcity: given men's wants and the character of external nature, they cannot satisfy their wants unless they spend the better part of their time and energy doing what they would rather not do, engaged in labour which is not experienced as an end in itself. Human need, whatever may be its historically various content, is rarely well catered for by unassisted nature. Some mammals get what they need easily, while for others life is an endless struggle for sustenance. Men would, apart from special cases, be among the unlucky ones, except that they, uniquely, can continually refashion their environments to suit themselves.[43]

Cohen's account is much more reminiscent of Smith's trans-historical propensity to truck and barter and to his view of labour as toil than it is to Marx's view of labour as the human species-activity that has taken on alienated forms in what he termed human pre-history, i.e. pre-socialist societies. Moreover Cohen's anthropomorphised 'lucky' and 'unlucky' animals are not seriously defended against conventional Darwinism, nor clearly explicated in any case; and he does not explain why his rational men have not moved *en masse* to the 'rare' locations where unassisted nature caters well for human need. On the whole, Cohen's contributions to analytical Marxism are less impressive than those of, say, the other contributors to Roemer's edited volume, because the methods of analytical philosophy, at least in Cohen's hands, are less determinate in themselves and less persuasive about the social world than the other techniques employed.[44]

Nor is Marx's concept of agency the almost wholly vague 'rationality' behind the preference profiles (of which economistic utility-maximisation is one) that Roemer mentions. Rather the very processes of conceptual criticism which Marx himself employs are the best candidates for his most general vision of human agency, since they come the closest to filling out the conception that he requires if the individualism that he so evidently presupposes can be rescued from the ravages of social determination, especially the determination of the individual by the predominating conceptual structure of commodity production. Whilst on the one hand individuals are virtual prisoners of the concepts that earlier generations have created in their progress from barter to capitalism, on the other hand, individuals have potential access to a realm of creative thought from which three things might emerge:

1. An analysis of our current position as prisoners.
2. A specification of the conceptual forms which arguably keep us trapped in disadvantageous ways.
3. An alternative array of concepts with a quite different inherent structure according to which new social forms could be progressively constructed.

This concept of agency has a creative and open-ended character in that it does not present humans as necessarily conforming to some biological or psychological form of inherent 'rationality', even one that somehow permits choices of preference profiles, never mind the cruder views that 'drives' and interests themselves are fixed or evolve in merely superficial ways. Obviously the claim that a critical and creative power of reason (rather than 'rationality') is at the root of human agency is a species claim; it need not appear in every individual for the view to be true, merely in some individuals in some ways over some of the time. Perhaps it is slightly embarrassing for Marx's free-ranging methods, employed in his many critiques, to turn up at the root of his view of human agency. However, it begins to bridge the gap between the way that the mode of production of material life conditions the general social, political and intellectual life process, and the claim that proletarians and communists could exercise the sort of agency that the overthrow of capitalism would require, given the tenacious grip the conceptual structure of commodity-production exercises on contemporary minds, not least through the sheer necessity it imposes on us to be agents of the utility-maximising type. The possibilities for alternative conceptions of productive social relationships were briefly sketched by Marx but never effectively pursued by him.[45] And the virtual requirement that the world's inhabitants change together is hardly encouraging, however sanguine he liked to be about world revolution.

Marx may have been telling us something important in his assertion that there is an inherent conceptual structure to commodity production, incorporating an opposition between use-value and value (whether value is defined by labour-time or not), yet we may not find ourselves persuaded by his presentation of this conceptual structure in detail and by his deductive arguments. His deductive analysis allowed him to forecast capitalist collapse, which was presumed to stimulate the agency that changes one structure of concepts for another.

If this forecast is wrong, then we are at present prisoners of commodity production but will not necessarily confront the kind of crisis that would necessarily stimulate us to escape. Even so, it is worth being told that commodity production is a conceptual structure – not the inevitable outcome of biological 'drives' which we could hardly hope to influence or psychological 'preferences' which we must respect as a matter of individual right. It would still be worth tracing this conceptual structure, if only to see precisely what it is and how exactly we are constrained. Some critical reconstruction of concepts may yet be possible in politics, and some social reconstruction of individuals and of our view of individual agency in actual practice. Individualism is very much what we make it, and Marx offers a theory how this is done.

Rational-choice explanations of selected phenomena may or may not be persuasive,[46] but there is a lot more than 'explanation' at stake here. What may or may not be possible in contemporary politics is the point at issue, and Marx tackled that at the deepest level of abstraction and from the broadest historical perspective. These 'grand' issues will not go away; hence the heat and light when he is invoked, criticised, interpreted and revisited. Participants in these debates have their own 'Marxes', to be sure, but none of these 'Marxes', on my contention, is anything like as precise and illuminating, so I hope, as the one I have explicated above. Analytical historical materialists, class-struggle theorists and rational-choice Marxists will continue to talk past one another until they look more creatively at Marx himself. The issues identified in his work are the ones that actually need debating: What is our relation to the production and exchange of external objects and of the human capacity to labour? What ought this relationship to be? How could the movement from one to the other be accomplished in politics? These are themes that I explore in chapter four, chapter five and chapter six below.

In my next chapter I examine Marx's work in *Capital* as a 'critique of the economic categories', probing for the exact points at which his critique differs from the political economy that is under criticism, and exploring exactly how Marx justifies his own contrary assertions. To make his critique meaningful Marx had to assume considerable overlap between 'forms of life', in the Wittgensteinian sense, and the theoretical concepts deployed in political economy. And to make it political, he had to depart from both the 'science' of economics in his day, and from the presuppositions of life in societies where market relations prevail. Given his background in the politics of satire and parody, current in the 1840s, and his situation in the politics of state harassment and socialist fragmentation of the 1860s, he unsurprisingly produced a puzzling text that defies a literal reading. I hope to show that the many layers of ambiguity are not regrettable but are rather a productive challenge to readers today.

Notes

1 Karl Marx, *Capital*, vol. 1, trans. Ben Fowkes (Harmondsworth, Penguin, 1976, repr. 1986), p. 128.
2 Marx, *Capital*, vol. 1, p. 139.
3 Marx, *Capital*, vol. 1, pp. 139–40, 154.
4 Christopher J. Arthur, 'Engels as interpreter of Marx's economics', in Christopher J. Arthur (ed.), *Engels Today: A Centenary Appreciation* (London, Macmillan; New York, St. Martin's Press, 1996), p. 196; Marx, *Capital*, vol. 1, p. 125.
5 Marx, *Capital*, vol. 1, p. 156.
6 Marx, *Capital*, vol. 1, pp. 156–7.
7 Marx's use of formal modelling and mathematical manipulations as a substantive device from which conclusions are drawn puts him closer in method at certain points to W. S. Jevons, whose *The Theory of Political Economy* was first published in 1871, and to the mathematical economics that he founded, than to 'classical' political economists such as Smith and Ricardo.
8 Marx, *Capital*, vol. 1, pp. 157–8.
9 Marx, *Capital*, vol. 1, pp. 160–1.
10 Marx, *Capital*, vol. 1, p. 162.
11 Marx, *Capital*, vol. 1, p. 181.
12 Marx, *Capital*, vol. 1, p. 199.
13 Marx, *Capital*, vol. 1, p. 209.
14 Marx, *Capital*, vol. 1, p. 209.
15 Marx, *Capital*, vol. 1, p. 209.
16 Marx, *Capital*, vol. 1, p. 241.
17 Marx, *Capital*, vol. 1, p. 280.
18 Michael Carrithers, Steven Collins, Steven Lukes (eds), *The Category of the Person* (Cambridge, Cambridge University Press, 1985), p. 300.
19 Karl Marx and Frederick Engels, *Feuerbach: Opposition of the Materialist and Idealist Outlooks*, Part 1 of *The German Ideology*, ed. C. J. Arthur (London, Lawrence & Wishart, 1973), p. 19.
20 Karl Marx, Preface to *A Contribution to the Critique of Political Economy*, in Karl Marx, *Later Political Writings*, ed. and trans. Terrell Carver (Cambridge, Cambridge University Press, 1996), p. 160.
21 Karl Marx, *Capital*, vol. 1, p. 92.
22 D. F. B. Tucker, *Marxism and Individualism* (Oxford, Basil Blackwell, 1980), pp. 11–12, 65.

23 Mark Warren, 'Marx and methodological individualism', *Philosophy of Social Science*, 18 (1988), 451–4.

24 See the helpful discussions on individualism and holism in Susan James, *The Content of Social Explanation* (Cambridge, Cambridge University Press, 1984), in David-Hillel Ruben, *The Metaphysics of the Social World* (London, Routledge & Kegan Paul, 1985), and on varieties of individualism in Steven Lukes, *Individualism* (Oxford, Basil Blackwell, 1973); see also Allen E. Buchanan's comments on Marx's individualism in his *Marx and Justice* (Totowa NJ, Rowman & Littlefield, 1982), p. 98, and Ian Forbes, *Marx and the New Individual* (London, Unwin Hyman, 1990).

25 Rom Harré (ed.), *The Social Construction of Emotions* (Oxford, Basil Blackwell, 1986), p. vii.

26 Harré, *Social Construction*, p. 32.

27 Marx, *Capital*, vol. 1, p. 92.

28 For a hostile view, see Ellen Meiksins Wood, 'Rational choice Marxism: is the game worth the candle?', *New Left Review*, 177 (1989), 41-88, reprinted in Terrell Carver and Paul Thomas (eds), *Rational Choice Marxism* (London, Macmillan, 1995), pp. 79–135.

29 For example, see Jon Elster, *An Introduction to Karl Marx* (Cambridge, Cambridge University Press, 1986), pp. 22–31; Alan Carling, 'Rational choice Marxism', *New Left Review*, 160 (1986), 24–8, reprinted in Carver and Thomas, *Rational Choice Marxism*, pp. 31–78; John Roemer (ed.), *Analytical Marxism* (Cambridge, Cambridge University Press, 1986), *passim*.

30 For a philosophical examination of these assumptions, see Daniel M. Hausman, *Capital, Profits and Prices: An Essay in the Philosophy of Economics* (New York, Columbia University Press, 1981), and (ed.), *The Philosophy of Economics: An Anthology* (Cambridge, Cambridge University Press, 1984).

31 See *New Left Review*, 184 (1990), 97–128, where Carling, Wood and Alex Callinicos hold forth.

32 In the first group I would put Roemer, Robert Brenner and Alan Carling; in the second, G. A. Cohen and Elster.

33 John Roemer, *Analytical Marxism* (Cambridge, Cambridge University Press, 1995), pp. 1–7, 191–201.

34 Jon Elster (ed.), *The Multiple Self* (Cambridge, Cambridge University Press, 1986), pp. 133–4.

35 Shaun Hargreaves-Heap and Martin Hollis, 'Bread and circumstances: the need for political economy', in David Whynes (ed.), *What Is Political Economy?* (Oxford, Basil Blackwell, 1984), pp. 28–9.

36 Roemer, *Analytical Marxism*, pp. 195–9.

37 Roemer, *Analytical Marxism*, pp. 194–5.

38 Roemer, *Analytical Marxism*, p. 2.

39 Roemer, *Analytical Marxism*, pp. 191–9.

40 See Marx's note on Hegelian contradiction in Marx, *Capital*, vol. 1, p. 744 n.

41 Marx, *Capital*, vol. 1, p. 127.

42 Karl Marx, *Capital*, vol. 3, trans. David Fernbach (Harmondsworth, Penguin/New Left Review, 1981), pp. 317–75.

43 G. A. Cohen, *Karl Marx's Theory of History: A Defence* (Oxford, Oxford University Press, 1978), p. 152.

44 For some similar criticisms see Derek Sayer, *The Violence of Abstraction* (Oxford, Basil Blackwell, 1987).

45 *Communist Manifesto*: 'In place of the old bourgeois society, with its classes and class conflicts there will be an association in which the free development of each is the condition for the free development of all' (Marx, *Later Political Writings*, p. 20). *Critique of the Gotha Programme*: 'In a higher phase of communist society … society [can] inscribe on its banner: from each according to his abilities, to each according to his needs!' (Marx, *Later Political Writings*, pp. 214–15).

46 This is very much Carling's position; see 'In defence of rational choice', *New Left Review*, 184 (1990), pp. 97–109.

CHAPTER FOUR

Mirror and irony:
Marx's critique

Redefinition and re-presentation

The first book of *Capital* is, in many respects, a work puzzling to the modern reader. Why, for example, was Marx so interested in 'the commodity' and its 'value'? Why did he not simply 'do economics' and deal with prices?[1] In this chapter I shall argue that the opening chapters of *Capital* make better sense if they are read as the work of a student of natural philosophy,[2] logic, history, and political economy, rather than as a work of 'economics', Marxist or otherwise. 'Marx's economics' seems to me a misnomer. I suggest instead that Marx aimed to re-present the economic theory of his day in order to reveal the constituent conceptions of capitalist society, and to rid the theory of logical and historical confusions, using arguments from natural philosophy. Though his distinctions were ingenious, the enterprise fails in certain respects, so I argue, because he relied on Ricardian propositions about value and labour that were and are adventitious to capitalist society, and because his use of natural philosophy to build on political economy was not persuasive in his own time, and is even less so now. Hence he came to conclusions about the meaning of value, and the nature of labour, that neither conform to constitutive understandings of those terms in everyday use, nor produce an extrinsic account that has been very effective intellectually or politically.

Marx's projected multi-volume study *Capital* (*Das Kapital*) was subtitled 'Critique of Political Economy' (*Kritik der politischen Ökonomie*), of which the first volume was entitled 'The Production Process of Capital' (*Der Produktionsprocess des Kapitals*).[3] Leaving aside the differences between Marx's work and modern economics (Marxist or non-Marxist), and suspending any suspicions as to the relevance and persuasiveness of Marx's re-presentation of political economy as a critical characterisation of capitalist society, the term 'critique' arises as a puzzle in itself. Where is the line in *Capital* between the author and the political economists? Is *Capital* in some sense a work of political economy, or is it a deconstruction of the genre? Criticising a school on its own terms is one thing when the results are various redefinitions and clarifications, but it is quite another if the 'performative' intention is to *épater* the whole enterprise and clear the ground for something else. Given that this question arises, it is evident that Marx himself was sufficiently ironic and 'double voiced' to create such a puzzle about the character of his critique, or at least some readers (myself included) find themselves in this position. John Seery draws attention to 'an implicit contention that we have systematically misread all of Marx, that we have read him far too literally', pointing in turn to the work of Dominick La Capra, who states the matter quite clearly with respect to Marx's re-presentation of the 'economic categories':

> But if one moves to *Capital* – the *locus classicus* of the 'mature' Marx for many commentators, even for those who would reinterpret it in the context of the *Grundrisse* – one has what is probably the most crying case of a canonical text in need of rereading rather than straightforward, literal reading geared to a putatively unitary authorial voice … The issue that should, I think, guide a rereading is that of 'double voicing' in the argument of *Capital*. Of the utmost pertinence would be a set of related questions circulating around Marx's indecision – at times calculated and at times seemingly blind – between a 'positivistic' assertion of theses and a critical problematisation of them. Among these questions would be the following: To what extent is Marx putting forth certain propositions in his own voice (for example a labour theory of value) and to what extent does he furnish an ironic deconstruction of the system of classical economics and the capitalist practice it subtended (including the assumption of a labour theory of value)? Does Marx himself simply have a labour theory value or is it part and parcel of the system he is criticising?[4]

And there are of course further points at issue. One could well be characterised as the parody/satire/reality problem: if a parody is fully convincing, the satirical barb is blunted, and the 'copy' looks too like the original. I am thinking here of the British impressionist Rory Bremner, whose portrayal, for example, of John Major, then Prime Minister, caught his physical and vocal mannerisms so perfectly, and matched so well with spoken lines of such utterly realistic banality, that the satire evaporated and the effect was about as funny and politically stimulating as watching Major himself. Perhaps the 'double voicing' here was super-subtle, and for subsequent viewers, Major then looked like, sounded like, and *was like* (i.e. was as seemingly inconsequential as) Bremner. Much the same analysis applies to the American film *Bob Roberts*, a satire on the mendacity of media-driven campaigns for elected office. The tawdry and bizarre behaviour of the fictional characters seems pale and unfunny compared with the surreal and unpredictable extravagances of actual electoral contests.

This is basically the point that Jean Baudrillard makes in arguing that 'Marxism' (which he construes as 'Marx') misfires as a critique of political economy and of capitalist society. Baudrillard contends that this is because Marx's critique mirrors too closely the economic rationality inscribed in political economy itself and in the dynamics of the kind of society which the political economists, with just a few exceptions and only very mild regrets, aimed to promote. On Baudrillard's view Marx's politics of proletarian emancipation is cast too much in terms of an anthropology that curiously dehistoricises labour and disastrously reifies class. Indeed, in my view, with respect to many literal-minded Marxists, Baudrillard's comments are rather well taken.[5]

Whether Baudrillard's own postmodern theorisations themselves function as a critique of, or a mere mirror to, late capitalism is not the question I am addressing here. What I am pursuing instead is an enquiry into how Marx can be productively re-read. Along with La Capra, Seery turns to Marx's *The Eighteenth Brumaire of Louis Bonaparte* for carnivalesque and performative language, and for ambivalent rhetoric that is ironically productive, an enterprise with which I have every sympathy.[6] In the present chapter below, however, I shall keep the focus on the opening chapters of *Capital* to see just where Marx and political economy overlap and become 'single voiced', and just where the 'double voicing' of ironic politicisation begins.

People and things

Marx's work in the opening chapters of *Capital* has been rather well characterised as anthropological (in a certain qualified and self-consciously anachronistic sense) by Paul Mattick, Jr, who writes:

> The starting point of Marx's research procedure in *Capital* is an attempt to see the categories of his own culture as foreign and strange. [Marx says in *Capital*:] 'A commodity appears at first sight an extremely obvious, trivial thing. But its analysis brings out that it is a very strange thing ...' ... The 'strangeness' of the commodity is not noticed by the economists who study it.[7]

Because Marx assigned to the mode of production the defining role in social development, and because he took the view that the categories of political economy 'bear the unmistakable stamp' of capitalist society as concepts in common use, he seems to be saying that a thorough critical exposition of contemporary economic science (not a rejection, nor a series of straightforward corrections) would lay bare the 'anatomy of bourgeois society', for which these categories are constitutive. For its 'microscopic anatomy' he turned to the category 'commodity', the subject of the opening chapter.[8]

In my reading, Marx is saying that the whole notion of a commodity needed explication and, moreover, that this was vital to the rest of his work, both in its textual and extra-textual senses. The opening chapters of *Capital* are closely and interestingly argued precisely because they present an elaborate thesis on the changing relations between people and things, not merely because the scope and import of Marx's account is different from the more quantitatively oriented studies pursued by modern economists, and different in political thrust from the largely apologetic accounts published by the political economists who preceded him. I shall first summarise my reading below, so that Marx's theory of the commodity, incorporating a labour theory of value, appears in an argumentative context. In the course of doing this I shall be discussing in a critical way where Marx obtained his raw material for his critique of political economy, why he chose certain concepts and theories for critical re-presentation, and how in clarified form they are linked together in an ingenious way in Chapter 1 of *Capital*. After that I shall explore a point in Marx's argument where he deployed a conception of 'labour' that improved on the political economists logically, but still shared their presuppositions in natural philosophy – or rather, presuppositions that Marx presumed he shared with them. At that point the parodic critique of political economy collapses into the terms of political economy itself as Marx saw it, and La Capra's question is answered. The question then for readers is how much of Marx's expository and argumentative strategy with respect to 'the commodity' and 'the labour theory of value' is compelling today, and I outline my own position on this.

Smith, Ricardo and Marx

For eighteenth- and nineteenth-century political economists concerned with explaining the production and distribution of wealth, and with accounting for the relative worth in exchange of what is produced and distributed, it seemed sensible to look for a substantial source and regulator of 'exchangeable value'. Something, they assumed, must account for the fact that at different times a given amount of one commodity is worth different amounts of another, in monetary terms. Moreover they assumed that in a given period the exchange-ratio between two commodities tends to be stable (or would be stable, except for temporary deviations). What seemed to require explanation was this: What gives commodities their value in exchange? What rule are we following when we trade one commodity for others of equal value? What accounts for significant changes in the monetary value of one commodity *vis-à-vis* the others? As money was presumed to be a quantitative indicator of value, money itself could not be the explanatory factor as to why some goods typically cost more than others.

Since the time of Adam Smith (and even earlier) various versions of a labour theory of value had been put forward. Such a theory had the attraction of a single-factor explanation for the phenomenon 'value-in-exchange', and for significant variations in it. Moreover, labour seemed a more substantial factor than the vagaries of demand or scarcity. That labour could not, in practice, be easily and precisely measured, did not seem a grave disadvantage at the time; rather it was taken to have a reality as a natural phenomenon – as body-in-motion – in a way that subjective or psychological phenomena – such as desire or preference – did not. The opposite argument – that money itself functions as a value-measure of demand as consumers choose amongst scarce goods and services – was not in circulation until the 1870s. For the political economists the labour theory of value seems to have had the character of a truth about natural phenomena intuitively and deductively grasped rather than a hypothesis about social phenomena that define themselves in terms of quantitative data. Adam Smith did not seem discomfited by having to admit that the 'real measure of value' could not itself be accurately measured. His theory of value (in one of its formulations) was re-stated by David Ricardo:

> It is of no importance to the truth of this doctrine, whether one of these commodities sells for £1,100 and the other for £2,200, or one for £1,500 and the other for £3,000; into that question I do not at present enquire; I affirm only, that their relative values will be governed by the relative quantities of labour bestowed on their production.[9]

At the beginning of his critique of political economy Marx chose to re-present what he took to be basic concepts and presuppositions of certain economic theorists (and, as I read him, concepts and presuppositions fundamental to the society which had produced the theorists). He started with the commodity – his context for unravelling the complexities involved in value – and worked up to money, capital, and eventually on to conceptions, problems, theories and issues which were less abstract, and closer to the visible intricacies of the capitalist economy, such as wages, circulation of capital, and profits. As he wrote to Ferdinand Lassalle on 22 February 1858:

> The first work in question is the critique of the economic categories, or, if you like, the system of bourgeois economy critically presented. It is the presentation of the system and, at the same time, through the presentation, its critique.[10]

The concepts and problems presented in modern textbooks of economics are frequently different from those of political economy, and political economy as re-presented in a critical way by Marx, though sometimes the terms involved are confusingly the same. It is probably mistaken to imagine that a nineteenth-century political economist or Marx himself would have seen the 'error' of his ways, had he been presented with a modern text. Certain terms are shared by political economists and modern economists, but the definitions and the presuppositions of the theorists now need careful contextual examination. Marx's critique of political economy does not resemble economics as practised today, since he developed many of his distinctions and arguments as narrative philosophical explanations rather than as relationships expressible and manipulatible in quantitative terms. Moreover it seemed important to him to present the principles and presuppositions that characterise capitalist, commodity-producing society in a way that was new in historical and political terms – in particular, how certain uncomplicated things and relations come to appear there in 'fantastic', 'mysterious' forms – before he dealt with the (for him) less consequential quantitative aspects of money, capital, and profit.

Exchange-value and money-commodity

Capital opens with an assertion about capitalist society as a historically specific period, not with an assertion about production and exchange in any or all human societies as a timeless practice:

> The wealth of societies in which the capitalist mode of production prevails appears as an 'immense accumulation of commodities'; the individual commodity appears as its elementary form.[11]

In capitalist societies, so Marx is saying, wealth appears as commodities. The contrast between capitalist societies and other societies, where wealth does not take this 'form of appearance' – as commodities – is developed later in his chapter.

A commodity, he notes, is 'an external object', 'a thing', and moreover a 'useful thing', which may 'be considered from a dual point of view, according to quality or quantity'. Quality–quantity is a traditional distinction in logic, and one of his basic tools in this analysis. The uses of things, he continues, and the ways in which they can be measured, are derived in part from human discovery or social convention, and from the nature of 'the thing itself', so both qualitative appraisal and ordinary quantitative measures have, in Marx's view, a basis in the social, material world. For Marx, working within the natural philosophy tradition, this is at once a world of natural properties and necessities, and of human discovery, invention, convention, transformation, and self-transformation.

The usefulness of a thing, he notes, makes it a 'use-value' or 'good', and 'use-values' (useful things) 'form the material content of wealth, whatever its social form may be'. In the particular type of society, however, that Marx has under consideration (capitalist, commodity-producing society), use-values are 'at the same time the material bearers of – exchange-value'.[12] For Marx it seems that, on the one hand, the notion of exchange-value and the practices of commodity production and exchange only arise in a particular type of society and have very particular effects. On the other hand, 'use-value', in his account, is simply a way of designating a useful thing. Hence 'use-value' could be mentioned in connection with any sort of society (though the term itself is modern), since people will always find some things useful, whereas exchange-value (and therefore the commodity) occurs in some societies, but not in others. In short, even though uses vary historically, some concept of usefulness is at the heart of Marx's conceptualisation of the relation between people and things, and it is as near a trans-historical and omni-cultural concept as makes any sense. Whether the relationship between people and things bears all the importance that Marx assigns to it in his larger historical scheme – a developmental account of the varying social structures of human civilisations – is another question (see chapter ten below).

Marx then presents the conventional view of exchange-value, and begins the task of clarifying – using the methods of classical logic and natural philosophy – the concept and the practice. My tactic here is not to collapse Marx's logical concepts into Hegel's as quickly as most commentators are keen to do, as the possibility that Marx is using non-Hegelian concepts simply disappears on that assumption, and conversely, the extent to which Marx and Hegel shared an understanding of pre-Hegelian logic vanishes as well (interpretative strategies with respect to Hegel and Marx are discussed in chapter nine below). For the moment, though, it is worth noting that in the various passages quoted in this chapter Marx employs terminology from pre-Hegelian logic (which also appears in Hegel's critique of logic up to his own time), but about which there is nothing particularly Hegelian in his use, e.g. 'form–content', 'substance–accident', 'abstract–concrete', 'identity/equality', 'contradiction in terms'.

My reading of these opening passages of *Capital* is that Marx discusses what *seems* to be the case, and later claims to reveal the 'necessary relation' or 'secret' hidden under this 'appearance'. Eventually he explains why he thinks this appearance arises, and outlines the conditions under which he expects it to disappear. There is thus a political content to the form of this discussion: a social life ruled by appearances must be less satisfactory than one in which realities are dealt with directly. As preparation to tackling the politics of this transformation, we learn how in capitalist society (and in classical political economy) things *appear* and *seem*:

> Exchange-value *appears* first of all as the quantitative relation, the proportion, in which use-values of one kind exchange for use-values of another kind. This relation changes constantly with time and place. Hence exchange-value *appears* to be something accidental and purely relative, and consequently an intrinsic value, i.e. an exchange-value that is inseparably connected with the commodity, inherent in it, seems a contradiction in terms.[13]

Marx tells us that exchange-value is not a quantitative *way* of stating an arbitrary relation; he claims that when we exchange commodities we are (according to accepted theory) trading interchangeable exchange-values in equal *quantities*. His reading of the 'bourgeois' theory of exchange entails the view that a commodity 'has' an exchange-value which can in principle be quantified and set equal to another such quantity; hence commodities are not merely *said* in accepted economic theory to 'have' an exchange-value – they are said *to be* exchange-values:

A certain commodity, a quarter of corn, for example, is exchanged with x blacking, or with y silk, or with z gold etc. ... But since x blacking, like y silk, like z gold etc. is the exchange-value of one quarter of corn, x blacking, y silk, z gold etc. must be interchangeable with one another or *be* exchange-values equal in quantity to one another.[14]

From that account of the conventional theory of commodity exchange Marx draw two conclusions about exactly what happens there. First: 'The current exchange-values of the same commodity express something equal.' Second: 'In general, exchange-value can only be the mode of expression, the "form of appearance" of a content different from it.'[15]

Marx explains his reading of 'bourgeois' theory by using an algebraic analogy, to which the expressions x blacking, y silk, and z gold lend themselves, and a 'geometric example'. His examples are not, however, acts of barter. Rather he gives a simplified, abstract account expressing the basis of actual practice in capitalist, commodity-producing societies: that is, an account of sufficient generality to cover all commodity exchanges, whether commodities for money, money for money, or commodities for commodities. Moreover, since his account uses terms from accepted theory, it attempts to explicate both a social practice and its theoretical expression. Saying that one commodity may be exchanged for another of equal value is equivalent, in Marx's view, to saying that exchange-values are traded in equal quantities, or that one quantity of value is exchanged for an equal quantity of the same. Unequal exchanges are not thereby excluded as a possibility. His claim is that in political economy the notion of value and the practice of commodity exchange are explained with reference to the rule 'one quantity of value for its equal', and that this rule is presupposed by exchangers in commodity-producing societies.

In Marx's view, then, the common 'content' in commodities (implied by accepted economic theory) cannot be the fact that they have a money-value expressible in price, since for Marx money is a complex, mystifying expression of the social relation (between people and things) or 'content' for which he is searching, and prices are very much a matter of circumstance and accident – they are not the direct expression of a defining relationship. Marx argues that money is neither logically nor historically a presupposition of exchange, but he does not conclude that money is a logical consequence of the social relation at the basis of commodity exchange merely because it has been developed gradually in practice as some kind of 'token'. Rather the argument is that money is a special sort of *commodity*, and that the paradigm case of commodity exchange must consist in an expression of the equal relation of any commodity to any other, as equal quantities of exchange-value:

> Let us take two commodities, e.g. corn and iron. Whatever the proportion in which they exchange, it may always be represented in an equation … e.g. 1 quarter corn $= x$ cwt. iron. What does this equation signify? That a common something exists, in the same quantity, in two different things … Therefore both are equal to a third [thing] which is, in and of itself, neither the one nor the other. Each of the two, so far as it [is] exchange-value, must therefore be *reducible* to this third [thing].[16]

Marx deduces the existence of a 'common something' from his *reductio* of commodity exchange to an equation showing equal quantities of exchange-value. But do his observations and arguments warrant this?

Unsurprisingly, given the way this demonstration employs the methods of natural philosophy, Marx turns to *the* natural philosopher – Aristotle – in order to better him on his own ground. As Marx points out, Aristotle looked at commodities in exchange and did not see a 'common content' or 'equal something'. Rather his view was that commodities are widely different, and only roughly commensurable (in terms of demand) with each other at first, and then later with money:

> such things as are the subjects of exchange must in some sense be comparable … Hence arises the necessity of a single universal standard of measurement … This standard is in truth the demand for mutual services, which holds society together … Money … is a sort of recognised representative of this demand … Money is therefore *like* a measure that equates things, by making them commensurable, for association would be impossible without exchange, exchange without equality, and equality without commensurability.

Although it is in reality impossible that things which are so widely different should become commensurable, they may become sufficiently so for practical purposes.[17]

Aristotle argues that money is *like* a measure that equates things. Equations of commodities to money, and hence of commodities to each other, are not equations in the strict mathematical sense, in his view, but useful expressions for a rough commensurability in terms of demand, a factor extrinsic to the thing itself. Marx, however, was sure that there was an 'equal something' in an equation of commodity exchange such as 5 beds = 1 house, and that he knew what it was:

What is the equal something, i.e. the social substance, which the house represents for the bed in the expression of the value of the bed? Such a thing can 'not, in truth, exist', says Aristotle. Why [not]? The house opposes to the bed an equal something, so far as it represents the real equal something in the two, the bed and the house. And that [equal something] is – human labour.[18]

Marx's argument by elimination which is supposed to confirm this 'fact' is very much the work of an old-fashioned natural philosopher:

This common something cannot be a geometric, physical, chemical, or other natural property of commodities. In general, their material properties only come into consideration so far as they [the properties] make them [the commodities] useful, hence into use-values. But on the other hand, it is precisely the *abstraction* from their use-values which manifestly characterises the exchange-relation of commodities … As use-values, commodities are, above all, of differing *quality*, as exchange-values, they can only be of differing *quantity*, hence they contain not an atom of use-value.

If we disregard the use-value of the material bodies of commodities, then there remains only one property, that of [being] the products of labour.[19]

In a similar way Marx argues that in the exchange-relation of commodities we are dealing with only an abstract, quantitatively equalisable aspect of labour, not the concrete, qualitatively distinct aspects of productive labour itself:

If we abstract from its [the labour-product's] use-value, then we also abstract from the material constituents and forms which make it into a use-value. It is no longer a table or a house or yarn or even a useful thing … It is *also* no longer the product of the labour of the carpenter or the labour of the builder or the labour of the spinnner or any other determinate productive labour. With the useful character of the labour-product there disappears the useful character of the labour represented in it, hence there *also* disappears the different concrete forms of that labour; they are no longer distinguished, but are all reduced together to equal human labour, abstract human labour.[20]

Marx's argument leads him quickly to two conclusions. First: the 'common something' in relations of equal exchange-value (of two or more commodities) is represented by value. Second: value can only be created by simple abstract human labour (i.e. by human labour in its quantitatively equalisable aspect), or rather, insofar as exchange-value is produced in a certain amount (in useful labour-products), only simple abstract labour counts as its substance and measure.

Labour and value

However, it is important to consider carefully just what human labour in its quantitatively equalisable aspect is really supposed to be. Human labour may be said – following a traditional distinction in natural philosophy – to have concrete and abstract aspects. Concrete forms of labour, Marx argued, are qualitatively different, e.g. tailoring and weaving, because they are conceptualised as different sorts of activities and produce correspondingly different results. With the development of commodity-producing societies, according to Marx, in which objects are produced for the market, an abstract aspect of labour becomes increasingly important in practice and (somewhat later) in theory. As productive labour becomes increasingly mechanised and simplified, it tends towards mere mechanical motion, and labourers themselves become, as the commonplace synecdoche aptly states, 'hands', rather than tailors or weavers. In its abstract aspect, human labour, according to Marx, is the

productive expenditure of human brains, muscles, nerves, hands etc. … human labour pure and simple, the expenditure of human labour in general … It is the expenditure of simple labour-power, i.e. of the labour-power possessed in his bodily organism by every ordinary man, on the average, without being developed in any special way.[21]

How persuasive is this analysis? While it may be said that the 'expenditure of human brains, muscles, nerves, hands etc.' underlies anything that we might want to count as productive labour, this is not saying much, as it seems unlikely that all the varied activities that count (at least at times) as productive labour have anything as physical and as unitary in common as the concept 'simple labour-power' seems to suggest. Moreover it is not at all obvious that a line can be drawn between productive and unproductive activities in themselves, particularly when Marx argues later in *Capital* that, in effect, demand on the market ultimately determines whether the products of such activities have any value at all, and therefore whether the labour-power expended on them is actually productive. Worse still, Marx goes even further and asserts that skilled or 'complex' labour 'counts only as intensified, or rather multiplied simple labour'. Marx's arguments in favour of this claim are a covert identification of abstract labour with unskilled labour, which, as he admits, varies (in concrete forms, I presume) among societies, and also a reference to 'experience' and a 'social process' (both unspecified) which allegedly confirm that a 'reduction' from complex to simple labour is 'continually' being made.[22]

That argument seems to me to be circular, as Marx initially claimed that commodities can only be equated as values-in-exchange because they have labour as a common factor, but then in establishing what sort of common factor this labour is, he appeals to the supposed equation of commodities to confirm that labour can be reduced to a unitary substance (of some sort) and measure (in some sense). On the other hand it may be that Marx is making covert appeals to the equation of skilled and unskilled labour by means of money-wages, using currency as a common factor, as in those terms one is treated as a multiple of the other. However, this seems counter-intuitive (does anyone really think that the labour market, even ideally, equates skilled and unskilled labour in exact gradations according to wage rates?), and indeed worse for the course of Marx's analysis as a whole (which was to ground market phenomena as 'appearance' in what he took to be more substantial relations within the social world). It might be that general perceptions of differences between skilled and unskilled labour are partly determined by wage rates, and partly determined by commonplace presuppositions about labouring activities of different sorts in a given society, but it seems unlikely that either Marx or anyone else would want to make this distinction solely in terms of wage rates – most bargaining takes this the other way around and argues from the character of the activity in order to change wage differentials.

In any case, the assignment of Marx's common factor ('expenditure of human brains', etc.) to all the activities commonly identified as labour is surely a category mistake. Do all forms of labour really have one (and only one) factor in common such that all forms are commensurable, even if only in theory? Is there really such a thing, even in theory, as 'mere work' or 'simple average labour'? Is there any way, even in theory, of rank-ordering (in multiples of this common factor) instances of the 'expenditure of human brains', etc.?

My negative answer is already apparent: mental energy (surely an almost wholly metaphorical use of the term 'energy') and physical actions of all sorts are involved in human labour. The activities commonly identified as labour have considerable 'family resemblances' in respect of subtle yet diverse similarities in the sorts of physical and mental capacities employed. But they have no unitary measure, and no common factor, except in the most approximate, tenuous and metaphorical senses. Arguments, for example, that an hour of a doctor's time represents the expenditure of very skilled – i.e. intense, multiplied – brain power are not serviceable.

The practice of commodity exchange and its theoretical expression in classical political economy are, on my reading of Marx, characterised by abstraction and reduction: abstraction away from concrete, material, qualitative differences between useful things and useful types of labour, and hence a reduction of these straightforward properties of things and of different sorts of labour to a quantitative equality founded on a supposed social substance – simple abstract labour. Marx does not use 'social' to suggest that labour is somehow non-material: the implication is that it is a substance which is part of the socio-material world, rather than the material world as it existed before or apart from human social life.[23] Commodities, in his view, present themselves as exchange-values, or values for short; or rather, in the paradigm case of commodity exchange (deduced by Marx from the accepted theory and presumed practice of capitalist society) only their abstract character as values comes into consideration in defining the relationship.

The idea that value is based on something more or less objective (abstract labour 'actualised' in labour-products) is correct, in Marx's view, but value itself is only an 'objective' (i.e. *supposedly* inherent – the scare quotes are Marx's) property of the commodity. Moreover, the objectivity of the labour-product as materialised abstract labour is said by Marx to be merely 'ghostly', since abstract labour represents an abstraction away from the concrete, qualitatively different kinds of human labour, and the reduction of those differences to something equalisable in quantitative terms. In his account, the labour-product is closer to the whole substance of things (since no abstraction and reduction away from its qualities is required), whereas the commodity-value has an objectivity that is 'purely social' – not based on the full socio-material nature of things, but abstract, conventional, and subject to alteration by humanity. One day, Marx hints, labour-time (as the substance and measure of value) will not rule the socio-economic world, but will be utilised in a consciously regulated scheme without any need for the concepts commodity, value and exchange-value as such (this conception is examined in chapter five below).[24]

Marx's *Capital* and political economy

Most of the overly critical commentary on Marx either rejects him outright as a political economist, hence not a modern economist, or rewrites him anachronistically as a modern economist, but rather an odd one. Most of the less-than-critical commentary merely follows along with Marx's own text, in which he takes political economy for granted in certain respects and then differentiates himself from it in others. I want rather to enquire critically into what Marx shared with the political economists, namely an approach to the 'economic categories', in order to evaluate his analysis of capitalist society on terms that are coincident neither with modern economics nor with natural philosophy.

Marx's reasoning in the opening book of *Capital* is an ingeniously, but not comprehensively, critical version of arguments developed by Smith, Ricardo, and others. Smith suggested that commodities *contain* value, and Ricardo used equivalent expressions. Marx rejected that view only insofar as it made value itself sound like an inherent substance or material property of labour-products. But his own view, in my reading, was only slightly different, though much more complicated. He held that labour-products function as commodities with exchange-value, according to the 'bourgeois' view of things, and that value itself is therefore *thought* to inhere in commodities. As he wrote in 1879–80, revisiting *Capital*, 'exchange-value is only a "*form* of appearance", the autonomous mode of presentation of the *value* contained in the commodity …'.[25] In contrast to Smith and Ricardo, Marx took the view that labour (its concrete forms and hence its abstract form) is 'realised' or 'actualised' in labour-products. Thus, for him, '[being] the products of labour' is some sort of 'property' of the 'material bodies of commodities', and so commodities are 'materialised' or 'vanished' labour or the 'static existence' of a force.[26] However, this is either a tautology – '[being] the products of labour' is a common quality of all labour-products – or it is a thesis that contradicts contrary views held in Marx's time that I see no reason to reject today.

While human labour (as a form of energy) can be expended on material things over time to produce changes in their properties, a theory that labour is 'materialised' in the 'material bodies' of commodities in some way (or that it *is* one of their properties, or that the material bodies of commodities *are* accumulated labour) seems to me to confuse energy with matter or with its properties. The expenditure of energy can alter the properties of material things, but the mere circumstance that that energy (whether human or otherwise) has been expended on them is not itself one of these properties. I do not think that Marx's view can be saved by drawing an analogy with the accumulation in matter of an electrical charge or other form of energy, since one is not the materialisation of the other, and Einstein's later equation of matter and energy (which, of course, draws no distinction between human energy and other forms) would not be helpful, either, as the creation of matter (or its dissolution into energy) is not a feature of the matter–energy interactions in which Marx is interested. In any case, Marx's view of human labour-power is precisely non-equational: labour-power has the ability, so Marx argues, to bring forth more value than was itself absorbed in its own reproduction. This supposed further 'property' purportedly distinguishes human labour-power from that of other power sources, whether animate or inanimate, but no arguments of whatever kind are offered by Marx, other than backward reference to the labour theory of value as formulated by the political economists, nor does he substantially claim that value-relations in capitalist society only proceed the way that they do because people make this particular presumption about human labour in contradistinction to other sources of productive energy (quite the reverse, really, given that Marx claims that this distinction is original to his own analysis). Marx himself uses the language of contemporary physics – read as consistent with the framework and methods of natural philosophy – when discussing labour as energy or force, so reference to the physical sciences, of his day and ours, is not, I think, out of place.

The Marxian equation of labour and labour-products might have been intended in a less literal sense, as Marx himself suggested in his comments on Adam Smith in *Theories of Surplus Value* (written before the first book of *Capital*),[27] but if so, then the thesis is only acceptable if there are good reasons for believing that the participants in a capitalist economy generally avowed that value is itself a substance, or that it represents something substantial, or if they could be shown in general to have presupposed such views in their social actions, either in Marx's time or ours. In my view none of these conditions has been fulfilled. Marx, however, may be right in claiming that in capitalist society some social relationships are perceived in the form of a thing (the commodity – if we accept that it differs somehow from a labour-product), and that this constitutes a mystification of the relationship between people and things and a fetishism in power relations as things control people. But insofar as he attempts to resolve the mystification by a re-presentation of the principle that value is created and measured solely by labour, his work misfires. There are three fundamental steps in Marx's presentation that I find unconvincing:

1. Marx has accepted the assumption of certain political economists that an exchange of commodities equal in value means that an equal quantity of value (determined by the amount of labour usually expended on that sort of commodity) is exchanged for an equal quantity of the same value substance. This objective view of *value* cannot, I think, be sustained.[28]

2. Marx has also accepted the argument that what commodities have in common (apart from their materiality) can *only* be labour of a certain sort, though his reasoning is more sophisticated than Smith's. I have already questioned the view that commodities have *labour* in common at all in the way that Marx claims. Hence I object to a step in his argument prior to the assertion that labour is the *sole* 'property' (apart from materiality) common to the 'material bodies of commodities', and that the simple abstract aspect of this labour is the substance and measure of value.

3. Marx, moreover, has argued that different sorts of labour are reduced by the process of commodity production and exchange to simple labour (since simple abstract labour must, according to his argument by elimination, be the substance and measure of the value of commodities). This is merely a refinement of a view held – but left unexamined – by Smith and Ricardo. Ricardo and Marx do not show that skilled labour is a multiple of simple labour, even in some sense that precludes precise, or even approximate measurement: they simply state it as a self-evident fact.[29]

Economics and politics

Taking the whole of Marx's *Capital* as his lifelong project, it is perhaps just possible that he intended his critical re-presentation of the labour theory of value (and his views on the society that produced and supposedly accepted that theory) as a hypothesis to be tested by a study of the exchange-ratios of commodities over time (to determine whether or not these ratios are, in general, regulated in proportion to the socially necessary labour-time 'materialised' in different commodities). But on the whole he has insulated his work from such treatment, merely referring to exchange-ratios as 'accidental and continually varying', and offering no practical help with the determination of a unit of labour-power in the abstract, so that simple abstract labour and its multiples could be measured. Not only does he deny (as Smith and Ricardo had done) that market prices always conform to values, but he also denies that average prices do so 'directly'; and he denies that value is equivalent to cost prices, or to price or cost of production.[30]

Marx does say that value is equivalent over 'longer periods' to the 'average' price around which market prices fluctuate, but he offers no guide to finding these averages prices other than Thomas Tooke's work in the *History of Prices* (6 volumes, London, 1838–57). Nor would these prices make his re-assertion of the labour theory of value testable, unless inputs of labour in some standard unit could be measured over time. In the *Grundrisse* Marx suggested that average or abstract labour could not be measured as such. There is, in Marx's view, no contradiction between his work in the third volume of *Capital* on the complex appearance of economic relations in capitalist society and his later, more abstract discussion of value and surplus value in the opening book. Value is said to be the secret hidden by the apparent complexity of capitalist economic phenomena; his work in the third volume is said to be vague and senseless unless deduced logically from his views on value.[31]

Marx's work is thus an attempt – using the methods of the natural philosopher and classical logician – to establish general truths about capitalist society, or rather to elucidate certain presuppositions (thought by Marx to be fundamental to that society) already expressed in an incomplete or inconsistent way by the theoreticians of that society, the political economists. One of those truths was their 'scientific discovery' of the labour theory of value. Marx provided arguments from nineteenth-century logic and natural philosophy intended, so far as I can tell, to confirm this 'discovery' or 'law' in physical terms (or on analogy with physical terms) and to explicate it as an important view actually held in capitalist society by theorists and presupposed by participants in the economic process. In that way he and the political economists speak in La Capra's 'single voice', despite the analytical, historical and political distinctions that Marx introduced into the genre.

Yet Marx's theory is still an interesting attempt to explain how a commodity differs from a useful labour-product. This is because it raises the question what is presupposed when a useful labour-product is treated as a commodity, something valuable solely or largely in terms of what can be obtained in exchange for it, or might be obtained in exchange. Marx's claim that this activity involves some measure of abstraction away from the immediately useful properties of the object is surely borne out from even a cursory, albeit hermeneutic analysis of market-oriented behaviour. Commodity speculators treat useful labour-products purely as values, that is, with maximum attention to what they will fetch in terms of other commodities or money (or what they might fetch), and minimum attention to their useful properties as particular objects, or objects of a particular type. Marx was right to raise the overarching question of value-in-exchange, right to question the social effects of treating labourers as commodities, and right to fight the trite assumption that relations of private property make exploitation a meaningless concept. Almost all of his discussion of capitalist society, therefore, remains immensely valuable, in my view. In capitalist society producers value objects which people have laboured to plan, produce, distribute, advertise, sell, regulate, tax, etc., not for what they are (objects of more or less utility to particular persons), but for what they will fetch in terms of money and other goods. Labourers in that society are treated in production as commodities with a cost in money-wages, rather than as human beings in the full sense described elsewhere by Marx. Indeed one reading of Marx suggests that it is this very alienation or inversion of human relations in the labour market (treating people as mere 'factors of production' and saleable on the market just like any other commodity) that requires the 'appearance' of money – a simulation of the social in a realm of things – very much as its forms are traced out in *Capital*.[32] In these ways, Marx's critique is 'double voiced', as La Capra puts it, and speaks to us politically today.

In the next chapter I move from Marx's reconstruction of capitalism, about which he was very famously prolix, to his view of communism, about which he was notoriously reticent, even though it was the solution to the dynamics of exploitation and economic crisis that his analysis portended. In doing so I look closely at certain textual surfaces, and at how the very surface of his text was construed, in different ways, by different commentators, and how this bears on the overall framework through which he has been commonly interpreted.

Notes

1 For a general characterisation of Marxist economics and critical discussion of its various schools, see Fred Moseley (ed.), *Marx's Method in Capital: A Reexamination* (Atlantic Highlands NJ, Humanities Press, 1993), introduction.

2 I take 'natural philosophy' to be 'the study of the spatio-temporal world' undertaken before the (full) emergence of modern natural sciences and employing a vocabulary derived from the classical and medieval tradition of logic and metaphysics; see *The Cambridge Dictionary of Philosophy*, ed. Robert Audi (Cambridge, Cambridge University Press, 1995), *s.v.* natural philosophy.

3 On the varying course of Marx's plans, see Terrell Carver (ed. and trans.), *Karl Marx: Texts on Method* (Oxford, Basil Blackwell, 1975), pp. 5–37. For a discussion of the variations in title and subtitle in the editions of the first volume in which Marx had a hand, see Christopher J. Arthur, 'Engels as interpreter of Marx's economics', in Christopher J. Arthur (ed.), *Engels Today: A Centenary Appreciation* (London, Macmillan; New York, St. Martin's Press, 1996), p. 177.

4 Dominick La Capra, *Rethinking Intellectual History: Texts, Contexts, Language* (Ithaca NY, Cornell University Press, 1983), pp. 270–1, quoted in J. E. Seery, 'Deviations: on the difference between Marx and Marxist theorists', *History of Political Thought*, 9:2 (1988), 320–1.

5 Jean Baudrillard, 'The mirror of production', in *Selected Writings*, ed. Mark Poster (Cambridge, Polity Press, 1988), pp. 98–118. Another point raised by enquiring into *Capital* as critique is the possibility and utility of reading it as simultaneously a critique of Hegel (in some sense) as well as of capitalist society; see Moseley, *Marx's Method*, chs 2–3.

6 Seery, 'Deviations', pp. 320–2. In his discussion of Marx, Seery suggests on pp. 307–8 that 'the point of irony, the subtext of its doubleness, has to do with the strategy of conveying obliquely to the reader the idea that the burden of interpretation has been left up to the reader … The reader as interpreter must, as it were, look beyond the confines of the text for the real point of the text'; see also John Evan Seery, *Political Returns: Irony in Politics and Theory from Plato to the Anti-Nuclear Movement* (Boulder CO, Westview, 1990).

7 Paul Mattick, Jr, *Social Knowledge: An Essay on the Nature and Limits of Social Science* (London, Hutchinson, 1986), p. 88; Karl Marx, *Capital*, vol. 1, trans. Ben Fowkes (Harmondsworth, Penguin, 1976, repr. 1986), p. 163; see also chapter one above, n. 46.

8 Karl Marx, Preface to *A Contribution to the Critique of Political Economy*, in *Later Political Writings*, ed. and trans. Terrell Carver (Cambridge, Cambridge University Press, 1996), pp. 159–60; Marx, *Capital*, vol. 1, pp. 90, 174–5.

9 David Ricardo, *On the Principles of Political Economy, and Taxation*, ed. R. M. Hartwell (Harmondsworth, Penguin, 1971), p. 86.

10 Karl Marx and Frederick Engels, *Selected Correspondence*, 2nd edn, ed. S. Ryanzanskaya, trans. I. Lasker (Moscow, Progress, 1965), p. 103.

11 Marx, *Capital*, vol. 1, p. 125. The quotation comes from Marx's previous work, *A Contribution to the Critique of Political Economy*, ed. Maurice Dobb (London, Lawrence & Wishart, 1971), p. 27.

12 Marx, *Capital*, vol. 1, pp. 125–6.

13 Marx, *Capital*, vol. 1, p. 126; my emphasis.

14 Karl Marx, *Capital*, vol. 1, ed, Frederick Engels, trans. Samuel Moore and Edward Aveling (London, Allen & Unwin, 1957), p 3; I cite this edition in preference to the Penguin one generally used in this volume because the translation seems much clearer in this instance; in further such instances I cite this edition as *Capital*, vol. 1 (Allen & Unwin).

15 Marx, *Capital*, vol. 1, p. 127.

16 Marx, *Capital*, vol. 1 (Allen & Unwin), pp. 3–4; my emphasis.

17 Aristotle, *Nicomachean Ethics*, trans. J. E. C. Welldon (London, 1902), pp. 152–4; my emphasis.

18 Marx, *Capital*, vol. 1 (Allen & Unwin), p. 29.

19 Marx, *Capital*, vol. 1 (Allen & Unwin), p. 4.

20 Marx, *Capital*, vol. 1 (Allen & Unwin), pp. 4–5; emphasis added.

21 Marx, *Capital*, vol. 1, pp. 134–5.

22 Marx, *Capital*, vol. 1, pp. 129–37.

23 I disagree with the view that for Marx 'social' is antonymic to 'material'; G. A. Cohen, *Karl Marx's Theory of History: A Defence* (Oxford, Oxford University Press, 1978), ch. iv.

24 Karl Marx, *Capital*, vol. 1, pp. 128–9, 138–9, 153–4, 171–3, 486–91; cf. this passage from Aristotle: 'But a substance exists in virtue of its quality, whose nature is definite, while quantity has an indefinite nature.' *Metaphysics*, trans. H. G. Apostle (Bloomington IN, Indiana University Press, 1966), 1063a28, p. 184.

25 Marx, '"Notes"on Adolph Wagner', in *Later Political Writings*, p. 242.

26 Marx, *Capital*, vol. 1, p. 143; cf. Karl Marx, *Grundrisse: Foundations of the Critique of Political Economy (Rough Draft)*, trans. Martin Nicolaus (Harmondsworth, Penguin/New Left Review, 1974), pp. 330–3, 359, 612–13.

27 Karl Marx, *Theories of Surplus Value*, vol. 1, ed. S. Ryazanskaya (London, Lawrence & Wishart, 1969), pp. 171–4.

28 Marx, *Grundrisse*, p. 446. Patrick Murray argues that Marx's move in defining the abstract labour that counts in value as only that labour which is 'socially

necessary' (thus building 'demand into the very concept of value' in a non-Ricardian way) means that Marx's 'theory of value cannot be construed as a labour theory in any ordinary or naturalistic sense' – despite the language in which it is couched (which I have analysed here). While I agree with Murray that Marx builds demand into his concept of value, it is unclear to me, however, whether a 'co-constitutive relationship between value and price' actually makes much sense or tells us anything useful about either; 'The necessity of money: how Hegel helped Marx surpass Ricardo's theory of value', in Moseley, *Marx's Method*, p. 50.

29 Moseley remarks on the continuing disagreement amongst Marx scholars on these issues, traces the history of this controversy briefly, and summarises two objections that I have attempted further to specify: 'the lack of an adequate reason ... for selecting labour as the common property of commodities that determines their exchange values, and the unresolved problem of reducing different kinds of skilled labour to equivalent quantities of simple abstract labour'; *Marx's Method*, p. 10.

30 Marx, *Capital*, vol. 1, pp. 269, n. 24; 680, n. 7.

31 Marx, *Grundrisse*, pp. 138-9; Karl Marx, *Capital*, vol. 3, trans. David Fernbach (Harmondsworth, Penguin/New Left Review, 1981), pp. 257–65.

32 Murray, 'Necessity of money', pp. 52–4.

CHAPTER FIVE

Technologies and utopias: Marx's communism

History and contradiction

After the collapse of 'communism' in the Soviet Union and in Eastern Europe, it is time to take the longer view. Communism has a history, and some version of that history is invoked whenever the term is used. Marx has become the most famous communist of all, and in his words: 'Tradition from all the dead generations weighs like a nightmare on the brain of the living.'[1] In the case of communism the nightmare is more than usually vivid. However, in order to grasp this lurid clarity we must examine carefully the tradition that the dead generations have left behind. This is because when the term is used in the present, the dead are made to walk among us. Rightly we must turn first to the earliest dead, as their work exposes numerous conceptual associations and contradictions that have fuelled subsequent political debate. Indeed the full texture of those debates, and the full irony of modern political practice, will not be visible unless we spend some time examining the origins and development of communist theory and politics.

In this chapter I propose to examine the conceptual history of communism at some length in order to situate Marx's version thereof within it. My reading of Marx's work in *Capital* takes the text as an extended political argument against capitalism, rather than as a deductive and mechanistic 'proof' that its collapse is inevitable. The conceptual structures that make the disjunctions and alienations of capitalist practice explicable and visible have been traced in chapter one through chapter four above. Replacing the mechanistic certainty that *Capital*, at least in some readings, and in some of its metaphors, seems to encourage, there must be further political arguments available, of which the terms of communism could be one. In the discussion below I use other theorists to help draw out what Marx, so it seems to me, did and did not have in mind. This exercise then focuses on one crucial passage, attributed to Marx, that seems out of line with the rest of his work. At the end I consider the political issues that arise in dealing practically with the proposals that Marx raises, and so set the stage for a consideration of his counter-capitalist political practice that forms the subject matter of chapter six.

Debates and discourses

Like all political terms, communism arose in the context of debate, although this seems to have begun so long ago that our guesses as to the nature of these discussions are more speculative than documented. The evidence, for Western thought, is that the debate was about possession or property, defined as the use or control of material resources. This could, of course, include people, insofar as slavery was practised, formally or informally. Whilst we cannot know what the original form of property was, it is widely assumed to have been a system of shared use that was rule-governed and normatively enforced. Through archaeology we have access to material artefacts, but in pre-literate cultures we do not have access to ideas, so we can have little knowledge of property relations in the earliest societies.[2] With literate cultures, such as that of Ancient Greece, we begin to have texts, and the evidence there suggests debate.

If the original or early form of possession was shared use within a community, no concept would be needed to describe it at all, as descriptions demarcate with respect to an alternative, something which the thing in question is not. A network of conceptual assumptions, perhaps rules and precedents, would be sufficient for practicalities, without an overall descriptive word or phrase. The political use of communism in the Western tradition begins with Plato in his text

The Republic (ca. 380-360 BC), at which point an alternative to shared use within a community was already clear. That alternative was 'private property' or 'individual ownership'.

Private property or individual ownership of material resources creates problems. Clearly it was an idea which disrupted traditional arrangements, which were most probably those of shared use. That 'sharing' was, of course, not necessarily amongst all individuals, nor amongst those who did the sharing was it necessarily equal in respect of use. Indeed the notions of 'all' and 'equality' may not have been operative, as community boundaries may not have been fixed, nor had standards of interpersonal comparison necessarily become available. Notions of the 'individual' as an agent or personality apart from the requirements or traditions of community life most probably developed within communities. The idea that communities formed from pre-existing 'individuated individuals' (Marx's ironic phrase) seems most improbable, though it must be said that various parables and theories, such as those in Smith's and Ricardo's political economies, have suggested that this has been in some sense the case.[3]

A notion of individuality, and of interests apart from or perhaps even at odds with community traditions and requirements, creates a debate. Arguably it also creates politics in its modern form as an activity for managing the interaction of self-conscious and self-interested individuals in such a way that some order within the group is, or at least could be, preserved. Obviously politics can also be pushed to the point where communities are radically reformed or even destroyed, as notions of what this order should be, and who should be responsible for it, come to differ.

The Republic, in my reading, is informed by Plato's revulsion at a constant conjunction of political interest in Athenian society. This conjunction was of individual ownership of resources, political control of the institutions of authority, and military might. We know this as political corruption, and it usually takes the form of military dictators who use the army to run the state, and then use this overwhelming advantage to secure material possessions for themselves, their families and their associates. In Plato's view, military might and institutions of authority were necessary to a degree for any community to exist, though his first discussion of the 'ideal community', where 'justice' or 'order' has been achieved, pares these requirements to a minimum. This is because his 'first community' produces no surplus or luxury goods, only basic necessities. There is thus no need for private property or individual ownership in any significant sense, as there is literally nothing to own individually that is not already available in the community. Within that first community, individuals cooperate to produce physical necessities and to enjoy leisure time. Though by definition they consume as individuals, they do not, as it were, pause to 'own' what they consume, nor to stockpile 'property' in order to provide things they might need later. The temptation for outsiders to attack such a community would be minimal, so Plato argued, as there were no desirable luxuries to steal, though some minimal defence against enslavement and sheer vandalism was required. This first community is based on a system of sharing or communal – as opposed to individual – ownership, and it also represents what we might describe as a subsistence or near-subsistence society. For that reason the audience in Plato's fictive dialogue rejects this community as 'fit only for pigs'. The audience wants surplus production, the production of luxuries, and with that requirement Plato manoeuvres his discussion closer to the realm of practical politics for his day and ours.[4]

Thus communism is in the first instance a proposal to reject a system of property relations in which individuals are allowed to use, control and own resources, in which these individuals can expect an organised and forceful guarantee of their property rights, and in which these individual rights have a priority such that community requirement, or the requirements of other individuals in the community, are not necessarily met, or met in full. Thus a communal system of shared use presumes community direction of resources as a priority, and the assignment of goods to individuals as a share that may be consumed or controlled individually, but not held individually in defiance of community decisions.

How the community is constituted, and how distributive decisions are reached, are of course further questions. These distributive decisions, including the distribution of obligations or other requirements to work as well as to consume, could flow from traditional practices or from decision-making bodies, and decision makers could be one individual alone or the whole group following a rule of consensus or some other mechanism of choice. What is crucial is that, on the one hand, there is no guarantee of individual rights to resources that the community must enforce irrespective of the needs of other members, but on the other hand, there is no danger to individuals that they will be abandoned entirely to the exercise of their own rights in securing material goods without any recourse to resources held collectively by the community.

Plato's discussion develops to encompass a 'luxurious' state in which the temptation to combine political, military and private interests is introduced and sharply escalates. To prevent the rule of corrupt, powerful and self-interested men (women were not rulers in Greece), he proposes that rulers should have a lengthy education and training to give them skills in abstract reasoning and knowledge of human affairs, an otherworldly perspective devoid of material self-interest, and a balance in their character and emotions. To keep them up to this mark he also proposes that they be forbidden family life and private property, so there would be no temptation for them to manipulate politics to their own advantage.[5]

In a surprising move Plato also argues for the admission of women to the ranks of rulers, and indeed the audience in the dialogue registers this surprise, no doubt to help the reader through it, though whether women are admitted on terms of precise equality with men, or whether the terms of rulership are themselves conceived in a masculine mode, are questions on which the text is ambiguous at best.[6] Within this 'guardian class' there are also military leaders, presumably subject to the same or similar strictures, as the temptations are the same. The economic and social arrangements of the rest of society are left undiscussed, but as luxury production is envisaged, it seems reasonable to assume that the individual incentive to material accumulation would require a system of private property in order to function.

In this way Plato's novel proposal that rulers should be forced to practise communism simultaneously enriched and confused the concept as he moved from his first 'ideal' society to his second 'luxurious' one. Much of the context outside and even inside the text has been lost, as selective attention, beginning with his pupil and critic Aristotle, has made Plato's recommendations notorious. The non-luxurious or 'primitive' community, in which communism is instituted for all, has been rejected on the terms ('city of pigs') given by the Platonic audience, which were not necessarily those of the author; the characterisation (in the quasi-authorial voice of Socrates in the dialogue) of the luxurious community as suffering from 'inflammation' has also been played down by later commentators. The introduction of women into political life as potential rulers has pleased no one, though for many different reasons nor has the requirement that rulers be absolute, because specially educated and trained 'guardians' are said to be as near trustworthy as any humans can be. Those against absolute rulers are seldom open about the intellectual or practical prerequisites of good rulership, and those in favour of absolute rulers have uniformly appealed to criteria other than education to justify such sweeping authority (which is usually derived from birth or divine intervention or both).

The Platonic state has been criticised as too unified, on the grounds that it is defined and maintained through the exercise of political and military authority by a self-selecting caste, thus neglecting the varied forms of institutions and interests that arise in a polity. And it has been dismissed as unduly divisive because it separates ordinary inhabitants quite markedly from any exercise of citizenship in choosing or influencing rulers, and because it institutes quite separate lifestyles and property systems for rulers on the one hand, and subjects on the other. The legacy of Platonic communism has been an enduring disjunction between the ideals of share-and-share alike in a community framework and a system of elite rule through unquestionable and ascetic authorities. It cannot be said that there has been any significant Platonic practice in politics, though one contemporary criticism of Plato was that he had borrowed the communal institutions and military training from the practice of nearby Sparta (of which little is independently known). That in itself was enough to condemn *The Republic* in classical Athens.

There is a decidedly more modern flavour to Thomas More's communism, outlined in his *Utopia* of 1516. This is because the context of political debate is again set in a communist alternative to a system of individual property rights, but with the addition of a concept of economic class moved well into the foreground. Again, like Plato, More shielded himself behind various narrative and dialogical devices in the text, so that it is more than usually difficult to attribute to him an authorial voice and personal view (which may, ironically, not be the same). However, within that framework it is clear that the appearance in England of 'vagabonds' or landless labourers was perceived as a problem, and in the eyes of some, this was seen as a consequence of moving from a communal system of mutual obligation (at least in theory) within feudal or quasi-feudal society to a system of individualised ownership of land and other resources in a commercial economy. Within that system it became possible to sever the link between persons or households and their means of livelihood (usually land), and the commercial advantage on doing so was defended (or at least tolerated) within the prevailing legal relations. Thus More seems to emphasise the futility of draconian penalties for theft, when theft seems to be the only alternative to starvation.[7] The discussion presumes that this problem is a by-product of individual rights to property and an economics of greed, and no exculpatory defence of individualistic commercialism is even attempted.

More's communist alternative is first and foremost a utopia, a word he coined, meaning 'nowhere', and its institutions and values are recounted in the genre of travellers' tales or 'tall stories'. Nonetheless, Utopia is no city of gold or land of luxury, so it is in a sense closer to Plato's non-luxurious or 'primitive' community than it is to the 'second-best' authoritarian state. Though Utopian society is rationalistic in the way that principles and ideals are uniformly instantiated, the values of the community rest on seniority and practical experience, a sexual division of labour, and considerable emphasis on religion. Whilst learning is venerated and scholarship merits time off physical tasks, rulership is exercised through (normally) male heads of households, then delegated representatives of those heads meeting at successively higher levels, and similarly with a priesthood. Agricultural and city-based pursuits are carefully rotated, money is unknown, and gold and other luxuries openly mocked.

As More's imaginary community produces and distributes necessities, and as all houses are permanently unlocked and periodically
reallocated, there is nothing material that is private and exclusive.
Sexual relationships are punished outside marriage, and the population
is kept regionally mixed and numerically in balance through a system
of exchange amongst cities and colonial foundations as necessary. Thus
individual incentive to accumulation does not exist, and leisure time is
individually consumed as planned production proceeds through a
schedule of rotated activities and tasks. The young and sick are loving-
ly cared for and any miscreants are punished with forced labour
as community slaves. Men and women undergo military training,
but the community also uses superfluous 'wealth' such as gold to hire
mercenaries. Wars, however, are fought only in self-defence or for
other morally justified reasons. Surprisingly, More's Utopians are not
Christians, though some undergo conversion as morally the Gospel
teachings are said to conform to their values. The sting in More's
implied critique is that, unlike contemporary Christians, Utopians are
tolerant of religious diversity.[8]

Intriguingly More chose to discuss the very issues that Plato seems
to ignore, namely the day-to-day life of ordinary folk in the community, the detail of their arrangements, and the structuring of their
values. In effect it improves considerably on Plato's sketchy 'city
of pigs' and redeems it for discussion. However, there is a price to
pay. The attractions of competitive individual accumulation and the
materially innovative consequences of commercial incentives are
completely foregone by the population as a whole. Perhaps in theory
communal values could favour and encourage individual innovation
for community rather than for private gain, but More chose to exem-
plify austerity, stasis and asceticism in his communist society. Whether
the limitation of production to what is merely necessary represents the
most desirable use of human resources is a question that he does not
choose to debate, arguing that luxury generates corruption. Hence
he presumes that the association between conflicting interests, perhaps
played out as class or at least mass action, and the achievement of
material 'progress' in society as a whole, is an unbreakable one. Because
More's communist society generates no individually held surpluses in

material goods, it prevents social problems arising from want and penury on the one hand, and greed and temptation on the other. Thus the authority structure has little to do politically, and needs only a consistent application of a commonsensical and rational code to sustain the community.

This line of argument – that communist society is non-luxurious – became difficult to sustain as commercialism and industrialisation took hold in European society. Thus the potential for the production of new goods, and for increased productivity in turning out familiar ones, overtook the old idea of austerity and made it look monastic. The diagnosis of the problem – known by the time of the eighteenth century as 'the social question' – remained very similar: how to prevent the poverty and worklessness engendered by commercial economies. The presumption was that this had happened because those economies severed links between labourers and the raw materials of their livelihood in order to institute and guarantee rights to private property. Confusingly, answers to 'the social question' were denominated 'socialism' as well as 'communism', sometimes interchangeably, and sometimes in distinction or even contradiction to each other. Thus any generalisation is at risk of serious inaccuracy, but it might be ventured that communists were often considered more extreme in their opposition to the status quo, and more likely to reject altogether a money system for exchange.

However, this is not to say that socialists, including communists, agreed on much amongst themselves even in terms of their criticisms of commercial societies. Socialism embraces almost any policy from mild redistribution of income and wealth within a capitalist economy to highly egalitarian revolutionary conspiracies to institute workers' control of the international economy. Perhaps by way of generalisation it might be said that socialists agree that 'society' exists apart from individual preferences and actions, and that it incorporates obligations and responsibilities to move resources towards those who cannot obtain a living through their own activities in the marketplace for goods and labour.

Specifically communist solutions to the social question were, in general, either directed to humanising the work environment or to minimising the time spent there. In that way communists engaged explicitly with issues of size and degree: large factories to gain the benefits of productivity, or small ones to reinforce affective ties and mutual help amongst works; continually advancing technology in order to gain the benefits of innovation, or emphasis on aesthetic craft-work and human-scale tools; national and worldwide solidarity, or small-scale 'utopian' communities. Perhaps the most radical vision was Charles Fourier's, as he merged work, aesthetics, pleasure and leisure together in small-scale 'phalansteries'. Contributions to production were to be arranged according to natural inclination, and rewards were communally allocated according to need and desert. Sharing applied to emotional and sexual relationships as well as to material goods and contributions, as only through the mutually agreed satisfaction of 'the passions' could social harmony be ensured.

In a rather different way ideals of Christian charity and self-efface-ment surfaced in organised movements to save souls from material as well as spiritual deprivation. Amongst the more extreme versions of this were the Shaker communities, in which sexual abstinence was an absolute rule, although mutuality in sharing productive tasks and con-sumption goods was the norm. Some communities pursued techno-logical innovation in order to maximise time for collective worship, and some were commercially successful in marketing seeds and other items, retaining surplus funds for communally determined use.

These examples could be multiplied many times in several direc-tions: there were elaborated schemes to be managed by authoritarian 'scientists of society'; paternalistic schemes for model factories and workers' communities; democratic plans for national workshops to equalise disparities between effort and reward; nostalgic efforts to revive the communal guilds of the middle ages; emigrations to distant islands to begin the world anew. Communist and socialist ideas and experiments flourished from the mid-seventeenth to the mid-nineteenth centuries in what has been described as a wonderland of practical experimentation on several continents. There was also a vast library of theoretically varied and innovative tracts, schemes and mani-festos in innumerable languages.[9] But by the later nineteenth century the verdict was in on most of the experiments, and the intellectual debate had solidified around one overwhelmingly influential communist doctrine: Marxism.

Marxism and communism

In a political partnership Marx and Engels devoted their careers to the communist cause, though one (Engels) worked for years managing his father's factories in order to support the other (Marx) through the tribulations of his vocation as publicist and theorist. Both were in sympathy from an early age with radical ideas concerning redistribution in response to the increasingly obvious difficulties of the agricultural and particularly the industrial labouring poor. Both were also enamoured of the power of modern energy sources and of the productivity of modern factory production. However, in certain terms they then distinguished themselves quite self-consciously from some aspects of the communist tradition, and in that way they functioned as systematisers more than innovators. Above all they were determined to enter, indeed create, an age of mass politics on a national and international scale.

In the context of mid-nineteenth-century Europe mass politics was in some places barely tolerated and was much more generally repressed. The French Revolution represented the most visible and highly publicised intrusion of mass participation and representative institutions into a politics of authoritarian kings, emperors and princelings. Marx and Engels aligned themselves in sympathy and doctrine with the normally clandestine and only periodically visible movement for constitutional rule, legislative assemblies, independent judges and responsible executives. Both expected this movement to grow and intensify on its own momentum; what they planned to contribute was an economic analysis critical of commercialism and the commercial classes.

Thus Marx and Engels took a systemic rather than merely redistributive view, and Marx in particular spent a lifetime analysing and documenting the proposition that monetary exchange is at the root of a self-replicating cycle of poverty amongst workers (or 'proletariat') and of accumulating surpluses amongst owners of productive resources (or 'bourgeoisie'). Neither was ever at all friendly towards 'utopians' for a number of reasons: Marx and Engels never favoured a politics of small-scale or 'experimental' schemes or communities, as opposed to large-scale nation-wide effusions of practical political activity; neither did they argue for the rejection of modern technology or against further innovations therein. Neither would have any truck with religious ideas or ideals, moral feelings or even ethical norms such as 'justice' in any but the most covert ways. Neither played the part of real or would-be leader or patriarch or founder. Neither was ever really dedicated to organisations, parties or even discussion groups, newspapers being the sole regular exception. The wonder is that anyone 'followed' them at all, as it was so difficult to find them politically in order to do so, and so little recognition of followership was ever forthcoming from either.

Against the above summary one particular text from Marx and Engels stands out as an exception, and it is one of the most often quoted and widely recognised. Neither ever said very much about communist society, and both insisted that communism was a movement already in existence, a movement of the present. This led them to comment extensively on the foreseeable future, which was not to be communism in its fullest realisation. Both stopped well short of the kind of guidance that would blueprint a future society, though both delivered brief statements of the general principles with which their short-term advice was supposed to be consistent. Thus these principles were said to guide their judgements about contemporary politics precisely because they were consistent with (an admittedly vague) conception of communism.

These statements of principle, and occasionally of proposed practice, have been extensively quoted and analysed, criticised and praised. Today the most famous among them is a short passage from *The German Ideology*, a manuscript work by Marx and Engels, written in 1845–46, but first published in 1924 in a Russian translation, and then in the original German in 1926. This passage is so well known and so extensively quoted that its omission from any study of Marx's work is worthy of notice, because it suggests that the commentator is unwilling to confront a difficult issue – the question of consistency in Marx's views on the relationship between industrial technology and communist society.

In the latest English translation, based on East German and Russian scholarship, we read:

> For as soon as the division of labour comes into being, each man has a particular, exclusive sphere of activity, which is forced upon him and from which he cannot escape. He is a hunter, a fisherman, a shepherd, or a critical critic, and must remain so if he does not want to lose his means of livelihood; whereas in communist society, where nobody has one exclusive sphere of activity but each can become accomplished in any branch he wishes, society regulates the general production and thus makes it possible for me to do one thing today and another tomorrow, to hunt in the morning, fish in the afternoon, rear cattle in the evening, criticise after dinner, just as I have a mind, without ever becoming hunter, fisherman, shepherd or critic.[10]

Commentary on this passage can be divided into four categories. In the first and second categories the passage is subjected to a straightforward reading but sharply contrasting evaluations. In the third category the passage, so I suggest, is significantly omitted. In the fourth, by contrast, the problematic aspects of the passage are raised, only to generate puzzlement. After exploring these areas of puzzlement, I turn to recent textual scholarship – relating very directly to the 'textual surface' – which suggests a surprising resolution to the difficulty that this passage seems to raise: Can the bucolic character of communism here possibly be consistent with the otherwise uniform view in Marx's writings that communism must incorporate, indeed further develop, the highly productive and mechanised technology that arises with the capitalist system?

First, there are writers who are sharply critical of Marx. They seize on these words as obvious proof that his concept of communism is poorly thought out, impractical, and – unbeknownst to himself – quite frivolous, because he has not characterised the division of labour in a convincing way nor established that it can be abolished in the rather fey manner suggested in the passage. These writers take it that Marx's intentions in this passage are serious, and they are not especially perturbed by any apparent inconsistency between the pre-industrial activities mentioned (hunting, fishing) and his professions elsewhere that communism must be based on modern industry, since they find those discussions no better. In this category I place Kostas Axelos, R. N. Berki, M. M. Bober, Bruce Mazlish, Alec Nove, and Peter Singer.[11]

Second, there are commentators, sympathetic to Marx, though in widely varying degrees, who also assume that he wrote this passage with all due seriousness. Like the previous group, these writers are not particularly worried by the undeveloped state of technology in the world of hunters and fishermen, but unlike Marx's strenuous critics, they are not so inclined to dismiss the view of communism presented in this passage. This is because they think that his critique of the division of labour – whatever the state of technology – is worthy of sympathetic yet critical exposition. In this group I place Allen E. Buchanan, G. A. Cohen, Graeme Duncan, Agnes Heller, Bertell Ollman, Paul Thomas, and Peter Worsley.[12]

Third, there are writers, similarly sympathetic to Marx, who omit discussion of this passage in contexts where we might reasonably expect it to appear. Most probably this is no oversight but rather a strategic avoidance of embarrassment at the patent naiveté of portraying communist society as a mixture of some activities that are pre-industrial (hunting, fishing) with others that are uselessly intellectual (criticising after dinner). Marx's comments elsewhere on communism seem better prospects for critical exposition, because they relate an expansion of individual autonomy and creativity to the continuation of modern industrial production – collectively planned and controlled, of course – and because they include comments on the division of labour that are at once more general and more defensible. In this category I place J. M. Barbalet, Isaiah Berlin, Jon Elster, Ben Fine, Alan Gilbert, Richard N. Hunt, Leszek Kolakowski, George Lichtheim, John McMurtry, Herbert Marcuse, Melvin Rader, William H. Shaw, Wal Suchting, John Torrance, and Allen W. Wood.[13]

Last, there are commentators whose sympathies resemble those of the writers in the second and third groups. They differ from the third group, however, in that they raise this passage from *The German Ideology*, instead of omitting it. They reward the reader by sharing their puzzlement at the apparent discrepancy in Marx's work between a pre-industrial vision of communism at one point and an industrially based communism at all others. This raises a spectre of incoherence in his views on technology in communist society that writers in the second group do not register, and so the exposition of his view on the division of labour in communist society seems fraught with difficulty. In this fourth group I place Louis Althusser, Christopher J. Arthur, Shlomo Avineri, Alex Callinicos, Michael Evans, William Leon McBride, David McLellan, John Plamenatz, Alfred Schmidt, and myself (until present writing). A close look at these views reveals the ambiguities inherent in the passage and the difficult issues it raises. These concern Marx's view on pre-industrial and industrial technology, the division of labour appropriate to each, and the kind of technology and organisation of labour that he expects in communist society.

Althusser associates *The German Ideology* with Marx's supposed 'break' from 'unscientific' humanism and his tortuous development of a 'scientific' perspective. For Althusser this perspective precludes, amongst other things, any naiveté about technology and the division of labour. He views the 'ambiguous role of the *division of labour*' in *The German Ideology* as evidence for his theory about Marx's intellectual development and therefore no longer puzzling.[14]

Arthur is more genuinely puzzled by Marx's words:

> This illustration maps pretty well the sort of working days Fourier outlined in his Utopian scheme. The pastoralism may well be ironical, since Marx already, in the *1844 Manuscripts*, criticised Fourier for taking agricultural work as exemplary. What is not ironical, apparently, is the general idea of such a solution to the division of labour. Yet one is struck by the fact that one does not overcome the present fragmentation of production by collating a heap of fragments.[15]

However, Arthur does not explain why Marx was being ironical, if indeed he was.

Avineri perceives no irony, but shifts his exposition to the division of labour in order to get away from the problem of technology:

> How these pastoral, bucolic occupations can serve as models for the abolition of the division of labour in a sophisticated, industrial society is, of course, a question to which an answer might have been expected, but an answer is not forthcoming in this or in any other of Marx's

writings. Marx's choice of such idyllic examples may indicate that he has sensed the internal difficulty of the relevance of his argument for a modern society. Yet if one accepts Marx's model of man as an other-directed being, a *Gattungswesen*, then one can envisage how the occupation of one individual can engender satisfaction in another ... thus even if a division of labour will after all be necessary, one man can find joy and satisfaction in another's occupation provided the social structure is oriented toward such possibilities.[16]

Callinicos adopts a similar strategy:

Commentators have often denounced this picture as Utopian. One can indeed wonder how literally Marx meant it to be taken, and it is worth noting that all the pursuits he lists are ones to be found in a traditional pre-industrial society. Nevertheless, there is a serious point underlying the passage, which is that the development of the productive forces under communism will be such as to free people from their existing role as cogs of the economic machine.[17]

Like Callinicos, I myself was unsure whether this view of communist society was taken seriously by Marx, and in any case how far it could be stretched to maintain consistency with his other views on the division of labour in communist society.[18]

Evans suggests that this passage in *The German Ideology* was intended seriously at the time, but that Marx changed his mind. Citing the much later *Grundrisse* manuscripts of 1857–58 Evans attempts to explain the puzzle by suggesting that Marx may have shifted his views on the division of labour – moving from a set pattern to an emphasis on choice – as well as on the necessity of an industrial technology in communist society:

Later, however, this Fourier-like picture changes: 'Labour cannot become a game, as Fourier would like it to be ...'

There were perhaps two reasons why Marx changed his mind. The viewpoint implied that a range of butterfly-like activities was best for all individuals. But if we think of the painter example [in *The German Ideology*: 'In a communist society there are no painters, but at most people who engage in painting among other activities'], for instance, it is evident that a painter devoted to his art would voluntarily spend the major part of his time painting. If there is any meaning to the notion of 'free activity', it must imply that the individual would have to choose for himself whether or not to engage in one major activity or a whole range of activities.

... Second, Marx accepted that large-scale industrial organisation requires differentiation of functions and roles: a technical division of labour must remain, though hopefully it will be functions rather than persons that will be specialised ... In *Capital* considerable emphasis is placed on the role of technological development.[19]

McBride merely refers to the passage as 'tongue-in-cheek' without elaborating on the point of the supposed joke. McLellan seems initially to have opted for the theory that Marx was parodying Max Stirner, the 'True Socialist' pilloried in *The German Ideology*:

Certainly Stirner seems to have been in Marx's mind when he was composing the section on Feuerbach in the *Deutsche Ideologie*. There are many references to Stirner and even a parody of him in the well-known description of future communist society ...[20]

McLellan does not cite a passage from Stirner, so one wonders why Stirner, rather than Fourier, is the supposed object of satire at this point in the text. Mazlish quotes a passage from Fourier in which the Utopian 'outlines a typical day in his phalanstery, listing an individual's activity at every hour ... "at 5½... a session in a hunting group ... at 7 ... a session in a fishing group ...""[21] Fourier continues by suggesting after-dinner cultural amusements at '9½' and bed at '10½'.[22] Subsequently McLellan seems to drop this theory and indeed any explanation at all. This is apparently because he finds the passage an oddity rather than a genuine puzzle:

The key factor in the establishment of communism was the abolition of the division of labour. But the only example that Marx gave of this here [in *The German Ideology*] was drawn from a rural community ... At least the means [abolition of the division of labour] to the end [communist society] was clear.[23]

Like Evans and the later McLellan, Plamenatz reasons that Marx's vision was serious at the time but was later abandoned, and he seems content to leave the matter at that:

The ideal described in *The German Ideology*, though never repudiated, is abandoned. The communist society will also be industrial, and production will be complicated and carefully organised, even though the organising of it will be done by the workers themselves.[24]

Schmidt suggests a departure from an 'early, romantic belief in the possibility of a complete abolition of the division of labour' because Marx moves in later works towards 'more concrete discussions of the question'.[25] As with Evans, the later McLellan and Plamenatz, this merely restates the problem – how to explain the apparent inconsistency between *The German Ideology* and Marx's vision, in all other texts before and after it (where the subject comes up), of communism as a society built on the achievements of modern technology.

Surface-text and sub-text

The German Ideology, Part 1, has recently been re-edited, and this new edition by Wataru Hiromatsu puts one of the most famous passages in all Marx's work in quite a new light.[26] The four previous rescensions, of which Hiromatsu is critical in varying degrees, arranged the textual fragments of the manuscript so as to produce continuous prose. These texts provided information on crossed-out material and handwriting on a highly selective basis, but none of the previous editions of *The German Ideology* gave the detailed information on this passage that appears in Hiromatsu's text. Hiromatsu has reproduced the German text column-by-column, page-by-page, sheet-by-sheet. Through notes and typography he shows the reader which words were written in Engels' hand, which in Marx's, which insertions can be assigned to each author, and which deletions. The manuscript has long been described as a mixture of rough draft, correction and amendment, fresh starts and fair copy. All this can now be followed in detail, word-by-word, in Hiromatsu's edition.

At the many points in the manuscript where individual words cannot be read with certainty, Hiromatsu provides his own reading and indicates the variants adopted by his predecessors. He offers an arrangement of material that follows his own views on where substantive discussion starts, stops and restarts on the sheets that survived the famous 'gnawing criticism of the mice' and other hazards, such as the German socialist Eduard Bernstein's predilection for crossing things out.[27] Because Hiromatsu has provided so much information about the handwritten text the reader is in a position to judge his suggestions and to form independent views. In future we should expect much more nuanced accounts of the way Marx and Engels thought and worked, individually and (here in *The German Ideology*) together – as individuals.

The overall pattern of composition within Part 1 of *The German Ideology* is now clear, though subject, of course, to many small variations. Engels seems to have provided a rough draft which Marx corrected, striking out individual words and phrases and inserting new ones, sometimes adding sentences and paragraphs in his own hand. Engels then provided some fair copy, incorporating these changes, occasionally making further changes of his own, subject to further amendment by Marx. However, even when handwriting has been identified, authorship is still open to some question. This is because the degree of collaboration on first draft and final copy (where it is extant) cannot be known with certainty. Ideas cannot necessarily be ascribed to one author or the other, because they may have been held independently before composition, they may have arisen in a mutual exchange, or they may have been adopted by one or the other on reading their separate contributions as they progressed (I explore some of these issues in chapter eight below). In any case Marx's handwriting was notoriously bad, so he used various friends (such as Engels and Joseph Weydemeyer) and his spouse (Jenny Marx) as amanuenses at various times.

However, the assignment of particular words to Marx or to Engels can on occasion be most revealing, and it behoves us to look closely at this in every case, so that we are not misled in the interpretation of particular passages by a blanket assumption that the work is a jointly written continuous text. For instance information on handwriting may lead us to interpret an apparently continuous passage, such as the famous vision of communist society, in a radically different manner, because it may reveal a debate between the two writers as they engaged in drafting their thoughts and noting amendments. This is precisely what I think took place. According to Hiromatsu's edition the whole passage is in Engels' hand, save for these few words inserted by Marx: 'or a critical critic'; 'criticise after dinner'; 'or critic'.[28]

This suggests to me that Marx, in reviewing and amending Engels' work, inserted these words and phrases humorously in order to send it up, and thus to reject it as a serious draft. In Marx's view, as I read the re-edited text, the hunter and fisherman were Utopian, naive, pre-industrial and an unconscious parody of Fourier by Engels. In drafting this passage Engels himself crossed out a further selection of vocations to be undertaken 'just as I have a mind', including being a shoemaker, a gardener and an actor.[29] The hunter and fisherman were reminiscent of the very pre-industrial Utopias that Marx despised. In his estimation, they represented a communist society fit only for 'critical critics', who were the butt of the satire and scorn in *The German Ideology* itself. Marx seems to have been telling Engels that this bucolic Utopia was just the sort of place where the 'critical critics' would be quite at home, because real production has become a folksy pastime and real intellectual effort has become after-dinner criticism. This is entirely consistent with the critical assessment that Marx made elsewhere of Fourier, praising his work for its attack on class-divided society, but noting that it was Utopian precisely because Fourier did not, indeed could not, incorporate modern industry into his scheme, owing to the undeveloped state of production at the time. The famous passage on communist society from *The German Ideology* cannot now be read as one continuous train of thought agreed jointly between two authors. To me it shows Marx sharply rebuking Engels for straying, perhaps momentarily, from the serious work of undercutting the fantasies of Utopian socialists. Marx considered most aspects of Utopian socialism to be a formidable distraction from the problems, political movements and solutions for which he wished to gain support, because of the outdated character of typical Utopian views on industry, and other faults.

Hiromatsu's edition has had little impact outside Japan for the unfortunate reason that the *apparatus criticus* is in Japanese only,[30] but readers should have known long ago that something in this passage was amiss. What were the 'critical critics' doing in communist society anyway? Marx's and Engels' attitudes to them were never any mystery. How could either have seriously promoted them to pride of place as communist exemplars? A scholarly edition of *The German Ideology*, such as Hiromatsu's, is essential to making plausible judgements in such matters of interpretation, but Marx's broad humour was staring readers in the face all along. Hostile critics of Marx will not now have such an easy time, since the full passage can no longer be ascribed to Marx or to Engels alone, or even to both working jointly. Indeed the full passage has no straightforward meaning now as a description of communist society in its technological aspect, since the comments by Marx on the 'critical critics' have cast the hunter and fisherman into sardonic oblivion. Those writers who took the passage seriously as a smoothly descriptive statement about productive activity and the division of labour in communist society will have some re-writing to do, because they will now have to present and assess Marx's views on the division of labour in communism independently of his pre-industrial vision. Other critics can return to this passage without embarrassment, if that was indeed the reason they avoided it, and those commentators who were puzzled were right to be so. Because Marx rejected the pre-industrial pastoral concocted by Engels, an overall consistency in Marx's views on the industrial character of communist society can be safely assumed, so it seems to me. But the relevance of this passage to the issue of a communist division of labour – however it is conceived – is now thoroughly compromised. The problems concerning Marx's views on the future organisation of labour, how 'in a higher phase of communist society' the 'subjection of individuals to the division of labour' will disappear, can now be more sensibly discussed, once this passage has been more productively re-read.[31]

Posthumous Marxism and revolutionary communism

Given that Marx and Engels refused to play any easy political game, and given that they gave everyone else so few chances to join or 'follow' them politically, it seems that there might have been a kind of mystery and allure in the very novelty of their approach, which was to pursue 'high theory' at a remove and trenchant commentary on the immediate. What linked these two activities was barely more than an idea – a communism based on modern industrial technology, but an inversion of the capitalist system. To these ends both Marx and Engels pursued popular journalism, though editorial control and state censorship restricted their ability to propagandise openly for their brand of communism, and audiences, whilst widespread in Europe and America, were comparatively small for any given series of articles. Up to 1850 Marx in particular aimed to put his views persuasively to relatively small circles of intellectuals, some of them communists or socialists (on various self-understandings of these terms), and some of them democrats moved by political inequalities or reforming radicals upset by economic inequalities (this political nexus is explored in chapter six below). Neither Marx nor Engels was at all focused on women as particularly oppressed in ways other than political and economic disadvantage conventionally understood, Engels' late attempts to respond to 'the woman question' notwithstanding (I explore Marx's work on gender and women in chapter ten below). My point here is that neither Marx nor Engels connected very successfully with the mass politics that arose after 1850, except late in life, and at something of a remove, when Engels took on the role of adviser to the Second International and to various national parties, so there is rarely any way to judge them as actors making practical links between communist principle and contemporary practice.

From the time of Marx and Engels onwards modern means of communication and increasing literacy allowed the practice of mass politics at a distance via the written word (Engels was quite fond of telegraphy in his advising role), and the apparent aloofness of these two German intellectuals is perhaps an effect of this growing disjunction. The communist tradition was not merely advanced in an intellectualised form; the activity of pursuing communism became itself an intellectualised endeavour. By the end of the nineteenth century the works of Engels, and numerous other systematic critics of existing society, became popular items of study for workers, and theory came to co-exist alongside and inside political organisations and movements as major activities. Thus Marx and Engels were amongst the first to move the masses beyond a politics of ideas to a politics of theory, and Engels in particular took on the burden of popularising the more forbidding tomes that Marx eventually produced.

Though denying that he was 'a Marxist',[32] Marx was fervently a communist, and in the context sketched above the association between his name and the avant garde of the movement became almost unbreakable. All Marxists were communists in some sense, and the chances of communism existing independently of Marxism became virtually nil. A further factor promoting this process was the internationalist perspective adopted by Marx and Engels from their earliest days, and this provides in part an explanation for their lack of personal involvement in partisan activity at the national level (a further reason was their lifetime exile post-1850 in England). Indeed, the two advised communists that they did not form a party independent of other democratic or specifically working-class parties (virtually all of which were illegal or clandestine before 1848), but were rather to work as individuals or in small groups to promote the constitutional revolutions of mass (or at least large-scale) suffrage and to push economic reorganisation on to the national political agenda. Instead the two almost always worked at the level of international information-exchange and cooperation in agreeing overall goals and definitions amongst allied groups and parties pledging to assist one another, and to ensure that working-class cooperation took precedence over the conventional 'ruling class' politics of national interest.

As communism and Marxism became synonymous, so the political agenda developed to promote the staged introduction of the new economic order, for which the founders provided notes rather than blueprints. Broadly speaking the 'battle for democracy' occupied the first attentions of communists, that is, the overthrow of authoritarian non-constitutional regimes that excluded working men from political power (women were not specifically included, and hence were typically excluded or marginalised). This was assumed to require violent struggle in order to resist the attacks or counter-attacks of authoritarian forces protecting the interests of large-scale holders of property or representing the interests of those aspiring thereto. A series of 'despotic inroads on the right to property', as it says in the *Communist Manifesto*, would ensure a redistribution under socialism of income, wealth, power and ownership to the mass of the people organised within a democratic state. Rewards would be proportional to labour contributed, but crucial to this system was the distinction between 'means of production' in land and in capital generally, which would be centrally controlled, and 'private property' in items for personal use and consumption, which would be safeguarded, indeed increased qualitatively and quantitatively for ordinary people.[33]

The line between this socialist stage and communism itself was deliberately vague, as the point of socialism was to create communism through practical activity and participatory politics, and individual interests were presumed to be converging on the collective good. At that point a labour contribution from individuals according to ability (rather than as a response to material reward) would be the norm, because technological productivity, planned production and consumption, reduced hours of work, and personal fulfilment through the productive and social aspects of the labour process would obviate the need for money as a mediator between working hours and consumption goods. The material means of life would then be distributed according to need.[34] Neither the political details concerning administration or any residual conflicts of interest, nor the economic details concerning the planning process for nation-wide schedules of production and consumption (and international arrangements mirroring these principles between countries), were ever spelled out. Nor was the political perspective of contemporary pre-literate or non-European peoples ever explored in depth by Marx *vis-à-vis* the forced introduction of trading relations and the domination entailed in colonial rule, on which he commented in his books and articles.

Even more seriously neither Marx nor Engels produced any useable theories concerning the organisation and mission of political parties at any stage, or of the principled criteria for intra-party or society-wide democracy, though there are sketches suggesting that Marx supported arrangements to institute workplace democracy and to vote in representative bodies to take decisions at successively higher levels (these issues are explored in chapter six below).[35] Thus the way was open for later theorists to fill these gaps in their own way, with their own personal predilections and political circumstances in mind. In this manner the political function of communism in the very late nineteenth century and throughout the twentieth century has come to deviate very sharply from the theories and practice of Marx and Engels, and even more noticeably from virtually all aspects of the communist tradition up to that time.

The more this deviation occurred, the more efforts were made on the communist side to invoke the authority of founders, and a mirror-like process of confirmation developed on the Western or non-communist side. Both sides generated a politicised form of scholarship and a curiously similar demonisation of ideas. Attempts to trace the roots or origins of twentieth-century communism in the ideas (most usually) or practice (very occasionally) of pre-twentieth-century communism became by the 1950s a sizeable academic and indeed political industry in the West. This was predicated on the view that criticism of current communists was not sufficient, as similar malpractices were bound to crop up unless communist ideas themselves were shown to be 'linked' to twentieth-century events and then 'refuted' once and for all. Thus many mid-twentieth-century accounts of the communist tradition suffer to varying degrees from a process of inscription – reading current political circumstances and judgements into what were presumed to be canonical texts, which were presumed to have forebears. With the collapse of the former Soviet Union and the dissolution of superpower conflict as an intellectual template, it is now possible to take a more dispassionate view.

Parallel to the association between Marxism and communism was a further association between the two and revolution. This was particularly influential through the developing world, most notably in China, Cuba and Viet Nam, where anti-imperialist struggles for national liberation took place. Very few successful revolutions were of the constitutional and democratic sort that Marx envisaged, although many participants may have associated themselves with revolutionary movements on the understanding that this would be the case. Nonetheless, through the late nineteenth century and on into the twentieth century, an apparatus of representative government has by now been widely established by various means, though stability has not been an overall feature, either within these regimes or between democratic and authoritarian models. Thus the original link between the need for popular revolutionary force and communist politics should well have weakened, and there is some evidence in the correspondence of the late Marx to suggest that he had taken peaceful transitions to socialism on board.[36]

Within the Marxist tradition, however, communism remained a doctrine of revolution, a guide for revolutionaries, the presumed authorisation for armed struggle. In part this association remained valid on Marx's terms, as anti-authoritarian movements and anti-colonialist peoples struggled for local democratic rule, though such societies were often far from instantiating the presumed benefits of modern material production that formed a necessary basis for the kind of socialist measures that Marx and Engels had wanted. The international cooperation between democratic movements that the two envisaged was almost never achieved either, as national and nationalist interests notoriously took precedence, rhetoric to the contrary. The most influential model for party organisation was derived from the writings of V. I. Lenin and from his experiences in fighting authoritarian rule in Russia, from his attempts to exercise political power in a war-torn society further troubled by civil war and foreign invasion, and from Stalin's consolidation of one-party rule and institutionalisation of highly centralised economic management. Elements of representative democracy within party and state structures evolved there, but in a sham-like way.

The totalitarian model as applied by Western commentators to communism underestimated the need for, and practice of, what are recognisably familiar forms of politics in an authoritarian system, but no model of democracy independent of self-description or elaborated excuses could save, then or now, the notion that the Communist Party of the Soviet Union, and the Soviet Union itself, was democratic. Nor did the communists of that regime, its satellites, or any other Marxist regime or movement of significance appeal to the non-democratic models of rule available within the communist tradition itself with any clarity or enthusiasm. As noted above, these included philosopher kings in Plato, patriarchal authority in More, or other versions of an administrative or religious elite. Thus it is difficult to see how one of the great political movements of the twentieth century conformed at all to any aspect of communism as a pre-existing tradition, other than to institute (amongst other things) redistributive policies of the sort that have sometimes emerged within the socialist programmes of representative democracies.

What divides redistributive socialism from Marx's communism, and indeed almost any other communism in the tradition, is the presumed continuance of the money economy, rather than the managed obsolescence of monetary exchange itself, i.e. the obvious and stated consequence of Marx's analysis of money (explored above in chapter one through chapter four). Nowhere in the 'communist' world was this ever seriously envisaged. The claims propounded by twentieth-century Marxist regimes, such as the Soviet Union, that, for example, 1936 marked the 'victory of socialism', that 1959 marked the beginning of 'the full scale construction of communist society', and that in 1961 the transition from 'socialism to communism' would be complete 'in the main' within twenty years, inspired little confidence inside or outside its boundaries.[37]

Indeed backtracking began in the 1970s, and by the beginning of the 1980s 'developed socialism' was said to be a lengthy historical stage, itself a whole historical epoch in which progress would be merely gradual. Comments on the relative unimportance of rosy futures suggested that the *communist* ideal had been officially shelved in the Soviet sphere. Furthermore it cannot said that dissidence within the various communist regimes flourished as much as it did because of any underground communist movement objecting on specifically and traditionally communist grounds either to the maintenance of monetary relations in society or to the undemocratic party and state structures that dominated the process of economic planning.

Clearly the abolition of private ownership of the means of production in itself did not even begin the process of socialising production through the planning process and readjusting consumption through the democratic process that Marx and Engels envisaged. Nor did the imposition of authoritarian rule via self-selecting (and self-purging) parties, and the accumulations of political and economic privilege (by cadres and apparatchiks), match any previous model of communist society. It is difficult to see how these arrangements, which have been described by their originators and participants as 'communist', could possibly conform to any notion of shared control and use within a cooperative community. If that is what communism has come to mean, then Orwellian language has indeed triumphed.

Future perfect

Communism still has a future as a critical perspective on an economic system based on private property, or so-called private property – enormous resources are now owned and controlled by 'artificial persons' or 'private' companies. The relation of these entities to an economic and legal doctrine of individual ownership and property rights is politically somewhat obscure and morally rather tenuous. The extent to which the current commercial system is founded on and indeed continually recreates wasteful and unjustified inequalities of income and wealth is always worth considering. The proposition that only effective demand, i.e. access to money or credit, is the sole necessary, efficient and desirable gateway to consumption goods has been in recent years loudly defended and politically manipulated. Some of the regulation and control of the 'means of production' that democratic states have come to exercise has recently been weakened or abandoned, and some of the redistributive measures giving access to goods on the basis of need (rather than monetary resources, however derived) has been dismantled. Insofar as the counter-arguments that society has a role in the productive process (beyond that of securing private property), and that the individual may claim resources on a basis other than commercial acumen (or charity), are still pertinent, then a critique of 'economic man' (*sic*) may rightly appeal to the communist tradition. After all, communists developed their systems for just this purpose.

The totalising or millenarian view amongst communists that competitive commercial individualism is fundamentally flawed, and that the wholesale substitution of communitarian relations is the sole logical and practical response, may have been a discursive strategy or trope within the communist genre. Critics who argue that communists are necessarily extremists who want to sweep away entire existing societies are not always reading the texts politically. Communists may well want to work within an existing democratic system to achieve their goals; notoriously they have sometimes claimed the right to do so. That said, there is also likely to be a continuing pattern of counter-cultural movements rejecting economic individualism and attempting to 'opt out'. In that mode the communist tradition runs within and alongside a recurring vein of religious and secular experimentation.

The use and control of material resources is a necessary and increasingly divisive feature of human society. How these resources are 'owned' and 'shared' will be continually debated, and communists have argued influentially against a thoroughgoing individualist view. The extent to which an individualistic economics and politics presides ideologically over what is in reality a 'socialised' apparatus of regulation and control is perhaps testimony to the necessity for at least some communism in practice, even in a world where luxury and surplus are the name of the game.

In the next chapter I explore Marx's place, in theory and in practice, in developing both liberalism and socialism, and in so doing I question the boundary line between the two. The extent to which, and the ways in which, democracy should or should not interact with the economic realms of production, distribution, consumption and exchange constitutes a major area of contemporary political debate – and if it does not, it should. In his own time Marx helped to construct the terms in which this debate is formulated, and he pursued political strategies that are worth revisiting. In that way I shall be claiming him as an important theorist in the democratic tradition.

Notes

1 Karl Marx, *The Eighteenth Brumaire of Louis Bonaparte*, in Karl Marx, *Later Political Writings*, ed. and trans. Terrell Carver (Cambridge, Cambridge University Press, 1996), p. 32.

2 For a highly sceptical view of the speculations constructed by archaeologists about social relations in pre-literate societies, see Michael Shanks and Christopher Tilley, *Social Theory and Archaeology* (Cambridge, Polity Press, 1987).

3 Marx, Introduction to the *Grundrisse*, in *Later Political Writings*, p. 128.

4 Plato, *The Republic*, ii.372A–374E.

5 Plato, *The Republic*, ii.375A–iv.434D.

6 Plato, *The Republic*, iv.445B–v.457A; Diana Coole, *Women in Political Theory: From Ancient Misogyny to Contemporary Feminism*, 2nd edn (Brighton, Harvester/Wheatsheaf, 1993).

7 Thomas More, *Utopia*, ed. George M. Logan and Robert M. Adams (Cambridge, Cambridge University Press, 1988), book I.

8 More, *Utopia*, book II.

9 Gregory Claeys, *Machinery, Money and the Millennium: From Moral Economy to Socialism 1815–60* (Cambridge, Polity Press, 1987).

10 Karl Marx and Frederick Engels, *Collected Works*, vol. 5 (London, Lawrence & Wishart, 1976), p. 47; for information on the manuscript, previous editions and English translations, see pp. 586–8, n. 7. For a selection of passages on communist society see David McLellan, *The Thought of Karl Marx: An Introduction*, 2nd edn (London, Macmillan, 1980), pp. 244–52.

11 Kostas Axelos, *Alienation, Praxis and Techne in the Thought of Karl Marx*, trans. Ronald Bruzina (Austin TX and London, University of Texas Press, 1976), pp. 257–8; R. N. Berki, *Insight and Vision: The Problem of Communism in Marx's Thought* (London, Dent, 1983), pp. 74–5; M. M. Bober, *Karl Marx's Interpretation of History*, new edn (New York, Norton, 1965), pp. 287–8; Bruce Mazlish, *The Meaning of Karl Marx* (New York and Oxford, Oxford University Press, 1984), pp. 94–5; Alec Nove, *The Economics of Feasible Socialism* (London, Allen & Unwin, 1983), pp. 46–7; Peter Singer, *Marx* (Oxford, Oxford University Press, 1980), pp. 60–4.

12 Allen E. Buchanan, *Marx and Justice: Radical Critique of Liberalism* (London, Methuen, 1982), pp. 22–4; G. A. Cohen, *Karl Marx's Theory of History: A Defence* (Oxford, Oxford University Press, 1978), pp. 132–3; Graeme Duncan, *Marx and Mill: Two Views of Social Conflict and Social Harmony* (Cambridge, Cambridge University Press, 1973), pp. 182–3; Agnes Heller, *The Theory of Need in Marx* (London, Allison & Busby, 1976), pp. 105–9; Bertell Ollman, *Alienation: Marx's Conception of Man in Capitalist Society* (Cambridge, Cambridge University Press, 1971), pp, 160–1; Paul Thomas, *Karl Marx and the Anarchists* (London, Routledge & Kegan Paul, 1980), pp. 148–9; Peter Worsley, *Marx and Marxism* (Chichester and London, Ellis Horwood, 1982), pp. 88–9.

13 J. M. Barbalet, *Marx's Construction of Social Theory* (London, Routledge & Kegan Paul, 1983); Isaiah Berlin, *Karl Marx: His Life and Environment*, 4th edn (Oxford, Oxford University Press, 1978); Jon Elster, *Making Sense of Marx* (Cambridge and Paris, Cambridge University Press, 1985); Ben Fine, 'Communism', in *A Dictionary of Marxist Thought*, ed. Tom Bottomore et al. (Oxford, Basil Blackwell, 1983), pp. 87–90; Alan Gilbert, *Marx's Politics* (Oxford, Martin Robertson, 1981); Richard N. Hunt, *The Political Ideas of Marx and Engels, vol. 1: Marxism and Totalitarian Democracy 1818–1850* (London, Macmillan, 1975); Leszek

Kolakowski, *Main Currents of Marxism: Its Rise, Growth, and Dissolution, vol. 1: The Founders*, trans. P. S. Falla (Oxford, Oxford University Press, 1978); George Lichtheim, *Marxism: An Historical and Critical Study*, 2nd edn (London, Routledge & Kegan Paul, 1964); John McMurtry, *The Structure of Marx's World-View* (Princeton, Princeton University Press, 1978); Herbert Marcuse, *Reason and Revolution: Hegel and the Rise of Social Theory*, 2nd edn (London, Routledge & Kegan Paul, 1955); Melvin Rader, *Marx's Interpretation of History* (New York, Oxford University Press, 1979); William H. Shaw, *Marx's Theory of History* (London, Hutchinson, 1978), W. A. Suchting, *Marx: An Introduction* (Brighton, Harvester/Wheatsheaf, 1983); John Torrance, *Estrangement, Alienation and Exploitation: A Sociological Approach to Historical Materialism* (London, Macmillan, 1977); Allen W. Wood, *Karl Marx* (London, Routledge & Kegan Paul, 1981).

14 Louis Althusser, *For Marx*, trans. Ben Brewster (London, Allen & Unwin, 1969), pp. 36–7.

15 C. J. Arthur, *Dialectics of Labour: Marx and his Relation to Hegel* (Oxford, Basil Blackwell, 1986), p. 137.

16 Shlomo Avineri, *The Social and Political Thought of Karl Marx* (Cambridge, Cambridge University Press, 1968), pp. 231–2.

17 Alex Callinicos, *The Revolutionary Ideas of Marx* (London, Bookmarks, 1983), p. 175.

18 Terrell Carver, *Marx's Social Theory* (Oxford, Oxford University Press, 1982), pp. 75–7.

19 Michael Evans, *Karl Marx* (London, Allen & Unwin, 1975), pp. 159–60.

20 William Leon McBride, *The Philosophy of Marx* (London, Hutchinson, 1977), p. 129; David McLellan, *The Young Hegelians and Karl Marx* (London, Macmillan, 1969), p. 132.

21 Mazlish, *Meaning of Marx*, p. 95, citing *Harmonian Man: Selected Writings of Charles Fourier*, ed. Mark Poster (Garden City NY, Random House, 1971), p. 13.

22 Nicholas V. Riasanovsky, *The Teaching of Charles Fourier* (Berkeley and Los Angeles, University of California Press, 1969), pp. 48–60 (this reference was kindly suggested to me by Paul Thomas).

23 David McLellan, *Karl Marx: His Life and Thought* (London, Macmillan, 1973), pp. 147–8.

24 John Plamenatz, *Karl Marx's Philosophy of Man* (Oxford, Oxford University Press, 1975), pp. 143–4.

25 Alfred Schmidt, *The Concept of Nature in Marx*, trans. Ben Fowkes (London, New Left Books, 1971), p. 146.

26 Karl Marx and Friedrich Engels, *Die deutsche Ideologie: Kritik der neuesten deutschen Philosophie in ihren Repräsentanten, Feuerbach, B. Bauer und Stirner, und des deutschen Sozialismus in seinen verschiedenen Propheten. 1. Band. 1 Abschnitt,*

ed. W. Hiromatsu (Tokyo, Kawadashobo-Shinsha,1974). I am deeply grateful to Professor Hiroshi Uchida of Senshu University, Tokyo, for informing me of this edition, securing a copy for my use and bringing the passage on communism to my attention.

27 Marx, Preface to *A Contribution to the Critique of Political Economy*, in *Later Political Writings*, p. 161; On Bernstein, see S. Bahne, '"Die deutsche Ideologie" von Marx und Engels. Einige Textergänzungen', *International Review of Social History*, 7 (1962), cited in Marx and Engels, *Collected Works*, vol. 5, p. 587 n.

28 Marx and Engels, *Collected Works*, vol. 5, p. 47; Marx and Engels, *Die deutsche Ideologie*, p. 34.

29 Marx and Engels, *Die deutsche Ideologie*, p. 34.

30 Professor Uchida has kindly undertaken translations for my use.

31 Marx, *Critique of the Gotha Programme*, in *Later Political Writings*, p. 214.

32 Karl Marx and Frederick Engels, *Selected Correspondence*, 2nd edn, ed. S. Ryazanskaya, trans. I. Lasker (Moscow, Progress, 1965), p. 415.

33 Marx, *Manifesto of the Communist Party*, in *Later Political Writings*, pp. 12–20.

34 Marx, *Critique of the Gotha Programme*, in *Later Political Writings*, pp. 211–15.

35 Marx, *The Civil War in France*, in *Later Political Writings*, pp. 183–7.

36 McLellan, *Thought of Karl Marx*, p. 209.

37 Martin Crouch, *Revolution and Evolution: Gorbachev and Soviet Politics* (Hemel Hempstead, Philip Allan, 1989), pp. 77–9.

CHAPTER SIX

Liberalism and socialism: Marx's democracy

Histories and theories

Does the collapse of Stalinism in Eastern Europe mark the 'end of history', as Francis Fukuyama from the Rand Corporation has proclaimed,[1] or the 'rebirth of history', as argued by the BBC correspondent Misha Glenny,[2] or the 'revenge of history', as diagnosed by the English Marxist Alex Callinicos?[3] First of all, however, we should ask, if these locutions make any sense. We are not going to know whether history is at an end or has been reborn or revenged for some time, so the truth conditions here are speculative. Most important, the term 'history' needs careful examination. Can these writers use it to refer in a commonplace way to 'what has happened'?

'What has happened' is of course a matter of selection, and necessarily so, but it is selection from what is already selective. No one has the totality of events on hand from which to select, and there is no totality of events in the first place. Events are not events till they are conceptualised, and there are arguably as many events as there are conceptualisers, even if many of them agree and even if they are eyewitnesses. Eyewitnesses notoriously disagree in practice in their descriptions as they conceptualise events; more academically, the search for a purely descriptive language – one that is independent of individual judgement and valuation – even for objects, never mind events, has been abandoned by philosophers, or at least thoroughly discredited.[4]

What does it mean, then, to talk about history? Using the term involves us in an interpretative exercise of some considerable complexity. Probably, and paradoxically, statements about history are really attempts to persuade people into making or accepting one future rather than another. Thus references to history are often future-oriented and political. Fukuyama, Glenny and Callinicos all have their hopes for Eastern Europe, the world, their domestic politics, as well as their careers, and their construction of contemporary events coincides with their various warnings and recommendations. This self-fulfilling circularity could not be otherwise, since I take it that future-oriented political discourse is one of the things, perhaps the main one, that distinguishes us from other animals. It represents the undoubted cause and supposed cure for the planetary problems that bear down on us as individuals.

Amongst the three accounts cited above we might find one more persuasive than another, at which point we should ask ourselves exactly why. Actually all three share a number of anodyne values and judgements, and make similar recommendations and give similar warnings. They differ on the finer points of what they would like to see occur in future, and on the role of soothsayers in the political process. Whilst all three writers have published for a wide audience, they undoubtedly have rather different ideas on where their most immediate influence might be: American policy-makers, the World Service audience, the European Left.

More controversially, these writers – and others on the subject – are bound to differ on what the situation 'is', as what it 'is' is constructed interpretively from claims about the past, using terms derived from past discourse. Indeed the present is necessarily only the past as far as it has yet occurred. The past, of course, exists as a matter of interpreted experience for each of us, and strictly speaking the present moment is always retrospective. Hopes, fears and recommendations are made persuasive through the marshalling of retrospection, otherwise known as history, and here I propose the join in the fray and offer a reinterpretation of Marx and also of democracy.

Fukuyama's triumphalism has been widely celebrated, but also denounced by innumerable writers, including Glenny and Callinicos.

This triumphalism is said to consist in gloating that 'the West has won' and that 'capitalism is the only workable economic system'; critics argue that these views are unhelpfully provocative and grossly over-simplified. While I would not disagree very much with this, I would like to offer a somewhat different interpretation of the recent political struggles. On the one hand I wish to be more triumphalist than any-one else, but on the other hand perhaps more despairing. At the same time, and as part of the same process, I shall apply the same terms of analysis to a reinterpretation of Marx's political career. This is not simply because Marxism is widely discussed in the context of the post-1989 political changes: Was it killed off entirely with Stalinism because the two were conceptually and therefore historically the same, or was Stalinism a deception practised on ideas and activities that were essen-tially different? Rather than get involved with this somewhat hermet-ic debate, I shall outline a reinterpretation of Marx's politics that will highlight the tenacity and complexity, the idealism and betrayal, of the struggle for democracy.

Democracy and democrats

In my view Marx was a democrat, and the tradition would be enriched if he were reclaimed as such. It is a complex tradition, but politicians find it to their advantage to simplify it. Marx's criticisms of 'bourgeois democracy' were trenchant, and they deserve re-examina-tion to see if there has been any progress since his time. Perhaps there has been less than we have been led to believe. Marx, and his political partner Engels, are chiefly known now as revolutionaries, but I shall argue that this aspect of their theory and practice has been vastly over-played. This was done by parties whose interests are at odds with, or are at least very marginal to, the sort of democratic politics that most people would find generally tolerable.

Since Marx and Engels are well known now as communists, it may sound surprising to relate that they supported, in theory and in prac-tice, national and international movements for representative and responsible government. However, it is also acknowledged in current biographical literature that they admired the ideals of the French

Revolution and were, at least at the beginning of their careers, democrats in some vague sense. My point is that what Marx and Engels shared with democrats of their own time, and – other things being equal – with ours, has been left unexplored, as it is thought to be obvious or off the point. Neither is true, and the events of 1989 highlight this quite dramatically. I would characterise the recent political changes in the former Soviet Union and Eastern Europe as revolutionary reconstructions with large, though varying amounts of popular participation. They are a further episode in the struggle for truly constitutional governments that dates back most notably to 1789 in France; the widespread spontaneous character of the popular outbursts in 1989 across Europe is also strongly reminiscent of the revolutions of 1848.

The political activities undertaken in the 1840s by Marx and Engels in various European localities – Cologne, Berlin, Brussels, Paris, London, Manchester – were part of the popular, if almost always clandestine, politics that led up to the outbreaks of mass anti-monarchical violence that occurred in 1848–49. During the revolutionary events themselves their travels extended as far afield as Switzerland and Vienna. As reporters and editors of a Rhineland paper they were able to relay news items to journals all over Europe, and to provide their own readers with similar coverage. In mass political action information and spontaneity are not at all inconsistent.[5]

My interpretative framework for comparing 1848 and 1989, and for analysing the political theory and practice of Marx and Engels, is necessarily very broad, yet I shall also try to be specific. It is not 'grand theory'. I take genuine constitutionalism to mean representative and responsible government, periodic elections, multi-party politics, an independent judiciary, and a multitude of rights that allow citizens redress against their rulers: rights to free intellectual inquiry, to uncensored publication on political subjects, to popular participation in all levels of government, to challenge governmental policy in the courts, to protect citizens from religious (or anti-religious) oppression, to self-government independent of foreign control. That list – which obviously overlaps the People's Charter of 1838 as well as Charter 77 and innumerable other documents demanding popular sovereignty – is something derived by me from the journalism of Marx and Engels.

A flysheet based on the jointly authored *Communist Manifesto* listing seventeen similar demands was widely circulated in Germany and in the German press, reaching an audience from London to the lower Danube. Marx and Engels signed the document, which called for a unified German republic, parliamentary government, universal suffrage, free legal services, an end to feudal obligations, complete separation of church and state, free education, nationalisation of productive resources such as mines and transport, state-sponsored mortgages and tenancies, state control of banking and currency, guaranteed livelihood and provision for the incapacitated, curtailment of the right of inheritance and the introduction of graduated rather than flat-rate taxation.[6]

However, what is generally not detailed now, as it was much more obvious to democrats of the time, was the nature of the enemy: authoritarian, non-constitutional monarchies. Amongst the myriad German states only four constitutions survived the post-Napoleonic reaction, and one of those was abrogated summarily in the 1830s. Otherwise monarchical or clerical authoritarian rule was the norm, sometimes dressed up with appointive or non-popular elective bodies with a 'consultative' role, but no real control. There was censorship, religious interference with conscience and education, arbitrary arrest and punishment, and a stifling conformity and stupidity that was both deeply resented and widely supported. These creaky structures were not up to the horrors of twentieth-century Stalinism, but they are not at all loveable in retrospect merely for the contrast. I think it safe to generalise that in 1848 as in 1989 they were perceived as outdated, inefficient and embarrassing by democrats, inconsistent with the ambitions of nationalists, and a focus for all kinds of discontent. All the 1848 revolutions were in a sense unsuccessful, in that reactionary, authoritarian or only mildly reformed regimes succeeded the popular meetings and constituent assemblies of the heady days of the '48ers. Constitutional rule did not reach Germany until the 1860s, France until the 1870s, and further east not until after World War I. It should quickly be said that these constitutions were not especially liberal by late twentieth-century standards.

During the 1840s Marx and Engels did not merely write but also spoke, and not just to workers. Workers were actually a difficult audience to reach as meetings were regularly broken up by the police (whether of Prussia, Belgium or France) as threats to public order. Arguably the more effective politics pursued by the two was with the various democratic societies that they joined and promoted; those societies of 'fraternal democrats' were, of course, semi-clandestine, as even semi-constitutional rulers in Belgium and France had little liking for such agitation. Thus Marx and Engels involved themselves in a dual strategy, playing both sides of the class divide. This is hardly more remarkable than the strategy pursued by other democrats who played both sides of a nationalist divide, making strategic alliances and temporary common cause with 'figures' or 'elements' or even 'cells' working for some form of liberation based on language, 'race' or ethnicity, or historic occupation of territory. This, too, should sound familiar to us as we assess 'what happened' in 1989 and subsequently; anti-Stalinism made common cause temporarily possible amongst the varied nationalities and political factions of Eastern Europe. Engels, more than Marx, was willing to play a nationalist card politically; but both were about as wholeheartedly committed to popular sovereignty as one could reasonably expect.

Where Marx and Engels differed from most of their democratic allies was in their economic policy, where even in the short term they argued for 'despotic incursions into the rights of private property', as the *Communist Manifesto* demanded.[7] Most of their strategic bedfellows wanted an expansion of rights to private property at the expense of feudalism both aristocratic and communal, and these propertied liberals were not interested in conceding resources or rights to the poor, working class or otherwise. Popular democrats, after pressuring their authoritarian rulers, also had a large stake in continuing public order and the legal system, so they had a strong incentive to cooperate with large elements of the surviving political structure; they did not need Marx and Engels or any other working class communists or radicals or idealists or utopians as allies at all in any continuing sense. This should also sound familiar in the present context when reformed and renamed communist parties and familiar political figures reappear in Eastern European politics with popular support or acquiescence, and as a sense of betrayal develops amongst those who had hoped, like Marx and Engels, to move the political agenda smartly forward in the direction of egalitarian and cooperative structures in the economy, or those who, rather unlike Marx and Engels, had wanted to push nationalistic demands for border adjustments and ethnic recognition or autonomy in cultural matters.

Constitutional government is difficult to achieve, yet solves few political problems, even in the longer term. But without it we get 'Absurdistans', which may paradoxically have had written and even very liberal-sounding constitutions. One very common thread of popular complaint during the recent risings in Eastern Europe was 'they treated us like fools', as respect for the ruled and redress against rulers was notably absent, and public untruth was the norm. It is heartening, and quite amazing, that people will turn out in large numbers and take ultimate risks to defend their dignity, and to interpret the recovery of that dignity in terms of participation in constitutional politics. Continuing demonstrations throughout Eastern Europe and the former Soviet Union continue to bear witness to this. Of course economic hardship, lack of material prospects and anger at falling behind in every way played a part in provoking mass action, as did the geopolitical shift represented by Mikhail Gorbachev's evident intent to dispose of the Soviet Union's European annex. But Soviet tanks were not the only threat to life and limb – many died in Romania, and economic decline can rumble on for centuries without widespread mass reaction. No rational calculator of self-interest in Eastern Europe could possibly have deduced an increase in individual economic advantage from turning out to support the candlelight demonstrations, human chains or mass occupations of public buildings. Constitutionalism implies power-sharing with citizens, and that implies respect for them and their views.

Any coalition for genuinely constitutional rule is very broad but necessarily temporary; Marx and Engels are correctly located within one, and their differences with their various temporary allies are no stranger or more sinister or outlandish or significant than the similar differences – over economic and nationalistic issues – that arise today. Participants in Civic Forum, New Forum, Citizens against Violence, or any number of other pressure groups for genuinely constitutional rule, are quite justified in having secondary agendas of their own and admitting to a merely temporary suspension of differences. Many of these coalitions were self-proclaimed 'non-parties' headed by 'non-politicians'. Some of these groups and some of the leaders made a transition to partisan politics; others did not. That was to be expected, and it casts no doubt on the original 'non-party' orientation, which was sincere enough and quite effectual. Marx and Engels considered the Communist League disbanded or necessarily moribund during the events of 1848, as they and their associates practised the kind of open-air, public-meeting, non-sectarian politics associated with the struggle for constitutional rule. At least one of their associates was elected as a deputy in the Frankfurt Parliament, which sat as a constituent assembly for Germany. Only at the end of the struggle, in the spring of 1849, did Marx and Engels take a partisan line, and then only in advising self-defence when workers' interests, and constitutionalism itself, were about to be engulfed by monarchical restoration. The knives were out at that point, and Marx and Engels freely vented their rage on democrats who struggled insufficiently or ineffectually against monarchical reaction, and then cravenly sought to protect themselves and what remained of their secondary agendas by compromising with or capitulating to the anciens régimes. But it is surely a disastrous over-simplification to see them as sectarians all through the process, and to disregard their respect for the political as well as the economic achievements of the somewhat liberal – if thoroughly commercial – classes that influenced the movement for constitutional government.

Communists and coalitions

Overwhelmingly the academic literature on Marx written or available in English treats him as an intellectual wrapped up from the very beginning in a world of books and ideas, most of which were 'philosophical', and derived from an encounter with Hegel (see chapter nine below).[8] Having undergone a 'conversion' to first to Hegelianism, and then to 'communism', Marx seems in these accounts to project his inward concerns outwards in publications of various sorts. Pretty uniformly in the literature these writings are taken to be records of his 'thought', and there is little detailed attention to the real and intended audience. Moreover there is little sense of debate, when Marx's *oeuvre* is recounted, and only a few commentators take seriously his peregrinations into practical politics – speeches, meetings, letters, editorial work – as genuine interventions, rather than as documents that record Marx speaking to himself and to us as posterity (for a discussion of Marx as authorial voice, see chapter eight below). Where Marx has a contemporary audience with which he interacts, it is generally conceptualised in the literature as internal to the communist 'League of the Just' and similar circles of 'believers'.

There are, however, certain exceptions to this rule, and I shall survey these briefly in support of my view here that Marx's career in coalitional democratic politics bears re-examination. Heinz Lubasz summarises the 'established thesis' that 'Marx's initial problematic was a philosophical one', and argues instead that from 1842 Marx was concerned with three political problems in Prussia:

> controversy about the possible introduction of representative government; the problem of poverty – the so-called 'social question'; and the struggle for the only political weapon available to the Prussian population at large, freedom of the press.[9]

Lubasz establishes something of a practical context for these interests and ideas, and his re-presentation of Marx's biography mirrors Marx's own autobiographical comments of 1859 quite closely; it also runs against the grain of Engels' biographical narratives, from which the – for my taste – over-intellectualised and over-Hegelianised tradition arises.[10] Lubasz writes:

> Working on the *Rheinische Zeitung* (from early 1842 to mid-1843), first as a contributor, later as editor-in-chief, Marx was plunged into a substantially different milieu from that of a student at the University of Berlin and a member of its Young-Hegelian *Doktorklub*. He now constantly came into contact with men of practical bent and immediate political purposes, and with these ... he weekly discussed the down-to-earth issues as well as the more purely theoretical matters which concerned them as political propagandists, commentators, and critics.[11]

While Richard N. Hunt's study is frankly directed at the political *ideas* of Marx and Engels, he does catch the consistency between them as communists, on the one hand, and at least some of the democratic forces of the 1840s, battling against the armed force of monarchical reaction, on the other:

> While some European democrats renounced violent revolution even under these circumstances [where peaceful efforts to broaden the franchise met with governmental indifference or repression], most did not, and precisely because they were democrats. Thus Marx and Engels' advocacy of popular revolution to overthrow the repressive oligarchies of wealth did not set them apart from the principles of democracy but, on the contrary, placed them squarely in the mainstream of the mid-nineteenth-century democratic tradition.[12]

Moreover he also occasionally catches the way that Marx and Engels interact positively with liberals, and how consistent with their strategy this was:

> In July 1846, Marx, Engels, and their new Brussels comrade, Philippe Gigot, signing themselves 'the German Democratic Communists of Brussels', publicly congratulated the English Chartist leader, Feargus O'Connor, on winning a seat in Parliament ... In October 1846, while disseminating his own tactical ideas among the German artisans in Paris, Engels defined the proper road to communism as a 'forcible democratic revolution'. A month later, in an article chastising the French democrat Alphonse de Lamartine for proposing *indirect* elections, Engels appealed to the legendary Constitution of 1793 ... [W]e may scrutinise the often-neglected 'Demands of the Communist Party in Germany', drawn up by Marx and Engels on behalf of the Communist League in late March 1848, when news of the revolution then sweeping across their native land made the formulation of specific demands a matter of urgency.[13]

Finally, Alan Gilbert, in a study that draws political action into an interpretation of Marx better than any of the others, finds similar things to say about the way that he pursued a strategy of conditional cooperation with, and intended persuasion of, democratic dissidents, chiefly in Belgium – where he was located and where this was possible – but also elsewhere, at least by correspondence. Gilbert writes that Marx

> forged a network of activists in London, Brussels, and Germany who agreed with his point of view and would fight for it during the democratic revolution of 1848.
>
> In Brussels Marx engaged the Communist Correspondence Committee in many-faceted political activity, prefiguring his organising in Cologne in 1848. Its members participated in the Brussels German Workers' Educational Society which had recruited 105 members by late 1847. Marx also involved the committee in joint activities with the Brussels Democratic Association. As a member of the Democratic Association's executive committee, Marx correspondingly encouraged it to concentrate its efforts on the Belgian working class and to uphold internationalism. As part of a democratic delegation, he journeyed to Ghent, the chief Belgian manufacturing centre, to set up a branch among French-speaking workers. After a first meeting in early 1848, the Walloon organisation attracted 3,000 people to its second meeting … [T]he Democratic Association corresponded with the Fraternal Democrats in London and saluted the Chartists' efforts to unite English and Irish workers.[14]

It must be said, however, that Marx and Engels themselves did little to remind anyone of their political practice as democrats or to incorporate much of their democratic views in their political writings. The theoretical support for constitutional democracy was embedded in their journalism, which presumed that the basic groundwork for constitutionalism was already receiving adequate publicity and that readers of the *Rheinische Zeitung*, or its successor the *Neue Rheinische Zeitung*, wanted or needed a radical but not impractical gloss on events and a stimulus to further direct action. Whether temporary coalitions for democracy succeed or fail, in later years the participants are more likely to be known for their differences than for their areas of substantive agreement. After all, controversy makes more interesting reading and exciting tale-telling, which is how 'history' reaches us. Narration has a logic or structure of its own, independent of 'events', even as these are conceptualised at the time. Writing 'history' from the point of view and state of knowledge of actual participants is an impossible task; participants do not know who is going to do what next, and no one knows how they are going to function in a narrative plot constructed years later when 'history' actually appears.[15]

After 1849 the situation with respect to the political theory and practice of Marx and Engels as democrats becomes even more difficult to assess, as effectively they cut themselves off from the coalition politics, mass action and press publicity in which it would be visible. Neither functioned as a direct participant in the constitutional struggles in Prussia in the early 1860s, by which time some of their younger associates were standing for elected office and beginning to win seats, and many others were pressuring politicians and parties for liberalisation of the political system, often through the trade union movement. Marx and Engels had little occasion to repeat the basic justifications for constitutional rule, as they did not participate in the coalitional politics necessary to get it going and to promote the further erosion of monarchical rights that genuine constitutionalism requires. Instead they gave advice at a distance through sectarian channels, that is, the workers' movements, national and international, and the nascent socialist parties of continental Europe and occasionally elsewhere. While in residence in England they contacted native socialists, but stood aloof from progressive coalitions, feeling unwelcome as foreigners. Circumstances were against their return to Germany; they had problems with citizenship, with finances, with family in England and in Prussia. They found it easier to stay on as émigrés in England and to visit Germany just occasionally for non-political reasons.

Frankly, though, if Marx and Engels had had the will to get back into German politics, they could have found a way. They could have pursued a non-party line on constitutionalism, as in 1848, or a partisan line within representative institutions, or a sectarian line as agitators pushing the political agenda towards economic issues related to class inequality – and pulling it away from the nationalist sentiments that cross-cut social class. Instead they offered advice by correspondence from London, a useful meeting place for international socialists needing encouragement, and theoretical works of uncertain immediate political value. It seems to me that Marx and Engels had no theory of the party in or out of revolution, no theory of leadership partisan or otherwise, no theory of the state or administration; nor is there any body of practical decisions taken or followed by them from which their views could be adduced. There are a few angry articles, occasional sketches, specific bits of advice and enigmatic generalities.

This can all be explained away, of course. Had they been practical politicians Marx would never have written his books (as much as he did), and Engels could not have supported him financially (and kept himself in the style to which he had always been accustomed). Both were bitter about what they regarded as betrayals in the politics of 1848-49, and neither wanted anything further to do with parties. Their participation in the German Social-Democratic Party (founded in 1875), before, during and after its period of illegality, was distant and minimal. Probably Marx did not want to put his wife and children through any more upheavals, expulsions and police surveillance; Engels never broke with his parents and siblings and seems to have had a fine regard for their feelings as burghers of Wuppertal. Increasing age was perhaps a factor, though the foundation of the non-Lassallean and pro-Marx German Socialist Party in 1869 coincided with Engels' retirement from business – at forty-nine years of age, and Marx was then fifty-one. This is not to berate them for the choices that they made, but to emphasise that their views – as they survive in the written record – must be read against a political background that includes their somewhat peculiar circumstances. From our point of view these texts are in dialogue with a 'silence' that requires interpretation; 'reading the words on the page' is never sufficient (on issues of interpretation, see chapter seven below).

Constitutionalism and democracy

Constitutionalism, however popularly supported, is not going to satisfy everyone in terms of economic policy, nationalistic aspirations and the mechanics of power-sharing. But it seems to me to be the key to the upheavals of 1989 and 1848, and altogether unfortunate to take it for granted, as do Fukuyama, Glenny and Callinicos. Anti-Stalinist it is, but it is no creation of the last fifty years. What disappoints me particularly is that there is so little consideration, in the literature on

Eastern Europe or elsewhere, of what might be done in specific terms to make constitutional rule more workable. Parliamentary systems and partisan politics are rather taken for granted, whereas they could be more excitingly redefined. Voting procedures, the mechanics of representation, unified or devolved government, referenda and consultation, the number of offices open to election, are what matter in practical politics in democratic countries. But too frequently constitutionalism is ossification, and the documents and legislation involved represent a low common denominator of agreement amongst partisan representatives. Party politicians are necessarily concerned to exclude citizens from the powers and rights that they wish to share out, concurrently or alternately, amongst themselves. The law of oligarchy is not necessarily an iron one, but it seems depressingly resilient. While the enthusiastic agreement on generalities that characterises mass politics must inevitably give way to disagreement on specifics, there ought to be some way to fuel compromise with idealism rather than cynicism. I do not think that we have got all that much further as democrats since 1848, and the fact that the second half of the twentieth century has witnessed the degradation of the whole enterprise in Eastern Europe, in which the 1848 Hungarian campaign represented the height of the struggle for democrats and radicals of that era, is a total disgrace for which great power politics is largely to blame.

I have argued that Marx and Engels were democrats of a largely undiscovered and somewhat reticent variety. Did their work undermine constitutionalism? In their own time, they supported it and probably had some effect; their criticisms of it were not influential on anyone with any great prospects for undermining it. Later, of course, their criticisms of 'bourgeois democracy' were highlighted at the expense of their support for constitutional politics as such. As this was done by other people for reasons of their own, Marx and Engels can hardly be held responsible. Yet they did argue that emerging forms of constitutional rule would prove inadequate in economic terms, as class struggle would be sharpened; yet class struggle within a constitutional framework could also force or win an amelioration of working-class poverty, and Marx and Engels promoted a socialist politics in their own time on this basis. The extent to which constitutional democracy is consistent with or indeed requires the unregulated, semi-regulated or welfare-supplemented market economy, is the issue that Marx and Engels separately raised in their works as early as 1842, and to which Marx in particular devoted his life.

This concern is reincarnated in present conceptualisations of 'market socialism', an area of debate that is precisely directed to assessing the extent to which democratically sanctioned economic regulation, and democratically validated decision making, are consistent with, or even required for, the present maintenance and future development of democracy into the next century and millennium. In this perspective Marx is a key figure in formulating a political theory that adamantly requires that economic affairs be considered within a 'democratic audit', rather than left to one side as 'private' or 'non-political'. From his earliest political concerns with furthering democracy in this fuller sense, he worked from national constitutionalism and democratic representation in the 'political' sphere through to an egalitarian system for the production and distribution of material goods and services. Thus he sought to move the political agenda in an economic direction, and to resist attempts to draw a line between democratic participation in politics and inegalitarian access to 'the market', whether this was the unemployment and exploitation characteristic of the labour market or the differential access to income and wealth characteristic of the market in consumption goods and capital. Along this continuum – from 'bourgeois' or 'merely political' democracy, in which prospects for freedom are delimited, redefined or subverted by differential access to wealth, all the way to the higher stages of communism (see chapter five above) – he posited various intermediate stages, sometimes distinguishing these as merely (though nonetheless progressively) 'socialist', rather than communist as such. As a stage-setter for, and early theorist of, 'market socialism', Marx has the best credentials of all.

Unfortunately the revolutionary sectarianism that succeeded Marx, and for which he has been unsympathetically delivered up to judgement, tends to push arguments away from substantive considerations into taxonomic ones – is an idea 'Marxist', or not? Just as there are multiple interpretations of Marx, so there is no one 'market socialism'. This presumption suits the following discussion, in which I use the sense of democratisation that I have attributed to Marx – moving from political representation to an egalitarian economic system – as a way of interrogating the fledgling tradition of theory and practice that can be loosely, though usefully, denominated 'market socialism'.

Market socialism

Since the 1980s market socialists have been talking the language of reconciliation, bargaining, negotiation, compromise:

> What is needed is a model of society where power is more evenly dis-
> tributed between ... groups; where the interests of owners of capital,
> of workers, and of consumers are all taken into account with none
> taking automatic priority.[16]

And they also appeal to the values of liberalism: 'The values I shall appeal to in defence of markets are welfare, freedom, and democracy.'[17] Market socialists are generally distinguished from liberals by an adher-ence to end-state or 'patterned' outcomes in terms of social justice[18] – which is therefore, on their view, not merely procedural – and market socialists also have a hefty commitment to equality and redistribution that weighs heavily in the balance against freedom and efficiency.[19] Distinctively market socialists have an urge to recommend the virtues of markets to socialists, and to make this their calling card. To be sure they also want to distinguish themselves from the New Right and lib-ertarian anarchists who argue for the expansion of market relations and contraction of the state – the removal of the 'mixed' from mixed economies. This raises certain questions: Why should socialists have to be reconciled with 'the market'? What made them hate it in the first place?

According to David Miller, socialists rejected the market for a vari-ety of reasons: nostalgia for pre-industrial conditions of production, or authoritarian attachment to the state.[20] In Miller's view, the former, however community-minded, is simply utopian; the latter, however well-intended, is disastrously anti-democratic. As utopians have never been very successful, and anyway have been off the scene for many years, they do not seem to me to make a good target; whereas statists – planners, apparatchiks, bureaucrats *et al.* – were on the twentieth-century scene, were visibly destructive in their policies, were clearly self-described as socialists (even the Nazis claimed to be 'socialists'), and were obviously destined for lingering historical ignominy, if not collapse (which was rather a surprise). Somewhere socialism took a wrong turn, according to Miller, but market socialists are not all that interested in finding out exactly where.

To do that would be to expose some inconvenient arguments which, judging by their language, they do not really want to address. Early socialism, particularly Owenism, was about cooperative production, common control of capital, equal opportunity to obtain differential rewards on merit, supervised conditions of work, and protection from exigencies of age and health. Elimination of middlemen, loan sharks, confidence tricksters and fraud marked a programme to clean up the market for consumers. The market in labour was to be reformed to allow for job security, education and training opportunities, paid vacations and reasonable wages even at the lowest end of the scale. Market socialism is not all that different.

Nineteenth-century liberals found this programme tough to take, as it interfered with rights to property and contract, and the immediate provisions of the *Communist Manifesto*, as mentioned above, promised to introduce such measures through 'despotic' means. Contemporary neo-liberals and libertarian anarchists have constructed defences against these measures on grounds of principle – freedom, justice, efficiency – rather than on the basis of self- or class-interest as such. But to them the package as a whole or in parts is surely socialism. Welfare liberals and social democrats have been canny enough to adopt the package, and then junk the label 'socialism'. I am not so sure that market socialists are as distinct from this group as they seem to think.

By contrast, More's *Utopia* (see chapter five above) held money up to ridicule and painted a picture of cooperative production and money-less distribution – though More also mentioned miscreants and sanctions, in contradistinction to Fourier's later phalansteries. These are presumably examples of the utopianism that Miller has in mind. Proudhon's 'labour money' scheme, so ridiculed by Marx,[21] occupies the middle ground that market socialists seem to want. This is the area between the cooperative management of monetary capital in production and consumer finance in distribution within a 'mixed' public/private money-economy on the one hand, and the moneyless distribution of goods and gratis production by able-bodied citizens in a certain kind of communist ideal on the other. In Miller's words:

> Like other market economies, market socialism provides incentives for producers to respond efficiently to consumer demand, but unlike capitalism, it places all workers in this position by linking incomes directly to the net receipts of each enterprise.[22]

What supposedly divides market socialists from welfare liberals is the common (neither individual nor corporate) control of capital, public (though not state) ownership of the means of production, a commitment to a redistributive (but not perfect) pattern of equality, and a programme of worker-participation and empowerment (with delegated authority to specialists). What divides Marxist socialists from market socialists is Marx's focus on money (see chapter two through chapter four above).

Market socialists talk the language of contemporary economics, attempting to show that it is compatible with a wide range of 'practical' institutions, egalitarian/interventionist/corporatist ones at that. Moreover, there is rather an air that adopting the language and values of the enemy is a clever move, once economics is shown to be consistent with certain arrangements that economists either ignore or deplore, such as worker cooperatives or public leasing of capital.[23]

However, perhaps this move is actually rather a large hostage to fortune. The insistence on the word 'market' suggests this, as it allows market socialists to envision a world where class-peace has supposedly been declared: the retail mega-mall. This is a world where individuals are equal as consumers, where they send significant messages to willing suppliers, where competition surrounds them with choice, where their consumption promotes, indeed defines, efficiency, and where they exercise an important freedom and create their identities.[24]

Casting money in a major role here would make the exercise sound grubby; 'market' is just that little bit sanitised, and there are plenty of encomiums in economics textbooks for ready quotation. It troubles me that 'the market' is conceptualised as 'choice', rather than restriction or rationing (which is what happens to individuals), and that its output is 'efficiency' (rather than accumulation and monopoly); that public planning is always a 'constraint' on citizens, whereas corporate decision makers are supposedly bound to the consumer interest; that public decisions are supposedly alien to the interests of the private person. Surely corporate planners plan our environment just as unresponsively as public planners. Surely production for the 'the market' excludes and pollutes just as 'statist' systems did. Surely we can identify directly with a public body that secures a public good. And surely we can be alienated by the consequences of individual choices, including our own.[25]

Of course there are problems with 'the market'; that is just what market socialism aims to fix. But if the problems are too atrocious or too fundamental, they are not fixable, and market socialists are out of a solution. To find out how good market socialism is, we have to reach the parts that it does not, by asking the questions that lurk beneath the discursive surface.

Markets and money

One of these problems is: 'What actually is a market?' Conventionally this is taken to be a domain in which prices adjust to meet effective demand, thus channelling resources most efficiently in terms of consumer preference. But is this the reality we experience, or merely an ideological veil? How often can we actually adjust the prices at which we buy our goods, or those at which we sell our labour? A Turkish friend of mine (a graduate student, then, in economics, as it happens) was most incensed and puzzled to find that bargaining was a not a UK norm in what he was told was a 'free market'. The excuse that bargaining works against efficiency because it is time-consuming rather contradicts the supposition that consumers have plenty of time to 'shop around'; no one has all that much time as it is, so it might well be better to spend the time in one place haggling. Job interviews do not end with these words, as in a market system they should: 'And what is the lowest salary for which you will undertake this employment?'

Rather, in modern 'mixed' economies we are looking at highly bureaucratised organisations ('private' and 'public' alike) for production and consumption, in which prices are largely set in advance at levels which keep the 'officers' and 'clients' roughly in touch. Further, so-called private and so-called public bureaucracies do not differ as much as economists pretend and market socialists accept, particularly Miller, who sees only the virtues of competition on the one side and the dead hand of legal monopoly on the other. Nove is rather good at making this point:

> The many American [and UK] senior company executives who award themselves annual incomes of $1 million and more surely do so because of their position at the top of the company's nomenklatura, rather than through successful entrepreneurship or exceptional marginal productivity![26]

Internationally and domestically there are highly segmented arrangements for connecting people to consumption goods; besides formal employment there are also innumerable legal and illegal strategies – from being unemployed or a claimant to undertaking criminal transactions or scavenging waste-tips.[27] No doubt there are some benign examples of 'ordered anarchy' in these arrangements,[28] but most are heavily patterned (e.g. sex-bias in unwaged domestic work, for instance) or formally incorporated as hierarchies of power and wealth (e.g. any multi-national corporation or domestic employer). Market socialists suggest that their proposed arrangements are neutral with respect to sexual or other forms of discrimination and thus these matters need not be investigated; whereas, I suggest, an investigation of these very issues would help to illuminate the way that their discussion in this literature is so skewed.

Market socialists have focused on transactions that are commonly commodified and thus involve money (e.g. retail shopping and waged employment); those that are not (e.g. subsistence agriculture and household labour) do not seem to merit much discussion. The general nature of human transactions is therefore not addressed, nor the specific character of commodified ones, nor the properties of money itself – precisely the subjects that Marx set out to explore in *Capital*.

It is in his work that socialism really took the turn, whether right or wrong, against money – and not merely against 'the market'. It was neither nostalgia nor statism, in Marx's case, that explains why he expounded socialism as he did. It was analysis (see chapter one to chapter five above). Marx's vision of communism is rightly maligned for its lack of detail in describing a hypothetical world no one could possibly ever enter or would possibly ever want, but it strikes me that 'the market', as defined by economists and promoted by market social-ists, is a fantasy that gets between theorisations that are usefully criti-cal, and life as people have to live it.

My aim in going over this material is to cast suspicion on the con-junction of terms in 'market socialism', and I reach an uncomfortably pessimistic conclusion: if we have money, we have to deal with the characteristic dynamics of capitalist or so-called market societies, and socialist ideals are necessarily incompatible with this. The abolition of money, on the other hand, contradicts virtually everything that people take civilisation to represent, and socialism is therefore a movement, as Eduard Bernstein famously suggested, of continuous critique. Critique has a rationale but cannot be a solution; what it is depends to some extent on what is there to criticise. That said, I am hopeful that close exposition of Marx will dampen enthusiasm amongst socialists for appeasement to 'the market', as socialists should not give up the criti-cal edge so easily. Ideals are one thing, but illusions are another.

As related in chapter three above, Marx's specification of the con-ceptual structure inherent in the concept 'money' is the centrepiece of his critique of political economy, and his critical model of the capital-ist economy. This is because he sees money as a conceptual and prac-tical development of the exchange of surplus goods, and a conceptual and practical pre-requisite for capital. Money is said by Marx – just to review the argument – to be a measure of equivalence in exchange-value, and to entail a quantitative expansion to infinity by its very def-inition (the 'Hegelian' aspects of this kind of claim are explored in chapter nine below). From these conceptual properties Marx derives the possibilities for human behaviour that characterise the socially constructed individuals of capitalist society, pre-eminently capitalists, who have the best chance to display the greed and selfishness that

appear at the conclusion to his discussion. Most social theorists, particularly economists and those, like market socialists, who rely on their vision, produce precisely the opposite kind of argument, moving from 'need' or 'desire', to 'interests' and selfishness. For Marx, workers are by no means excepted from this greedy and selfish behaviour, though he is not at pains for political reasons to stress this. Market socialists merely presume these commonplace assumptions. Whilst these assumptions appear in descriptive-sounding prose as 'mirrors' to capitalist society, they are actually assumptions constitutive of the behaviour through which such a society is constituted. They are a crucial site in which meaning is constructed, and Marx rightly directed his critical analysis at the 'economic categories'.

Marx relates the structure inherent in socially constructed concepts to the possibility for individual agents to act on their own volition in certain ways:

> The hoarding drive is boundless in its nature. Qualitatively or formally considered, money is independent of all limits, that is, it is the universal representative of material wealth because it is directly convertible into any other commodity. But at the same time every actual sum of money is limited in amount, and therefore has only a limited efficacy as a means of purchase. This contradiction between the quantitative limitation and the qualitative lack of limitation of money keeps driving the hoarder back to his Sisyphean task: accumulation.[29]

According to Marx, individual actions have cumulative social consequences:

> There is a contradiction immanent in the function of money as the means of payment ... This contradiction bursts forth in that aspect of an industrial and commercial crisis which is known as a monetary crisis ... As the hart pans after fresh water, so pants his [the soul of the bourgeois] after money, the only wealth.[30]

From the above, I deduce that Marx is committed to a view that a commodity-producing society is by definition one in which useful goods are valued for exchange in accordance with some measure – money, a standard of price. For Marx, concept anticipates action, indeed creates the possibility for actions of certain types that simply could not exist other than as an instance of the concept he claims to discern. This conceptual structure is said to have been initiated in the rudimentary exchanges of social groups he could not observe, and because they were presumably pre-literate, it seems unlikely that evidence of the earliest kinds of exchanges could ever be found against which his view might be challenged. The upshot of this is that Marx's social theory is crucially dependent on a structure alleged to inhere in concepts such as money, and the way those concepts provide possibilities for individual and social development along certain lines, as and when agents undertake it.

On the one hand Marx has conveniently established acquisitive behaviour as historically developed and potentially malleable; on the other hand the entire course of civilisation, on his account, is bound up with the logic of surplus production and therefore necessarily with monetary exchange, if we assume that his historico-conceptual deductions outline our situation. If there is a socialism that does not accept the continued necessity of monetary exchange, then it is going to be very hard work even getting it a hearing. But there is no point in confusing this with the statist regimes that described themselves as socialist: they never abolished money nor ever attempted to secure any genuine break, voluntary or otherwise, with the history of commodification. If socialists intend to accept the monetary economy, however cooperativised and democratised, then they had better come clean as social democrats and welfare liberals. At least that way they could perhaps start to build effective political alliances – and so slough off the analytical and historical burdens of twentieth-century 'socialism'.

Theories and struggles

Marx was far ahead of his time in theoretical terms, and perhaps it is no surprise that his participation in practical politics, whether in terms of coalitions with democrats or particularistic contacts with communists, was so limited. There is little reason to think that he expected these issues – the extent to which democratisation is consistent with, or conflicts with, the 'market forces' of capitalism – to be resolved in some extra-constitutional way; indeed the sketch he drew of the 'true secret' within the confusions of the Paris Commune encompasses an orderly body of representative institutions with considerable control over the economic structures in which most citizens were located. His sociological and political assumptions about contemporary French politics may have been self-delusory, and his sketch is not only hypothetical but also not a fully-fledged constitution. *The Civil War in France* was a eulogy for an event that he did not want to happen; earlier he had warned the 'Paris proletariat' against delusion in pursuing the 'national souvenirs of 1792', when radicals had formed the original Commune de Paris.[31] And he was too much the populist to fancy himself as Lycurgus the Lawgiver or as Rousseau's Legislator, delivering ready-made solutions from on-high, although as I have indicated above in this chapter, I find his aloofness from practical politics in later life rather difficult to excuse. But at least in his pamphlet of 1871 there is some brief attempt to expand the theory of constitutional democracy in specific ways.

This material is discussed by Callinicos, but in very stale terms such as workplace democracy; even Engels took on board the fact that there are domestic workplaces largely staffed by women, something which the revised Trotskyism that Callincos promotes has evidently not yet considered. Fukuyama and Glenny are instead obsessed with a sort of post-Marxist emphasis on economics – the organisation of employment and delivery of goods and services within the international context, where multi-national trade and finance determine the fate of small countries – an interesting contrast with 'market socialists', who raise the international context rather reluctantly. Marx's own writings on contemporary politics are rather more broadly political than that, more exploratory of ideas, and more revelatory of personalities. Engels explained, some years after Marx's earlier work on French politics, *The Eighteenth Brumaire of Louis Bonaparte* (1852), that Marx had not had time to gather the economic information that would have 'proved' his analysis correct and 'justified' it as a deductive exercise; I think that Engels is wide of the mark there on Marx's method. Marx was an acute commentator on political events as they unfolded; it is a shame he had so little chance to turn his talents to shaping events themselves, and to rework his ideas in response to practicalities.

We can be triumphalist about European constitutional democracy and its resurgence; it is genuinely valued by a mass of quite ordinary people who see its terms as essential to their dignity in daily life. I think we can be in some despair about great power geo-politics, which is worse than it was in Marx and Engels' time, and about the contemporary class struggle, which balances social democratic amelioration in some nations against environmental degradation internationally. It is regrettable that Marx and Engels are to us so silent on the basic elements of constitutional politics, and that by reputation they represent such an exclusive focus on the economic issues that arise within that framework. It has to be said that they were not fight-to-the-death revolutionaries, and it is distinctly unfortunate that they became leading lights – unbeknownst to themselves, of course – for authoritarian revolutionaries and Stalinist regimes. This twentieth-century phenomenon was the result of an enormous amount of interpretation (of Marx and Engels, to be sure, but also of quite a lot else) – all of it quite at odds with the one I offer here. I take the international politics of democracy to be the best context now for interpreting the work of Marx and Engels, and I have used their experiences with it as an aid in commenting on contemporary struggles, in which theories come to life, or at least attempts are made to do this. Treating Marx and Engels as 'history' in this context comes over to me as a distancing device, a way of consigning issues or movements to the back-burner, if not the dustbin. While this may appear to be a move merely on the textual surface, it seems to me that we live in a world of surfaces, and they need careful watching.

In the next chapter I explore the way the textual surface that we take to be 'Marx' is constructed through translation. In doing so I consider the presumed distinction between translation and interpretation, and how this affects not merely texts as translators produce them, but readers when they take them up. Texts are not just what is on the page, nor is Marx just what he was when he was corporeally extant. Democratic politics is constructed from ideas not just by 'citizens', but by 'readers', who have a complex and active role in making Marx ever-meaningful.

Notes

1 Francis Fukuyama, 'The end of history', *The National Interest*, 16 (Summer 1989), pp. 3–18.

2 Misha Glenny, *The Rebirth of History: Eastern Europe in the Age of Democracy* (Harmondsworth, Penguin, 1991).

3 Alex Callinicos, *The Revenge of History: Marxism and the East European Revolutions* (Cambridge, Polity Press, 1991).

4 Richard Rorty, *Contingency, Irony, and Solidarity* (Cambridge, Cambridge University Press, 1995), ch. 1.

5 See David McLellan, *Karl Marx: His Life and Thought* (London, Macmillan, 1973), ch. 4; Terrell Carver, *Friedrich Engels: His Life and Thought* (London, Macmillan, 1989), ch. 6.

6 Karl Marx and Frederick Engels, *Collected Works*, vol. 7 (London, Lawrence & Wishart, 1977), pp. 3–7.

7 Karl Marx, *Later Political Writings*, ed. and trans. Terrell Carver (Cambridge, Cambridge University Press, 1996), p. 19.

8 Leszek Kolakowski opens his account of Marxism, linking ideas to movements and events, with the words 'Karl Marx was a German Philosopher'; *Main Currents of Marxism: Its Rise, Growth, and Dissolution, vol. 1: The Founders*, trans. P. S. Falla (Oxford, Clarendon Press, 1978), p. 1.

9 Heinz Lubasz, 'Marx's initial problematic: the problem of poverty', *Political Studies*, 24:1 (1976), 24–5.

10 Terrell Carver, *Engels* (Oxford, Oxford University Press, 1981), ch. 5; Terrell Carver, *Marx and Engels: The Intellectual Relationship* (Brighton, Wheatsheaf, 1983), ch. 4.

11 Lubasz, 'Marx's initial problematic', pp. 25–6.

12 Richard N. Hunt, *The Political Ideas of Marx and Engels, vol. 1: Marxism and Totalitarian Democracy 1818–1850* (London, Macmillan, 1975), pp. 134–5.

13 Hunt, *Political Ideas of Marx and Engels*, vol. 1, pp. 136-7.

14 Alan Gilbert, *Marx's Politics: Communists and Citizens* (Oxford, Martin Robertson, 1981), p. 112. I cover similar ground in a similar way with respect to Engels in *Friedrich Engels*, pp. 185–8.

15 On these issues see Hayden White, *The Content of the Form: Narrative Discourse and Historical Representation* (Baltimore MD, Johns Hopkins University Press, 1987); and Alex Callinicos, *Theories and Narratives: Reflections on the Philosophy of History* (Cambridge, Polity Press, 1995), ch. 2.

16 Julian Le Grand and Saul Estrin (eds), *Market Socialism* (Oxford, Oxford University Press, 1989), p. 23.

17 David Miller, 'Why markets?', in Le Grand and Estrin (eds), *Market Socialism*, p. 29.

18 Raymond Plant, 'Socialism, markets and end states', in Le Grand and Estrin (eds), *Market Socialism*, pp. 74–5.

19 David Miller, 'Markets and equality', unpublished paper for the 'Markets and Political Theory' meeting of the Conference for the Study of Political Thought, Williams College, Williamstown MA (18–29 April 1992); Julian Le Grand, 'Markets, welfare and equality', in Le Grand and Estrin (eds), *Market Socialism*, pp. 193–211; Alec Nove, *The Economics of Feasible Socialism Revisited*, 2nd edn (London, HarperCollins, 1991), pp. 245–6.

20 Miller, 'Why markets?', pp. 27–9.

21 This is discussed in Patrick Murray, 'The necessity of money: how Hegel helped Marx surpass Ricardo's theory of value', in Fred Moseley (ed.), *Marx's Method in Capital: A Reexamination* (Atlantic Highlands NJ, Humanities Press, 1993), pp. 37–61.

22 Miller, 'A vision of market socialism', *Dissent* (Summer 1991), 408.

23 Miller, 'Vision', pp. 409–13.

24 David Miller, 'Why markets?', pp. 25–49; see Alan Carling, 'In defence of rational choice: a reply to Ellen Meiksins Wood', *New Left Review*, 184 (1990), 106, for a challenge to socialists concerning the market and freedom.

25 Keith Graham, *The Battle of Democracy* (Brighton, Wheatsheaf Books, 1986), ch. 6.

26 Nove, *Economics of Feasible Socialism Revisited*, p. 259.

27 Alec Nove, 'The role of central planning under capitalism and market socialism', in Jon Elster and K. O. Moene, *Alternatives to Capitalism* (Cambridge, Cambridge University Press, 1989), pp. 100–1.

28 Michael Taylor, *The Possibility of Cooperation* (Cambridge, Cambridge University Press, 1989).

29 Karl Marx, *Capital*, vol. 1, trans. Ben Fowkes (Harmondsworth, Penguin, 1976), pp. 230–1.

30 Marx, *Capital,* vol. 1, pp. 235–6.

31 Marx, *The Civil War in France*, in *Later Political Writings*, pp. 181–7.

CHAPTER SEVEN

Translation and interpretation: Marx's words

Words and meanings

It is widely appreciated that 'translation is interpretation'. What is not so widely understood is that all interpretation is translation. Even in situations where the reader is a native speaker of the language in which the text is written, the activity of reading – deriving meaning from words – necessarily involves a process of translation. That is, reading is an active process through which various forms of difference are negotiated, so meaning – not just language – is 'translated'. The outcome of these negotiations, perhaps surprisingly, is not sameness or similarity or 'non-difference', but rather difference yet again, often rather self-deceptively and one-sidedly disguised as 'agreement'.

'When we understand at all, we understand differently.'[1] This is a principle that comes to us from the linguistic philosophers Paul Ricoeur and Hans-Georg Gadamer, and in this chapter I mean to develop its application in connection with my recently published translations of classic texts by Marx.[2] These are the first genuinely new, line-by-line retranslations of works variously put into English between 1888 and the 1930s. A number of new editions done from the 1960s onwards contain differences in translation but are not what I consider to be serious attempts to look at the original texts (which have themselves undergone scholarly changes) and to recast the thoughts therein for a contemporary audience.

This brings me back to the practical implications of the

Gadamer/Ricoeur principle, and the development in the 1980s of 'reader–response' criticism which elaborates some of the consequences.[3] Interpretation is translation, precisely because in any act of reading the reader must form some judgement as to what the text is saying, most usually a translation into one's own words of 'what the author meant', or 'what the text means to me'. A mere recitation of text, whether from memory or from reading aloud, is generally rejected as an indication of understanding, and therefore of having read a text. This a clue to the plausibility of my claim that interpretation is translation. Readers are not mirrors or receptacles for meanings that are supposedly fixed in the words from which a text is constructed. A mere download of data is not a 'reading', even in apparently paradigmatic and allegedly trivial usage: STOP signs are read and interpreted, indeed translated to the reader's own context, from which the appropriateness of various courses of action is judged: screeching to a halt, gliding through, target practice for bottles or bullets etc. More complicated texts merely complicate the process, most usually by raising questions of authorship, intent, genre, history, culture and politics.

Authorship, intent, genre, history, culture and politics can all be interestingly debated with respect to the classic texts by Marx. This is because, amongst other reasons, some of them (though actually only three major ones) were jointly written with Friedrich Engels, in various senses of the word 'jointly'. Authorial intent, so it has been argued by Quentin Skinner, is ultimately inaccessible, as even living authors view their texts in different ways at different times, saying rather different things about them.[4] Indeed an author who always said the same thing about a given text would seem to deny that as the world moves, so readers (including the author) tend to view texts differently and derive new meanings from them. In any case, post-structuralist philosophy provocatively declared the author dead and located any meaning that a text might contain within the heads of readers, thus pluralising understanding and taking authority away from authors.

Liberation for the reader is not perhaps quite the gift that it sounds, as universalising difference and celebrating plurality have sent some readers (though not me) rushing headlong for their chains, longing for a world of certainty in which authors know what they want to say, their texts represent just that one meaning, and readers either get it or they don't. On that understanding of things, someone needs to tell readers whether they have got it or they haven't, and there are plenty of commentators ready to strike the authoritative or even authorial pose, standing in for the author, and pronouncing on the correctness or otherwise of such understandings as readers have expressed. The post-structuralist approach, by contrast, did not so much kill the author as declare everyone a reader, and thus democratise interpretation amongst authors, commentators and readers. My understanding is that all these readers are at liberty to negotiate their different understandings through dialogue with each other, and that what results is a further airing of difference, rather than an understanding that is supposedly authoritative and definitive, even if numerous readers happen to agree with each other at any one point. Following on from that, what I want to do in this chapter is to blur the supposed distinction between interpretation and translation even further by detailing what any reader of Marx must do, even if the reader's German is perfect. (Marx did write occasionally in French and English; I am concentrating here on German texts.)

Any reader confronting Marx must form some view about the author, the author's intention in writing or publishing the text (with or without signing it), the presumed audience and political context, and any amount of further contextualisation ranging from 'background' – concerning political parties and relevant personalities – to 'foreground' – concerning what particular words are thought to have meant at the time, given events and usage to that point, and conversely what they could not have meant, given intervening events and linguistic changes.

The opposite strategy is also possible, but no less a reading, that is, to assume that the text is an artefact in the reader's own time, and that such meanings as can be derived relate to the reader's own context, dialogical community, and politics. Whilst only a few readers feel sufficiently empowered to exclude the author and (presumed) authorial context quite so rigidly, and indeed to push aside the weight of historical commentary and scholarship that inveighs against anachronism and 'ignorance' of history, this approach at least has the merit of acknowledging that reading is an activity in the present, done presumably for present purposes, and that reading on behalf of people long gone, as if one could re-enter their world, is a distinctly odd idea, usually captured as 'antiquarian'. Most readers, I suspect, are actually taking both approaches and producing very mixed results.

My readings of Marx are no exception. I bring 'background' contextualism to my readings, and these understandings are derived selectively from commentators and amplified with imagination. But if I did not think that these texts have something to communicate to present-day readers about the present, I would not be reading them at all. What that something is, is a personal construction about politics that is deliberately associated with Marx, though this has disadvantages. Having satisfied canons of scholarly and commonsensical honesty, I often wonder if Marx is a useful sign under which to write politically? On balance I think he is, but persuading others of this requires in my terms a newly contextualised Marx as well as freshly re-read texts, and considerable thought about translation.

All of this is going on in the actual process of translation, or at least it was in mine in ways that I am pleased and interested to acknowledge. With other translators, however, I am not sure that this is really the case: either that they were aware of the active and multi-faceted process that constitutes a 'reading,' or that if they were, they cared to acknowledge it publicly. Being really honest, I would say that in as much as translation highlights the way that any reader exercises power in constructing an interpretation, readers who actually write the texts – to which they bring their politics, and from which they construct it – are in a very powerful position indeed. They find themselves in the happy position of ventriloquist, making a dummy person say what they want 'the author' to say. This is what occurs in the usual sense of translation, i.e. re-producing a text in another language.

As with power in any form, this power held by translators is potentially constructive, and not solely destructive. I think I have avoided, more than the previous English translation (and variant editions), language that is neither English nor German, awkward and verbose expressions, stilted phrases and inapposite metaphors, loss of alliteration and muddled syntax, and most important of all, a reading of later philosophical doctrine into earlier political texts. On the other hand, I have allowed Marx to sound like a foreigner, chiefly by keeping his sentence length (which is sometimes extreme, even by German standards), and by following his ideas through certain grammatical constructions that are (or were) more common in the German he chose to write than in the English generally written today. (Much the same concerns arise in producing, say, seventeenth-century English texts for a contemporary student audience, and again, this for me counts as translation in the wider sense.) In the same way I have helped Marx to sound like 'a man of his time' by choosing terms and expressions that would not be out of place in nineteenth-century English usage, but I have also very occasionally played on the inevitable drift in meaning that late twentieth-century readers would be likely to experience (e.g. 'witchhunt' and 'smear' – see below). Thus there has to be a determination as to what sort of English Marx is supposed to be speaking, given that he was a nineteenth-century German, living in England, writing for an international German-speaking audience, and expecting to be translated. While not wanting to re-write Marx as a rap artist, I also did not want him to sound alien and incomprehensibly 'other'. After all, in my view the text still speaks to concerns that readers of Marx's time, and since Marx's time, have in common, even if the full realm of association differs for the two groups. Indeed who is to say that all late twentieth-century readers are going to pick up the same associations anyway (whatever my intentions), and the same applies retrospectively to Marx's readers, now long out of dialogue with us. In the remainder of this chapter I shall recount a number of examples illustrating these points, and then offer some concluding comments on Marx and the politics of translation.

Texts and translations

Perhaps the most famous paragraphs attributed to Marx are the opening ones of the *Communist Manifesto*, as standardly translated for English readers (by Samuel Moore, with Engels' assistance, in 1888):

> A spectre is haunting Europe – the spectre of Communism. All the
> Powers of old Europe have entered into a holy alliance to exorcise this

spectre: Pope and Czar, Metternich and Guizot, French Radicals and German police-spies.

Where is the party in opposition that has not been decried as Communistic by its opponents in power? Where the Opposition that has not hurled back the branding reproach of Communism, against the more advanced opposition parties, as well as against reactionary adversaries?[5]

First of all I had to address the strongly held view that this English text, being blessed by the translator of *Capital* and friend of Marx, and by Marx's political partner of some 40 years, is simply sacrosanct, and that, if there were any defects of translation that could be remedied, the time had long since passed, as the text was so well known and so influential in the socialist tradition. In other words, the English *Manifesto* simply is the *Manifesto* for English readers, and so reference back to German texts at all is really misguided. While there are, of course, good reasons for remembering that 100 years of textual history will not go away, and indeed need not go away, I took the view that there are other considerations relevant here, namely that there does not have to be just one English-language *Manifesto*, just as there is no single German one. While the publication-history of the *Manifesto* is too complicated to go into here, and indeed there is serious doubt and controversy concerning the order of the earliest editions, suffice it to say that there are two pamphlet-style renditions from the period 1848–51, and that versions of this text were re-published in German from 1872 onwards.[6] These German versions incorporated both ambiguous slips and changes (that may or may not be attributable to printers), as well as corrections and notes written or authorised (in some sense) by Marx and Engels variously. The original manuscript and printer's copy have never been recovered.

In other words, two things happened to this text in German: it wandered away from its origins, which are themselves textually disputed and defective in various ways, and it also acquired a doctrinal status, in that footnotes and introductions were added to explain its supposed enduring messages. Anyone who has looked at the rather scrappy, twenty-three- and thirty-page editions from the earliest days must be struck by the contrast with the edition of 1890, in which Engels' notes purport to reconcile the *Manifesto* with Marx's critique of political economy and materialist conception of history – as Engels understood them, writing some seven years after Marx's death. Marx's own approach to re-publishing the *Manifesto* in 1872 was rather different, noting that it was a historical document which 'we have no longer any right to alter'.[7]

Rather than merely tracing Engels' well-trodden path yet again, I resolved to produce an alternative *Manifesto* in English, one based on the editions of 1848–51, and published without Engels' later framing of the text with introductions and doctrinal 'corrections' in footnotes. My intention was to present a text based on the earliest published versions in order to bring to readers a sense that the work itself was hot off the press. I am not arguing that the development of the German and English texts after 1872 was in some sense wrong; rather I am proposing to offer readers an English rendition of the pamphlet-style *Manifesto* which emphasises its role as a political intervention. While not denying the importance of studying the development of Marxism, I am denying that that is the only way to approach the text, and I am also arguing that there may very well be gains in seeing a more political, less doctrinal *Manifesto* in English. Whether this is really productive in any intellectual or political sense is up to readers to judge; obviously it is an approach that I thought worth trying, and at the moment I certainly prefer it. In any case such a text in English is not otherwise available.[8]

With those considerations in mind, then, what did I do with the two famous paragraphs when I sought to translate them, i.e. derive meaning from a text?

> A spectre stalks the land of Europe – the spectre of communism. The powers that be – Pope and Tsar, Metternich and Guizot, French Radicals and German police – are in holy alliance for a witchhunt.
>
> Where is the opposition that has not been smeared as communistic by its enemies in government? Where is the opposition that has not retaliated by slandering more progressive groups and reactionary opponents alike with the stigma of communism?[9]

In the traditional translation, 'spectre', 'haunting', 'holy alliance', and 'exorcise' all seem to go together, following a metaphor of spooks and ghosts. In the second paragraph 'has not been decried' is an apparently obvious translation of the German, though the phrase 'hurled back the branding reproach' surely falls into my category of language that is neither German nor English. My approach to these passages was to take them as an integrated argument, as the succeeding line states (and here I agree with tradition): 'Two things follow from this fact.' In terms of an integrated argument, it seemed to me that this small army of metaphors should be mobilised together, and march in formation towards the reader. If the verb is 'haunting', then perhaps the subject should be 'ghost', as after all, *ein Gespenst* could be either. Unfortunately it is difficult to see *geht um*, a pretty colourless verb of motion, as anything like 'haunting' (see chapter one above). Clearly ghosts haunt and spectres stalk, preserving something of the alliteration of *ein Gespenst geht um*, even though 'stalk' is rather more unusual and sinister in English than 'goes about' or 'moves around'; another option – 'is at large' – would be needlessly vague and verbose.

'Holy alliance' seemed to me quite a reasonable historical allusion, given that Marx mentions the Russian Tsar and the Austrian reactionary Prince Metternich, even if the German text, taken literally, does not quite make this connection. Rather 'holy' is attached to *Hetzjagd*, where the sense is that of hunting, coursing, running to hounds, mad rush, etc. A *Zeitungshetze* is a press campaign. Rather than follow the text literally ('bound together in a holy hunt for the spectre') I opted for 'are in holy alliance for a witchhunt', reckoning that 'witchhunt' would convey to modern English readers the sense of a staged and purposeful political panic, and taking Marx's present perfect ('have entered into') as more to do with the present than the past.

Just as Marx's language played on historical associations that he presumed were available to his readers, so it seemed to me to be defensible to introduce historical associations (albeit anachronistic in terms of the 1840s) that are arguably parallel to Marx's construction of events (viz. the McCarthy period of late 1940s/early 1950s), when a rather similarly spectral communism stalked the USA. Following that line of reasoning, and wanting to produce a snappy text in English (even though the analogous 'punchy' effect is produced in nineteenth-century German through rolling periods and sheer verbal weight), I opted for 'smeared' rather than 'decried' (*verschrieen* is rather more 'shrieky' than 'decry'), and for 'retaliated by slandering ... with the stigma' (as opposed to the quite unintelligible 'hurled back the branding reproach'). 'Exorcise' in the traditional version seemed to me to confuse the metaphor of the occult, as to exorcise implies cleansing whatever has been spiritually possessed. Thus exorcising a spectre misconstrues the sense; the German merely says that reactionaries are in league 'against' it.

My efforts at re-translating these paragraphs are neither more nor less literal than the previous version. Rather my goal was to produce coherent thoughts in modern English. However, the thoughts are not what Marx's contemporaries thought when they read it, and there were as many readings at the time as readers. Readings today are going to be different yet again. However, I do not think that these readings are going to be of much use unless there is some semantic coherence in the text, or at least more than there has been in English. This coherence is largely, though not wholly, a matter of subjects, verbs and objects, tense and word order. Metaphor, allusion, alliteration, puns and innumerable other forms of word play flicker throughout the texts that translators construct, not all of it under their conscious control, no doubt. But translators who do not organise this around some meaning which they find in the 'original' are not going to produce a text from which readers derive very much at all, other than a judgement (very common in the case of Marx, and in his case a judgement of considerable political import) that the author was confused. Marx's translators have rather a lot to answer for.

The Eighteenth Brumaire of Louis Bonaparte is a classic in this respect. The narrative is notoriously difficult to follow, and curiously students of Marx seem far more willing to engage with the daunting philosophical complexities of works such as his *Critique of Hegel's 'Philosophy of Right'*, or with recherché polemics in *The German Ideology*, than they are with a historical episode as well documented and politically pertinent as the events of the second French republic and empire. Even as a way of testing the large-scale generalisations about politics and history that Marx offers in the *Manifesto* at reasonable length, and in his 1859 Preface to *A Contribution to a Critique of Political Economy* in brutally abbreviated fashion, very few commentators address his detailed commentary on stirring revolutionary events and a depressingly regressive aftermath. Even Engels, writing a preface to the work in 1885, was rather nervous on this subject. On the one hand, the way that Marx has been framed within the political and scholarly traditions has worked against reading the *Brumaire* at all, and on the other hand, English readers are particularly ill-served by the traditional translation, which derives from an American version of 1897, because it blurs so very badly what Marx had to say.

In any case, even if we assume that readers contemporary with the publication of the *Brumaire* in 1852 were familiar with the current political context, there are still formidable problems of interpretation – that is, deriving meaning from a text – in the original pamphlet as it came out from the publishers in New York. Marx wrote in German about events in France, using a mixture of German words, loan words from French into German, and French words in order to describe French institutions: *konstituirende Nationalversammlung, legislative Nationalversammlung, parlamentarische Versammlung, Konstituante, Assemblée, parlamentarische Republik, bürgerliche Republik, demokratische Republik, Bourgeoisie,* and *Proletariat,* to list but a few. He was writing for an audience of émigré Germans in the USA, in the first instance, and he and his associates ensured that copies of the pamphlet were also on sale in London. From police records it is known that some reached Germany, then in deepest political reaction against the revolutions of 1848.

Along with the *Manifesto,* the *Brumaire* was one of only a few of Marx's works to be re-published in his lifetime (in Hamburg, in 1869, when the political situation had altered substantially). Given the slippage between the way German democrats (of either period) were likely to have understood Marx's 'take' on French democracy, what then of further slippage between that and what an English-speaking, i.e. English and American, audience could possibly make of it? The Congressional and Parliamentary systems are not all that similar, and it is difficult to know what English and American audiences today are going to make of : 'constitutent assembly', 'legislative national assembly', 'parliamentary assembly', 'parliamentary republic', 'bourgeois republic'. Democratic institutions flowered only very briefly in Germany between 1848 and 1849, and by 1852 there were none left, in the full sense of representative and responsible government. The French Assembly, by contrast, has a virtually continuous history from 1789 onwards, but under a variety of names, and for a variety of purposes, constitution-writing amongst them. Hence it was not always clear, even in French politics, what exactly the representative body was doing, and in what sense 'the people' ruled through it.

Marx, of course, was most intrigued with the question of who 'the people' actually were, in terms of social class, and how that very large issue related to electoral suffrage and to the policies that various governing agencies actually pursued. Anyone who surveys the contemporary Anglo-American literature on 'democracy' can see at once that this is still a topical and stimulating question, even if hardly anyone is pursuing it to much effect. I actually wanted to eschew 'bourgeoisie' and 'proletariat' in the text, as they now seem to me to reek of the museum, and the rather rarefied Marxist wing at that. 'Propertied' or 'commercial' classes, and 'labouring' or 'working' classes, would have made Marx's point, so I argued (to various authorities involved with the re-translation), but to no avail; I thought I was winning other battles and so conceded that one in order to consolidate my gains. Overall I am suggesting that in the *Brumaire* Marx is still about 150 years ahead of his time, and so one cannot rely on an Anglo-American audience today understanding his discussion very readily in conceptual terms, never mind following his scathing satires on political personalities long forgotten even in France. Much of the *Brumaire* consists of biting polemic against political positions that ought to be familiar, even if all the personal and institutional names are not, but this is far from clear in the traditional English text, which is itself 100 years old.

One of the best examples of Marx's savage and unforgettable irony is not actually mangled in the traditional English version. Marx denounces those in 'the party of order' whom he sees as complicit with anti-democratic activities, and particularly with Louis Bonaparte's authoritarian use of the Presidency of the Republic in the events leading to his *coup d'etat* of 2 December 1851. At that point the republic was effectively overthrown, and the way was open for his

declaration of empire the following year. Marx writes, with dry under-
statement:

> Thus the *party of order* itself, though as yet still the cabinet, and not yet
> the national assembly, denounced the parliamentary regime. And it
> protests when 2 December 1851 banishes the *parliamentary regime* from
> France!
>
> We wish it a pleasant journey.[10]

However, very little else in the standard translation achieves that
level of clarity. While my view, as sketched above, on the way that individual readers reach 'difference' as they derive meaning from texts,
would seem to exclude any concept of clarity, this is not quite the case.
'Difference' in what readers derive from texts is one thing, so long as
this 'difference' produces meaningful dialogue, but texts that consist of
semantic fog are quite another. The familiar English version of the
Brumaire falls into that category, in my view, not simply because the
English wording needs improvement here and there (as was for me the
case with, e.g. the opening paragraphs of the *Manifesto*). Rather the
narrative in the *Brumaire* is itself an intricate interlocking mechanism
of quite precisely formulated thoughts. These thoughts involve both
complexities of detail in terms of personalities and events, and multiple levels of irony in the authorial voice (see chapter four above and
chapter eight below). Because of that, any little slip in the way that
Marx's thoughts are made to fit together starts to make it even more
difficult for the reader to follow the text along, deriving meaning from
the narrative. In that way a semantic fog creeps in – highly ironic in
virtue of the fact that 'Brumaire' was the month of fogs in the French
revolutionary calendar.

A few examples will illustrate how this process begins – just where
the traditional translation slips out of focus – but I stress that the effect
throughout a reading of the *Brumaire* is cumulative, and I rely on readers' extrapolating onwards in order to imagine the full effect. I imagine that amongst readers of this chapter there are at least a few who
have finished the *Brumaire* wondering, 'Just where did I lose the
thread?'

The conventional text attempts to deal with historical complexity
by means of footnotes, which I was not allowed in my edition, rather

to my relief, as in a physical way they break the narrative flow. I have attempted to keep the reader apprised of the precise chronology constructed by Marx through the use of square brackets which do not impede the flow of the sentence, and I have also attempted to do the same with other kinds of detail (usually about personalities or events), in order to bring out the force of Marx's arguments as I understand them, again without disrupting the flowing prose. I am sure that this cannot be entirely successful for every reader, but I have adopted it as a complement to my general strategy of finding a sharp, crisp, intelligible thought in every sentence of a classic – but unfortunately rather under-appreciated – text by a very accomplished German stylist.

Sometimes the traditional English translation is merely fuzzy and needs sharpening up to catch Marx's venom. Compare the literal and insipid traditional text:

> Thus, so long as the *name* of freedom was respected and only its actual realisation prevented, of course in a legal way, the constitutional existence of freedom remained intact, inviolate, however mortal the blows dealt to its existence *in actual life*.[11]

With the sting in the tail as re-translated:

> Hence so long as freedom is *nominally* respected and only its actual exercise is hindered, in a very legal way you understand, then the constitutional existence of freedom remains undamaged, untouched, however much its *commonplace* existence is murdered.[12]

At times in the traditional version one is left wondering what at all is going on:

> Thereby they [republican constitutionalists] merely made the impotent attempt still to exercise, when only a parliamentary minority, as which they already saw themselves prophetically in their mind's eye, a power which at the present moment, when they commanded a parliamentary majority and all the resources of governmental authority, was slipping daily more and more from their feeble hands.[13]

Sorting this out was not too difficult:

> At a time when they [republican constitutionalists] controlled a parliamentary majority and all the resources of governmental author-

ity, they saw themselves prophetically as a parliamentary minority, and made only an impotent attempt to exercise a power, which was day by day slipping from their feeble grasp.[14]

My overall point here is that after even two or three such passages, in as many pages, the intricacy of Marx's thought is blurred. Marx is scathing about the naiveté of the National Assembly, damning about Bonaparte's character, and clear about the would-be dictator's craftiness. Virtually all of these vital shades of judgement and their relation to the thrust of the narrative are lost in the first passage below, and (I hope) captured in the second, in which I straighten out the syntax, but also update the language somewhat from the quaintness (e.g. 'rascally') and obscurity (e.g. 'reviews') of the late 1890s.

The traditional text:

> Bonaparte, who precisely because he was a Bohemian, a princely lumpenproletarian, had the advantage over a rascally bourgeois in that he could conduct a dirty struggle, now saw, after the Assembly had itself guided him with its own hand across the slippery ground of the military banquets, the reviews, the Society of December 10, and finally, the Code pénal, that the moment had come when he could pass from an apparent defensive to the offensive.[15]

The re-translation:

> Because he was such a bohemian, and such a prince of thieves, Bonaparte had the advantage over bourgeois grafters of fighting dirty; once the national assembly itself had escorted him over the treacherous terrain of regimental dinners, army reviews, the Society of 10 December and finally the criminal law, he saw that the moment had come to go openly on the offensive.[16]

This raises the crucial issue of Marx's audience in an English translation of his topical exposé. Is it an English-speaking audience of the 1850s, of the 1890s, or of the present? My contention that there is a Marx for the present, constructed within a translation of what is necessarily a historical document, underpins my view that the text should signal all the following things to the reader:

- Marx as a political writer of the 1850s

- Marx as a German
- Marx as a strong stylist
- Marx as a re-published and translated 'late Victorian'
- Marx as an angry pamphleteer of his time and ours.

How much of the following tale from within the *Brumaire* rings familiar in outline if not in detail, and why should we not find similarities between that situation and later ones? Some of the language in my translation below was unavailable in the 1890s, never mind the 1850s, and the allusions in my English are there specifically for the modern audience. Though Marx wrote (famously, in the *Brumaire*) that 'tradition from all the dead generations weighs like a nightmare on the living',[17] I presume in my version that he is still writing for the living – precisely to wake them up. For purposes of comparison I insert certain words from the traditional translation into my re-translation below:

> On 20 December [1850] Pascal Duprat [the Orléanist deputy] cross-examined [cf. 'interpellated'] the minister of the interior on the 'gold bars' lottery. This lottery was blessed by the Elysée, as Bonaparte and his faithful henchmen had brought it into the world, and Carlier the prefect of police had taken it under his wing, although in France all lotteries, with the exception of charitable raffles, were illegal. Seven million tickets at a franc apiece, the profits supposedly earmarked for the transportation of Parisian riff-raff [cf. 'vagabonds'] to California. Partly the idea was to replace the socialist dreams of the Paris proletariat with dreams of glistering gold [cf 'golden dreams'], and the guarantied right to employment with the seductive prospect of the grand prize draw. Of course workers in Paris did not see through the blaze of California gold to the plain old francs winkled [cf. 'enticed'] from their pockets. But in the main it was just a straightforward swindle. The riff-raff wanting to open up the gold mines of California without the trouble of leaving Paris were Bonaparte himself and his debt-ridden cronies. They had partied [cf. 'squandered in riotous living'] through the three million authorised by the national assembly, and the cash box had to be refilled one way or another. Bonaparte had vainly launched a national subscription for so-called workers' towns, putting himself at the head for a substantial donation. Meanminded bourgeois awaited

this with grave suspicion, and when of course it was not forthcoming, the socialist 'castles in the air' crashed to earth [cf. 'fell straightaway to the ground']. The gold bars were a better draw. Bonaparte & Co. were not satisfied with pocketing part of the profit from the seven million over and above the cost of the prize bullion; they fabricated false lottery tickets, issuing the same number 10 on fifteen or twenty tickets, a financial scam [cf. 'operation'] in keeping with the Society of 10 December.[18]

Neither authors nor translators have control, in any very strong sense, over the meanings (plural) that readers (plural) derive from texts that they publish. Moreover, publication occurs in a purposive context about which readers have to make up their own minds, not just about why texts are produced, and re-produced, when they are, but why they themselves are reading these texts, and what they intend to do, if anything, as a result. It is from understandings of the past that the present is continuously constructed, by individuals, but largely from common materials. Hence it makes sense to revisit these materials, to reinvent them as common experiences, as they are re-read, and revitalised meanings are then derived. Quite a lot more of Marx is due, indeed overdue, for re-translation, but please, only if an interpretative context is thought through. There is an audience out there, English has moved on, and politics has changed – though after re-reading Marx afresh, perhaps not all that much.

In the next chapter I take a more detailed look at the 'Marx' who is being translated, in particular the 'voice' that is presumed to reside in the text. Presumptions about voice are an integral part of the way that meaning is constructed by readers. Marx was evidently aware of this, and had a number of different authorial strategies. While in chapter five above I noted that the dead walk among us when ancient words are used in the present, in chapter eight below I observe how the dead also speak to us in voices from beyond the grave.

Notes

1 See Paul Ricoeur, 'Metaphor and the main problem of hermeneutics', in *A Ricoeur Reader: Reflection and Imagination*, ed. Mario J. Valdés (London: Harvester/Wheatsheaf, 1991), pp. 303–19.

2 Karl Marx, *Later Political Writings*, ed. and trans. T. Carver (Cambridge: Cambridge University Press, 1996).

3 See Jane P. Tompkins (ed.), *Reader-Response Criticism: From Formalism to Post-structuralism* (Baltimore MD: Johns Hopkins University Press, 1980); see also Terrell Carver and Matti Hyvärinen (eds), *Interpreting the Political: New Methodologies* (London, Routledge, 1997), introduction.

4 See James Tully (ed.), *Meaning and Context: Quentin Skinner and his Critics* (Cambridge: Polity Press, 1988).

5 Karl Marx and Frederick Engels, *The Communist Manifesto*, in Marx and Engels, *Collected Works*, vol. 6 (London: Lawrence & Wishart, 1976), pp. 481.

6 See Karl Marx and Friedrich Engels, *Das Kommunistische Manifest*, ed. Thomas Kuczynski (Trier, Karl-Marx-Haus, 1995), pp. 29–225; also Terrell Carver, 'Retranslating the "Manifesto": new histories, new ideas', in *The Communist Manifesto: New Interpretations*, ed. Mark Cowling (Edinburgh, Edinburgh University Press, 1998).

7 Karl Marx, *The Communist Manifesto*, ed. Frederick L. Bender (New York, W. W. Norton, 1988), p. 44.

8 Hal Draper's 'New English Version' of the *Communist Manifesto* follows very closely what he terms 'the Authorized English Translation of 1888'; as explained, I depart very considerably from this kind of assumption about the 1888 text, and therefore I produce a new translation that differs considerably from Draper's. Hal Draper (ed.), *The Adventures of the Communist Manifesto* (Berkeley CA, Center for Socialist History, 1994).

9 Marx, *Later Political Writings*, p. 1.

10 Marx, *Later Political Writings*, pp. 51-2.

11 Karl Marx and Frederick Engels, *The Eighteenth Brumaire of Louis Bonaparte*, in *Collected Works*, vol. 11 (London: Lawrence & Wishart, 1979), p. 115.

12 Marx, *Later Political Writings*, p. 43.

13 Marx and Engels, *Collected Works*, vol. 11, p. 117.

14 Marx, *Later Political Writings*, p. 45.

15 Marx and Engels, *Collected Works*, vol. 11, p. 157.

16 Marx, *Later Political Writings*, p. 86.

17 Marx, *Later Political Writings*, p. 32.

18 Marx, *Later Political Writings*, p. 85; Marx and Engels, *Collected Works*, vol. 11, p. 157.

Writing and reading: Marx's voices

Authors and voices

Meaning is constructed in practice, or re-constructed in reading, on presumptions about who is speaking and why. The 'why' generally relates to purposive assumptions and hence to other individuals in some performative context. Most things that are said are said to another or to others, hence the context is 'dialogical', and dialogues are generally in aid of something, hence the performative dimension. Few interchanges are just trading words.[1] Frustratingly the dialogical context for many texts was presumed at the time, and not stated by either authorial voice or audience recipient. Personal letters are notoriously difficult in this respect – few correspondents go through a performative context already presumed between two parties, all for the benefit of a third – but the point is more general respecting of other forms of communication. In any case the parties to the (presumed) dialogue need not have agreed with each other completely at any point as to what was being said and why, as understandings between communicators are almost always necessarily approximate (here I follow out the arguments introduced in chapter one and developed in chapter seven above).

Readers today are aided by, but very dependent upon, contextual reconstructions, to which they are recommended to turn, and which have themselves been passed down to become a tradition. Mostly the reconstructions relevant to Marx centre on him as if he were a person (actually he is presented as 'an author') and tell us his 'story', in the first instance, and thus build up a picture of who is speaking (at the time and down the ages) and why in general he does this (again, rather muddling 'why' at the time and 'why' down the ages). Thus readers get a sense of Marx's voice and why it was one and the same with himself – supposedly. This happens through the biographical frame into which commentators on Marx insert what it is they have to say about his 'thought', itself a canonical exploration of texts. Very often this biographical frame also presents a physical image of the author, to whose imagined voice the reader will be listening. Marx's is all too familiar, and as with most biographical practice, presents a 'master image' dating from late in life, when the master's 'thought' is presumed to have matured from germs of intimation traceable in early writings. This practice has two deleterious effects: first, it validates visually a teleological reading of an author's work, valuing early materials just as 'steps on the way' to something only fully realised at some presumed culmination; second, in Marx's case, the presumed culmination has, since Engels, been conceptualised as a doctrinal system issuing forth from a scientist/philosopher. The stiffly formal character of Victorian portrait photographs is perfectly suited to this reading, and these are the images of the 'mature' Marx – including, of course, the literally stony monument at Highgate Cemetery – that appear on the cover of standard biographies. Just for a change, try imagining an authorial Marx aged 18 or 21 – these unfamiliar images are readily available, just not much used – and extrapolate from there to the '48er, who was only 30 at the time of the revolutionary events (the next extant image dates from 1861 when Marx is already too recognisably 'himself' at 43).[2]

The Marx canon has been dramatically revised on occasion, as with the 'discovery' of the 1844 'early manuscripts' in the 1960s, when English-language commentators took them up. No one has dared to interpret these texts without characterising their author, and everyone is happy to re-evaluate a text when its authorial attribution changes, as happened with the historical work *Revolution and Counter-Revolution in Germany* (from Marx to Engels), with the satirical *Last Trump of Judgement Day for Hegel the Atheist and Anti-Christ: An Ultimatum* (from Marx to Bauer), and with the letter that supposedly proved that Marx wanted to dedicate *Capital* to Darwin (from Marx to Edward Aveling, though Marx did send Darwin an inscribed copy of the second German edition, which Darwin left unread).[3] As with many other forms of academic commentary, political theory is a genre that relies heavily on a canon of writers, treated as the origin of ideas still of interest. These origins are themselves explored as an interpretative activity producing texts directed to the presumed interests of contemporary audiences. My point here is that some biographical narrative is a required, unexceptionable, and indeed unremarkably normal (and so virtually invisible) part of the genre. Presumptions about voice emerge as these biographies are constructed and handed down through 'the literature' from which present-day audiences learn their 'Marx'.[4]

Marx is particularly interesting in this regard, because his biography has always embodied a partnership with Engels, and Engels was also his first biographer, so the story also originates with him – Engels – as a privileged voice in a narrative that underwrites this privilege. In his (exceedingly brief) autobiography Marx also recounts various things about Engels and how he saw their respective works. Interestingly he does not actually characterise their relationship (e.g. as a partnership, on some understanding of the term), but proceeds in a rather cool and factual way through their separate paths to the same conclusions, their decision to collaborate on a joint work (*The German Ideology*), and their further joint authorship of the *Communist Manifesto*.[5] Marx is also on record as finding it strange that a journalist referred to the two of them together, as if they were one person, and in a letter to Engels he complains: 'It is exceedingly odd, the way he speaks of us in the singular – "Marx and Engels says", etc.'[6] Is Marx presuming that a plural verb would mean separate identities for each? He says nothing positive there or elsewhere at any length about the parameters of separation and overlap between the two. We are left in a domain of inference.

Thus the narrative tradition about Marx inevitably engages with his relationship – textual and personal – with Engels, who – unlike Marx – became keen to characterise this relationship in volubly general terms. I have argued elsewhere at considerable length that Engels himself defined the intellectual terms through which Marx as a 'thinker' is understood. Moreover I have also argued that some of these terms are crucially set, or are finally made clear, only after Marx is dead. Engels as literary legatee, family executor, and political survivor thus found himself in a new relationship with the man to whom he played 'second fiddle' (Engels' own description) when the presumed 'first fiddle' was extant.[7] This is a complex and controversial argument, and I shall not be repeating its various claims and defences once again. My point here is that as a result of these narratives constructed by Engels, and in particular as a result of the narrative tradition constructed by writers – either pro- or anti-Marx – who readily turned to 'the partner', it is not clear in textual terms if Marx is one person or two, and therefore precisely whose voice – so we imagine – is speaking to us through the texts we read, and with whom we are, in our internal narratives at least, in dialogue.

Even supposing that we take Marx to be one person, there is considerable variation in the kind of material through which he is supposedly speaking to us. There are works of rhetorical and somewhat fictive persuasion – at one extreme – such as *The Civil War in France*, an address (written in English) in which Marx idealises the Paris Commune of 1870–71, writing in the indicative about how the situation might have been, and – at the other end of a discursive spectrum – there are volumes of 'excerpt notebooks', in which Marx copied out long extracts from other writers, leaving the dialogical context unclear (though there are often links to other materials he wrote later). Intriguingly he sometimes either miscopied his source (in that textual discrepancies abound), or seems to have reformulated or even contradicted the author's thoughts, without flagging this clearly to his (posthumous) readers. In the mountain of text left to us there are some thousands of personal letters between Marx and Engels, and to and from third parties (well over ten thousand items altogether), as well as a range of manuscript and published works, ranging from the overtly polemical (e.g. *The Poverty of Philosophy*) to the forbiddingly yet ironically theoretical (e.g. *Capital*, vol. 1). After 1850 it becomes very problematic to determine just who Marx's intended audience really was – or audiences, assuming he had multiple strategies and deliberately wrote texts that would be read in different ways by different kinds of reader. Saying that he generally wrote for an international socialist community somewhat begs the question, as Marx's most analytically challenging works are written rather differently from his speeches and messages to the individuals and groups affiliated to the International Working Men's Association, for instance. In any case there is a large amount of journalism written by Marx where the content must have been tailored to editorial expectations, but a subversive authorial voice can never – pre-eminently in Marx's case here – be ruled out. These are all problems that thoughtful readers and alert commentators encounter with other social theorists in the canon; it is just that with Marx it seems that virtually all of these problems get a look in at some point in the story – or they should, anyway.

On the whole my complaint about the better sort of commentary is that it contextualises along over-familiar lines, following a rather tired genre of intellectual biography. This tends to duplicate the paradoxical 'Man of Action' BBC Radio series (most guests seemed to be intellectuals and civil servants), in that the rough and tumble of political engagement seems to get smoothed over as the commentator engages with 'thought' and thus makes the biography properly 'intellectual'. My complaint about the worse sort of commentary is not necessarily that it is so hostile as to preclude any 'fusion of horizons' between commentator, subject, and audience (with Marx there are, of course, many examples of this), but rather that poor commentators seem to feel that Marx always spoke in the same authoritative voice, uttering doctrinal pronouncements whatever the text. On that view even gestures towards personal and political contexts hardly count, and texts get strung together without any consideration of argumentative sense and dialogical context. Marx thus speaks in a lapidary mode, just as his gravestone suggests.

Singularity and plurality

What happens when two authorial voices join? Despite the biographical tradition of lifelong 'partnership' initiated by Engels, Marx and Engels only produced three major works together, and interestingly all three works were produced in different senses of 'together'. *The Holy*

Family (published in 1845, their first collaboration) has separately signed individual chapters, and is also by 'Engels and Marx', as Engels had an international reputation as a journalist and socialist at the time, whereas Marx had little readership outside the Rhineland and few publications to his name. Engels complained at the time of writing (1844–45) that Marx's contributions had swamped his, thus casting doubt on the sense in which a 'jointness' between the two was equal in the way that authorial attribution might imply.[8]

After that the two worked together on *The German Ideology*, which was planned for publication but never completed, as Marx famously relates in his autobiographical remarks of 1859. Apparently, Marx and Engels reached self-clarification (according to Marx, does 'self' here really refer to two people? or to the same clarification?), and the large 'printer's sheets' on which the two had scribbled were abandoned to 'the gnawing criticism of the mice', a typically mordant joke from an ironist of considerable savagery, and someone who was always in debt and awaiting publishers' advances. As detailed in chapter five above there are passages in *The German Ideology* in which I read dialogue and debate, rather than two writers groping to agree a 'smooth' text (as generally presumed by editors, except Hiromatsu), and in any case, given Engels' role as Marx's amanuensis (notwithstanding lengthy passages in Marx's hand as well), the manuscript presents irresolvable hermeneutic difficulties. When is Engels speaking for himself? When is Marx speaking through him, together with him (and vice versa)? When is Marx speaking for himself against Engels (was there ever any vice versa)? In any case there is now no way to order the various starts, re-starts and re-writes that reside on the surface of the manuscript sheets, which were themselves divided up in various ways (usually into two large columns) and then filled in at different times in what appears to be a set of odd sequences, accompanied by much crossing out. Reproducing the material as it lies on the page is clearly the best editorial strategy, but then that merely reproduces the textual conundrum: what are these people saying? to each other rather than to readers? to readers in agreement with each other? However, of all the various works attributed to Marx (one way or another), it seems fair to say that *The German Ideology* rates very highly for sheer originality and stimulus, and the raggedness of the text hardly gets in the way. It is very much the origin of what Marx termed 'our outlook', and textually there is considerable overlap with the 1859 'Preface' and other works.[9] The *Communist Manifesto* is the joint work with the fewest authorial problems, in that we have two earlier versions by Engels (a Communist 'confession of faith' written in a catachetic style, and a draft on the principles of communism for a party congress), and surviving documentation indicates that Marx worked on a final draft up to (late) submission for publication in early 1848. A textual comparison between Engels' draft 'principles' and the final text suggests where Marx's influence lay, but no one, not least the two themselves in subsequent comments on the document, disputes that both had a hand in the final version. Engels did write in 1869 that the work was essentially Marx's, as was his wont when presenting himself as 'second fiddle' yet Marx's authorised 'voice'. Somewhat contrarily I have argued that the historical passages, for instance, have far more to do with Engels' voluminous earlier writings than with Marx's considerably thinner and more theoretical output. It also seems unlikely that the two authors agreed the final draft whilst actually working together, Marx being presumed from circumstantial evidence to have worked on the text as the 'last hand' on his own. Nonetheless everything about this work suggests an unambiguously joint effort – though what is lacking are joint signatures, as the Manifesto appeared anonymously for obvious political reasons.[10]

The real difficulty here is not the joint authorial voice in the *Manifesto*, but the multifarious character of the audience – the document was written to satisfy a committee incorporating known individual views in order to weld together diverse, less well-known communists who met only occasionally, and then only to advise and educate each other rather than to embark on any concerted campaigns or covert actions. There may very well be silences in this text – areas too controversial to cover – and ambiguous formulations to please different people differently. By the late 1860s and early 1870s both authors were willing to 'own' the Manifesto and to have it republished with full authorial attribution and a jointly signed introduction. But by then they could also frame it as a historical document and plead other preoccupations in order to forestall any suggestion that they should have updated it or written another manifesto instead.

While Marx and Engels were both alive their primary authorial strategies were to sign themselves singularly as themselves (Engels had a rather long history of pseudonyms in his days pre-Marx), and to refer respectfully if slightly distantly to each other (from the contemporary perspective) as a distinguished author of one's acquaintance. Engels' *Anti-Dühring*, for example, appeared as his own journalism in 1877–78, in the first instance, and then shortly after as a volume with an introduction to the work as Engels' own in which Marx was quoted and advertised as a mentor and influence. But in the second edition, published in 1885 two years after Marx's death, the partnership motif appears, and the reader encounters the joint subject 'Marx and I' in a narrative shift. Engels also proudly recounted that Marx had contributed a section on 'economics' and that he had adjusted his text to reflect this joint if rather retrospective input. After Marx's death Engels provided numerous introductions and prefaces to new editions of Marx's works, all in the same vein, and Marx emerged from Engels' narrative as the presumed 'senior partner' once Engels had self-identified as his 'junior'.

This 'Marx' is a voice that Engels used very effectively to recount the 'materialist interpretation of history' (not a phrase Marx used) and to create the 'imprimatur' that drives the partnership narrative in its most stringent form – perfect agreement – or its slightly less stringent versions – eventual convergence in a 'deterministic' system, or 'division of labour' in complementary fields.[11] In the 1885 Preface to *Anti-Dühring* Engels relates that he read his entire manuscript to Marx, and so he – Engels – feels confident that it says what Marx agreed with. But why was Engels *reading* to Marx? (Marx could read!) And if he was reading aloud, was Marx listening? Curiously Engels does not report Marx speaking for himself about *Anti-Dühring*. Obviously quite a lot would depend, then, on what Marx is supposed to have said, so mysteriously this is a case where Engels fails crucially to give Marx a voice, and this 'silence' becomes a blank cheque. Marx did write a (very short) introduction to *Socialism, Utopian and Scientific*, itself extracted from *Anti-Dühring* and published (in French) in 1880, and Marx indeed recommended the pamphlet to readers for its 'political' content, interestingly limiting his endorsement to something narrower than Engels ever claimed, and not spelling out exactly what he meant. Even here, however, 'voice' is an issue – Marx signed this not over-enthusiastic and rather qualified endorsement of Engels' first major work for many years with someone else's name, that of Paul Lafargue, his (Marx's) son-in-law. Engels, so I have argued, was a genius at consciously taking on complexity in some context and then unself-consciously creating ambiguity out of it. The notion of Marx's 'imprimatur' is a characteristically Engelsian construction. It raises the issue of whether one person is right to speak for another, and if so, whether they speak with one voice. Once one of the parties is dead, the issue becomes unclear. Engels made Marx live on not only by giving him a voice of his own, but also by constructing a narrative such that when Engels spoke, Marx seemed to speak, too.[12]

Summarising the position, I see the following voices lurking within the Marx–Engels 'partnership', and I note the usual consequences amongst commentators:

- separate signed voices, as in *The Holy Family* – generally ignored in commentary
- joint anonymous voices, as in the *Communist Manifesto* – generally attributed by commentators to Marx, rather than Engels
- debating voices, as in *The German Ideology* – almost universally homogenised in commentary as 'Marx and Engels'
- 'His Master's Voice', as when Engels regurgitates Marx in reviews and articles – Marx's silences about this activity are read by commentators as 'consent' ('tacit', rather than 'express')
- the 'resurrected voice', as when Engels makes the authorial Marx speak from beyond the grave – commentators read this in conjunction with the 'partnership' narrative, on Engels' own terms.

Revoicing the voices

Much of the Marx that has come down to us derives from commentary on Engels' Marx, a notion that Engels himself encouraged in (not very) private correspondence, suggesting that his own works made easier reading than the triumphs of the master.[13] Many millions more read *Socialism, Utopian and Scientific* and (eventually) *Dialectics of Nature* (edited posthumously from Engels' manuscripts), then ever tackled *Capital*, vol. 1, or even *Value, Price and Profit* (written by Marx in English for workers' meetings). But even when commentators are explicating works by Marx, there has been an overwhelming tendency to revoice Marx as Engels constructed him. Engels framed Marx in a biographical narrative about Hegel and dialectical philosophy, thus implying that Marx's aim was system-building in some comparable manner, and portraying him as a 'scientific materialist' to rival Darwin, as Engels said in his 'Graveside Speech'.[14]

It is interesting that the major texts by Marx which are cited in conjunction with Engels' claims are often footnotes and tangential remarks. The 1859 Preface to *A Contribution to the Critique of Political Economy*, for example, contains a 'guiding thread', which Engels revoiced as a lapidary doctrine, beginning with his book review of the same year. Marx himself consigned these few sentences of text to a footnote to *Capital*, vol. 1, surely not the place for one of the scientific discoveries of the age. Originally it came from a hastily drafted preface and was intended merely to guide the reader; as a footnote to another text it seems exactly that – a footnote – except when taken, for example by analytical Marxists, as 'Marx' *simpliciter*. Possibly there is a highly ironic authorial strategy in Marx which reverses footnotes to text in terms of speaking to the reader, but as a way of reading Marx, in my view, this focus on footnotes and odd sentences tends towards the cabalistic. References to Hegel are similarly cast by Marx himself in a prefatory and comparative vein, typically in the second preface to *Capital*, vol. 1, in which he comments at length on *someone else's* comparison of his (Marx's) method with the one employed by 'that mighty thinker' (Hegel). (I deal more extensively with Hegel's role in the Marx narrative in chapter nine below). There are very few references indeed to 'dialectic' in Marx, and none to its centrality to explaining anything and everything. Marx merely comments that he 'coquetted' with Hegelian terminology in the opening chapters of *Capital*, vol. 1 (see chapter two through chapter four above), and makes a limited number of qualified comparisons elsewhere in the text. My point here with respect to commentators is that these remarks and passages are not so much 'taken out of context' as put into a context supplied by the Engelsian tradition. Another Marx appears in commentators' texts, another voice, re-voiced from Engels.

Voices and lives

Teleology plays a large part in traditional biographical narrations, in that the young Marx and the young Engels seem destined for each other in their early lives, and their first meetings are invested with world-historic significance. Commentators are generally so uninquisitive about the narrative conventions of the genre in which they write that it is unthinkable to imagine querying the tradition and possibly presenting the tale another way. The 'first meeting' invariably sits within an autobiographical and biographical frame which Engels established. In 1895 (some fifty-three years after the event) he wrote to Marx's biographer Franz Mehring, saying that the first meeting between the two (in 1842) was 'rather cool', an admission that is paradoxically useful in a hagiographical account. Fortunately the story picks up again in late 1844 after Engels and Marx have corresponded, and they not only meet but agree to collaborate – on *The Holy Family*. In that way they are re-voiced in a narrative recounting the founding moments of the partnership, a narrative that benefits from the suspense generated by the near-abortive first encounter. Had they gone their separate ways in 1842, what would have happened? One can hear the bio-pic voices ringing through the biographies as these originary encounters are re-visited, re-enacted, and re-voiced.

The 'perfect agreement' and 'eventual convergence' theories on which the 'Marx-Engels' school relies require the unitary voices detailed in the typology above. The other variant in the 'partnership' narrative – the 'division of labour' thesis – requires something different in terms of voicing Marx and Engels. Engels suggested, once Marx was off the scene, that scientific and historical questions were assigned to him, largely though not wholly – after all, Marx had left publications and notebooks on these subjects. In this way at convenient moments the voices of the two can be conveniently different – saying compatible things about different subjects, presumably by agreement – and also conveniently the same – overlapping and making use of each other's materials. Obviously this keeps the voices in time and in harmony – where the commentator requires this – and at these moments the commentator, in whose voice the narrative proceeds, rather conveniently disappears. A common authorial strategy in commentary is to write from a position of presumed scholarly authority and to follow the manuals of style which advise crisp declarative sentences and avoidance of the pronoun 'I' – perhaps just lapsing into an indeterminate 'we', rather inveigling readers into the illusion that they, too, are helping to write the text as well as reading it. Readers do write texts as they read, in my view, but for them to have to do so hand-in-hand with commentators seems an unnecessary renunciation of the authorial voice that readers should retain, independent of commentators who wish to create a 'partnership'. Over-inclusive commentators attempt to make readers into their 'junior partner' and so subsume their voices into one that is authorial and authoritative. Engels did much the same with Marx.

Dead authors/living texts

The *Marx-Engels Gesamtausgabe*, better known as MEGA[2], is one of the major academic monuments of the mid-twentieth century, or at least it should have been. Planned in over a hundred double volumes, and benefiting from the seemingly limitless funds and person-hours that only East Berlin and Moscow could provide, the operation was carried out – from the 1960s until about 1990 – in staggeringly pedantic textological terms. The remit was to publish everything that survives by Marx and Engels in the original language, and to catalogue any missing or doubtful items, as well as to include third-party letters, other items of interest, and a mountain of information about the manuscript production, publication history, and contemporary reception of every work. Only the purest scholarly principles and procedures were employed, and the *Apparat* volume accompanying each volume of text gives details of variants, line by line and word by word. A fundamental tenet of the operation was that chronology should play a crucial part in ordering the materials presented, and that copy-texts for each item would be chosen with that in mind. Obviously for any given work, the earliest manuscript draft does not necessarily or even usually represent the copy-text to which early drafts can be related, and from which variant copies, authorial notations after publication, further editions and translations can be tracked. Sometimes the choice of copy-text can be a matter of judgement and therefore subject to debate and dispute, but the sort of arguments involved follow well-established lines, and the whole exercise often has the marks of a necessary but boring aridity.

Unsurprisingly, though, for a series produced (till the early 1990s) under orthodox Marxist regimes, there was some considerable investment in finding Marx and Engels to be in 'ideological' terms what tradition already decreed them to be, whilst also maintaining the reputation of the editorial section as purely 'scientific'. In editorial terms Marx and Engels are treated in MEGA^2 as separate individuals producing separate works, but also working together and collaborating from time to time, just as surviving documentation indicates. *The German Ideology* presents special difficulties that I have already discussed (see chapter five above), in that an apparently collaborative work, interpreted as the production of a single-voiced 'smooth text', comes into question once readers are equipped with an apparatus that identifies each individual's handwriting, and so a variant interpretation becomes possible – some passages become a debate in which one author contradicts the other. Although material from the opening of *The German Ideology* was included in the MEGA^2 *Probeband* of the early 1970s, the full text has not yet appeared, possibly for reasons of this sort, i.e. an unwillingness amongst certain parties to probe too deeply into the particulars of the unitary, joint 'voice' that is presumed to be speaking form the authorised version.

At a certain point in the Marx–Engels story, however, all this breaks down. As MEGA^2 has advanced through the *Nachlaß*, in which 'economic works' relating to the published volumes of *Capital* are treated separately (from all other works, from letters, and from notebook materials), the editorial team (reorganised and refunded since the mid-1990s) has reached *Capital*, vol. 3. This work is problematic in that it was edited by Engels for publication after Marx's death, and it appeared in 1894 as authored by Marx and edited by Engels. But the manuscripts from which Engels worked were written by Marx in 1861–63, before the final manuscript draft of *Capital*, vol. 1, was started. Engels' text is known to depart from Marx's manuscripts at numerous points, and a number of commentators have begun to voice disquiet. The manuscripts have themselves been published in MEGA^2, working chronologically through Marx's materials. Since these manuscripts have become available, it is not too difficult to compare Marx's thoughts with Engels' published version of *Capital*, vol. 3, which of course appeared as the third volume of the masterwork, and the last that would appear. The volumes of supplementary materials published later as *Theories of Surplus Value* count as volume 4 of *Capital* only in a supplementary sense, rather than as a continuation of the analytical presentation of the 'economic categories'. Undertaking this comparison of Engels with Marx, Norman Levine has complained that Engels 'Hegelianised' the text at certain points, and Christopher J. Arthur has argued that Engels introduced the concept 'simple commodity production' to the detriment of Marx's argument.[15] This type of work has complicated matters for MEGA^2 considerably.

In MEGA^2 terms the problem is the copy-text of *Capital*, vol. 3. Is it the 1894 text as edited and published, indeed 'completed', by Engels, to which Marx's manuscripts of 1861–63 are a precursor in a rough-and-ready sense? Or is the *ur-Capital*, vol. 3, really the 1861–63 manuscripts as Marx left them, to which Engels' editorial emendations and additions are exactly that – variants of a text that can be judged independently as 'coming from another hand'? Everyone agrees that Engels' voice in *Capital*, vol. 3 as published is that of an editor, speaking first to readers through an introduction, and then helping readers through a text in which Marx speaks as author. The problem that has arisen is the extent to which Engels' voice is *additionally* so nearly authorial that the published text is not merely a joint production, but actually an act of clairvoyance, in which Engels – as medium – allows Marx to speak through him from beyond the grave.

Extravagant as it sounds, the latter characterisation is the one that suits the 'true believers' in the orthodox tradition (which encompasses both biographical narrative and doctrinal substance), and precisely the 'fact' they need in order to finish the tale – that of the Marx–Engels 'partnership' – most convincingly, in order to safeguard the 'ideology' that is 'truly Marxist'. What could be better proof that two voices spoke as one than universal recognition that one voice in the ultimate instance was as good as the other? The matter is 'ultimate' both in terms of *Capital* as a sequential work and in terms of Engels' career – he died just a year after this final volume was published.

Conversely, those arguing for an assumption that unity between the two cannot be assumed but must be established evidentially instance by instance, are in a strong position to unravel the narrative on which so much Marxist orthodoxy depends, by working backwards from the differences that textual comparisons between Marx and Engels can plausibly establish. These differences, so the sceptical analysis runs, are so striking, and so divergent from the tenor of Marx's analysis, that a presumption of doubt becomes more strongly justified than ever. Blanket presumptions of 'partnership' thus become even more damaging to fresh and stimulating readings of Marx, and indeed to new ways of challenging capitalism politically that might be developed outside the 'orthodox' framework of assumptions and 'laws'.

What would satisfy 'the orthodox' is an admission from MEGA[2] that Marx's 1861–63 manuscripts are forerunners of a copy-text, which ought to be *Capital*, vol. 3, as published by Engels. This text would therefore be authorially established by Engels, not merely editorially constructed, though quite how clear this elision of distance – between editorship and authorship – would have to be made is not as yet very helpfully addressed by those arguing for the 'orthodox' view. Can Engels be viewed as both author and editor without contradiction? Contrarily, those in MEGA[2] who see advantages in preserving a clear distinction between editorship and authorship, and hence between Engels and Marx as 'voices', where circumstances suggest that this is the case, need do little more than stick with the chronological principle and hold the line, already visible, between the author's hand (in the 1861–63 manuscripts) and the editor's work (in the 1894 edition). This is just as the MEGA[2] text would helpfully indicate, provided that the 1894 edition is actually produced in line with the series as currently progressing. It may very well be that some readers will do the textual comparison (between the 1861–63 manuscripts and *Capital*, vol. 3, as published in 1894) and conclude that that Engels did an excellent job re-writing Marx, and that Engels' 'economics', whether conceptually 'Hegelianised' or not, is an improvement on Marx's manuscript thoughts, which in any case antedated the real beginning of the critique in its worked out form. It could also be that other readers will conclude that Engels meddled unnecessarily and unhelpfully with Marx's thoughts, which in the 1861–63 manuscripts are really more in line with the sequential thrust of *Capital* than they are with Engels' version of Marx's methodology and consequent emendations to his text.[16] My point is that MEGA^2 should continue to make it easy for readers to choose, rather than adopting a view that erases, or tends to erase, the different sorts of readings that readers might want to construct.

Interestingly in 1859, when Engels began giving voice to Marx in earnest, he never actually wrote a promised third section of his review of Marx's *A Contribution to the Critique of Political Economy*. Having produced a political biography of Marx in order to put the first instalment of his economic critique into context, and having discussed what Engels termed the 'historical' and 'logical' methods that Marx supposedly employed, the advertised summary of the critique itself – a digest of Marx's critical re-presentation of the economic categories – did not ever appear from Engels' hand. After Marx's demise, however, and due to very widespread pressure on Engels as literary executor, Engels evidently overcame this reluctance to engage with Marx's multi-layered analysis and difficult modes of conceptualisation about 'economic' matters. The results can now be evaluated, provided that Engels retains an editorial – rather than authorial – voice, and one person of the pair does not turn into the other. Otherwise we risk a *midrash* version of *Capital*, vol. 3 – something that seemingly looks like Marx, seemingly sounds like Marx, seemingly is Marx – but isn't. Or put it the other way round – if Engels speaks for Marx at the end, I think it is going to be hard work making Marx meaningful if we have to work backwards through the *oeuvre* on the assumption that he was really Engels all along.

In the next chapter I consider the Hegel–Marx relationship in a similar way. Everyone agrees that there is a Hegel–Marx relationship, but the contextual narratives surrounding that one are rather different in structure from the polarities to which the Marx–Engels relationship has given rise. The Hegel-Marx relationship is conceptualised much more variously and ambiguously in documents and commentary than the Marx–Engels relationship, not least by Marx himself, and I shall explore below some of the reasons why this is so.

Notes

1 Quentin Skinner, 'Reply to my critics', intro. to James Tully (ed.), *Meaning and Context* (Cambridge, Polity Press, 1988).

2 A complete collection of images (with dates and ages) of the Marx-Engels 'clan' is available at http://csf.Colorado.EDU/psn/marx/Bio/Photo/

3 Terrell Carver, *Friedrich Engels: His Life and Thought* (London, Macmillan, 1989), pp. 73–4, 217; David McLellan, *Karl Marx: His Life and Thought* (London, Macmillan, 1973), p. 42; Terrell Carver, 'Darwinism', in Tom Bottomore *et al.* (eds), *A Dictionary of Marxist Thought*, 2nd edn (Oxford, Basil Blackwell, 1991), p. 131.

4 This view about political theory as a genre, and the biographical genre on which it is dependent, is developed at greater length in Terrell Carver, *Gender is Not a Synonym for Women* (Boulder CO, Lynne Rienner Publishing, Inc, 1996), ch. 3.

5 Karl Marx, *Later Political Writings*, ed. and trans. T. Carver (Cambridge, Cambridge University Press), p. 161.

6 Karl Marx and Frederick Engels, *Collected Works*, vol. 40 (London, Lawrence & Wishart, 1983), p. 64, quoted in Christopher J. Arthur, 'Engels as interpreter of Marx's economics', in Christopher J. Arthur (ed.), *Engels Today: A Centenary Appreciation* (London, Macmillan; New York, St. Martin's Press, 1996), p. 199 n. 2.

7 Terrell Carver, *Marx and Engels: The Intellectual Relationship* (Brighton, Harvester/Wheatsheaf, 1983); see also Terrell Carver, 'Marx-Engels or "Engels v. Marx"', *MEGA-Studien* (1996/2), 79–85.

8 Carver, *Friedrich Engels*, pp. 175–80.

9 Carver, *Marx–Engels Intellectual Relationship*, ch. 3.

10 Carver, *Marx–Engels Intellectual Relationship*, ch. 3.

11 Carver, *Marx–Engels Intellectual Relationship*, intro.

12 Carver, *Marx–Engels Intellectual Relationship*, ch. 5.

13 Carver, *Marx–Engels Intellectual Relationship*, ch. 5.

14 Carver, *Marx–Engels Intellectual Relationship*, ch. 4.

15 Norman Levine, *Dialogue within the Dialectic* (London, George Allen & Unwin, 1984), ch. 4; Christopher J. Arthur, 'Engels as interpreter of Marx's economics', in Arthur (ed.), *Engels Today*, ch. 8.

16 Carl-Erich Vollgraf and Jürgen Jungnickel, 'Marx in Marx' Worten', *MEGA-Studien* (1994/2), 3–55; Wolfgang Jahn, 'Über Sinn und Unsinn eines Textvergleichs zwischen der Engelsschen Ausgabe des dritten Bandes des *Kapital* von 1894 und den Marxschen Urmanuskripten', *MEGA-Studien* (1996/1), 117–26.

CHAPTER NINE

Philosophy and politics: Marx's Hegel

Whose Hegel? Which Marx?

Hegel and Marx did not just happen. Nor are they like Gilbert and Sullivan, Beaumont and Fletcher, or even Marx and Engels. They never met, and they never corresponded (Hegel died when Marx was 13). Marx referred many times in his voluminous works to Hegel, but then he also referred to an enormous number of writers – an almost unbelievable number. If there were a citation count, it is possible that Hegel would win, at least amongst philosophers, though this would hardly do more than start a discussion on why this is important, and what it is supposed to mean. If Marx is to be linked up (or married off?) philosophically, there are alternative candidates – Aristotle is one.[1] But then it seems to me that Marx constantly draws on the early nineteenth century remnants of medieval and early-modern 'school philosophy', deploying distinctions such as essence–appearance, motion–stasis, potential–actual, quantity–quality, and no doubt many others, without citing any particular author or source (see the discussion of Marx and 'natural philosophy' in chapter four above). I will be exploring these issues, and others in both philosophy and politics, as my aim is to stand back from the Hegel–Marx pairing as it has been transmitted to us, and to try to get it into a new perspective. I shall be arguing the following, hoping to clarify with complexity:

- The Hegel–Marx pairing is a construct or narrative, not a

conceptual reflection of a 'fact' that cannot be otherwise than it has come down to us through the literature.

- Hegel's work is rather different in different texts, and the texts themselves changed over time in terms of what they were thought to say, and how important individual items in the corpus were supposed to be.
- Hegel as a figure has meant different things to different people politically at different times, including our own.
- Marx and Engels had rather different views about Hegel and his texts at different times, and in my view, they are most interestingly regarded as two different people whose exact agreement cannot always be assumed.
- The most productive use of Hegel in scrutinising Marx is the most specific citation, linking text to text and sticking to what is peculiarly 'Hegelian' about Hegel, and I aim to provide an example of that.
- The least productive use of Hegel in scrutinising Marx is the most general overarching type of contextual claim that presumes a timeless Hegel ever-present as such in each text and for each reader.
- There is a case for divorcing Hegel from Marx almost completely as a reading strategy just to see what Marx looks like without him, and there is no case for presuming that Marx must always be viewed in a 'Hegelian' context.
- It does not follow that this strategy of 'minimising Hegel' coincides with the rational-choice Marxist reading (in Jon Elster's hands), which substitutes positivist presumptions as the only alternative to what is said to be 'Hegelian', construed in pejorative ways.
- 'Minimising Hegel' as a strategy leaves open the possibility of putting him back in, if doing so produces a Marx that readers find interesting and productive.

The Hegel–Marx pairing, and the familiar 'contextualisation' that goes along with it, is a narrative – a construct. It is not a chronicle of 'what happened' (as if that kind of narrative were ever 'objective' and uncontroversial) but rather an even more tenuous interpretative move. It was created by a particular person, at a particular time, for particular reasons, in a particular way, and it has been taken up by others and repeated or reinterpreted for varying reasons.[2] That is all fair enough, and just what one might expect, but as a reading strategy, it has attained a certain majesty as 'what is'. We have forgotten that it was made up, and, of course, as usual, we forget that we forgot. G. A. Cohen's *Karl Marx's Interpretation of History: A Defence* is the *locus classicus* for this kind of unconscious, or at least uncommunicative, presumption that Hegel and Marx are forever joined as a Holy Family. Cohen's opening chapter, 'Images of History in Hegel and Marx', just begins the Hegel–Marx story without prelude or question. Cohen identifies Hegel with 'German philosophy', outlines what he takes to be Hegel's philosophy of history, and then tells us that Marx (amongst others) was 'captured' by this vision. Thus in Cohen there is really no discussion of the Hegel–Marx relationship as if it could possibly be problematic or even very complex or varied, and his conclusion is suitably simple: 'We said that Marx's conception of history preserves the structure of Hegel's but endows it with fresh content'.[3] I think that there is really rather more to say than that.

Citing Hegel politically

Marx had an intellectual relationship with Hegel of great complexity, and it unfolded as he read and re-read, remembered and re-visited the texts. We have a record of this, of sorts, in the textual citations and allusions that Marx produced. Hegel, however, was rather larger than the sum of his published texts (some of them edited up from lecture notes by his students during Marx's lifetime). He was adopted by various political factions, given varying interpretations to match, and frequently deployed discursively in what passed at the time for political contexts. Thus there were not only many Hegels, but also a vague omnipresence, on which Marx – and anyone else – could draw. References to Hegel could mean something very general and topical, and something quite specific and scholarly. Needless to say, it is not always clear from surviving texts what to make of the Hegelian discourses in which Marx participated – along with a great many others, which may have been more to do with other ideas, other thinkers, other problems, than with Hegel, writ large or writ small.[4]

As indicated above, it may be that in citing Hegel or Hegelian thought Marx is really drawing on ideas that Hegel and Hegelians already had in common with previous philosophers, and which, in the manner of immanent critique, both Hegel and Hegelians, and also Marx, accepted and rejected in suitably complex ways. In other words, for Marx, Hegel and Hegelians were conveniently to hand as repositories of ideas that actually came from elsewhere. As many of these scholastic ideas are now somewhat strange to us, I think that there is often a tendency to assume that they are peculiarly 'Hegelian', or that the peculiarly Hegelian reading is the one referenced by Marx or his contemporaries – but this is not necessarily the case. It just looks that way to us.

As Hegel aimed to recapitulate and rearticulate all previous philosophy (and history, science, etc.), he was indeed a useful source on 'knowledge' up to his own time. Indeed he wrote longer and shorter encyclopaedias, which were his idea of popularisations. But if this divergence between Hegel and his predecessors is not explicitly investigated, we can easily end up with an overly Hegelianised and overly philosophised Marx, or at least so it seems to me. It is actually quite difficult to break out of this particular hermeneutic, as German-language commentators cite Hegel rather the way I am suggesting that Marx did – in a larger context, and as part of a familiar tradition. For English-language commentators Hegel is a great (and in analytical circles unmentionable) 'other', a 'difficult' philosopher not in the analytical or empirical tradition, and a special hurdle, so it emerges, that must be surmounted, before the postulant can tackle Marx. Metaphorically those in the English-speaking world are always advised and warned when 'Continental' philosophy looms ahead, as if in a fog on the far side of the Channel.

In the 1830s and 1840s in the German kingdoms and princely states, politics was necessarily an elite affair conducted in code, that is, insofar as politics tended towards anything like criticism, rather than adulation and confirmation of traditionalist rule. These states were non-constitutional, authoritarian regimes, sometimes with 'consultative' representative bodies, but no genuinely free press, no interest in public mobilisation of opinion (unless suitably obsequious), and they were overtly intolerant, albeit somewhat inefficient in terms of surveillance and repression. Such toleration of free expression as there was tended to be confined to the universities, and from time to time these were purged amid resistance. As the self-professed foundation of these states was historico-theological, mythologies were essential, analytical enquiry considered subversive, and religion at the heart of authority. Any form of philosophy that touched on the great questions of existence was up for criticism from doctrinal Christians, and the ambiguous and coded language of Hegel and his school was an unsurprising result, given the atmosphere of narrow-minded bigotry. Hegelian language is deliberately difficult to interpret, for political reasons, not just philosophical ones. Moreover it is a philosophy, not just because the thinkers were that way inclined, but because any critical consideration of society would have to take place in a suitably circumscribed and abstract frame. The curious cross-over between philosophy, theology and politics that Hegel attempted was itself a political move in about the only way possible for him, yet still allowing access to publishers and a livelihood.

This political streak, coupled with a necessary ambiguity, is something that commentators do not necessarily appreciate today, as by the 1860s public life in something like the modern sense had emerged in Germany. By contrast, in the 1830s and 1840s, philosophy lectures and philosophy books were the political currency that intellectuals could safely (at least more or less safely) exchange. David-Friedrich Strauss, of course, lost his job at Tübingen, and was chased out of Switzerland for writing a book about the historical Jesus, and Ludwig Feuerbach never worked at a university again, after publishing his doctoral dissertation 'Reflections on Death and Immortality', which was taken to be atheistic.[5] So there were limits on what could be thought, published, analysed and questioned, even in universities, never mind in wider circles and the media. That Hegel was easily subjected to both conservative and liberal readings was hardly an accidental authorial strategy. He became a great philosopher and attained the highest levels of state-sponsored academic achievement. But, as is well known, there were two distinctly different readings of his *oeuvre*, dividing along political lines.

Before the 1850s a 'Hegel-Marx' narrative would have looked odd or otiose. Of course Marx was involved with Hegel, as who in a political context was not? But then, Marx's involvement was within the Young Hegelians, or rather on the edge of them – or so he chose to place himself. Marx was rather lucky to have met up with the one Young Hegelian who would really suit him – Engels – as Engels was both clear on the atheism issue, having no truck with mystical pantheism and wet-minded humanism, and also farseeing about technology, being really taken with practical activities connected with wealth, or lack of it, and with industrial productivity, and exploitation.[6] None of the others had those attractive qualities, and lacking Engels, Marx would very likely have stayed at the margin in terms of publicity and impact, being even less effective than he was.

Once past 1848 and into the 1850s a Hegel-Marx narrative was really required, as the politics of Hegelian intellectual codes had faded out. What is immediate does not need to be explained, as the context is assumed; when ideas and motives are no longer so current, readers need the benefit of 'background' and 'help'. In the 1850s Marx still wrote in an idiom reflecting his reading of Young Hegelianism, having decided to apply it to a critique of political economy. He was in a certain sense rather old fashioned and out of date, after 1848, and not just in terms of intellectual approach. His political strategies never really got to grips with the party politics and (limited) constitutionalism that arrived in the 1860s; nonetheless *Capital*, vol. 1 (1867) was supposed to be the political book of the age. I find it rather mysterious exactly how this formidable tome was supposed to connect with what kind of political movement, and indeed it is famous as one of the greatly respected but little read books of all time.

Gospel according to Engels

The Hegel-Marx narrative was created by Engels to explain away this problem, by arguing that Hegel was still relevant, and by enabling Marx's audience to get in touch with his message, once the Hegelian context had been set. As the story emerged in Engels' book review of August 1859, Marx appears as Jesus to Hegel's John the Baptist (almost!). Or at least Marx appears as the successor German philosopher, and revolutionary inverter of philosophical truth. Rather unfortunately the Engelsian mixed metaphors were themselves Young Hegelianism revisited. These were magical kernels and mystical shells, turning Hegel upright so that he stands on his feet, inverting an idealist dialectic to make it materialist and so on.[7] It is all rather mysterious, or simple-minded, though not nearly so bad as the infamous 'thesis-antithesis-synthesis', which an early commentator and populariser – Heinrich Moritz Chalybäus – inflicted on the undeserving master, and which some commentators – the lowest of the low, in my view – further visited on Engels and Marx.[8] One is tempted to turn to the *Theses on Feuerbach* (written in 1845) for clarification of Marx's 'philosophical' position vis-à-vis Hegel, as indeed Engels did, when he published them in edited form in 1888 – but then it is almost difficult to remember now that they are theses on *Feuerbach*! Feuerbach is currently read, if read at all, as an add-on to Hegel (in a context set by Marx), quite the reverse of the historical position and contemporary Left Hegelian view to which Feuerbach was central and 'transformative'. At that point he was, of course, not the pre-cursor of Marx, but rather the author of the *Preliminary Theses on the Reform of Philosophy*, and *Principles of the Philosophy of the Future* (both published in 1843).

In the 1830s and 1840s Marx's engagement was overwhelmingly with the Young Hegelians, and with 'the master' only rather indirectly. Where Marx does address Hegel directly, it is 'Hegel' in the title that makes these texts now seem so central. Possibly one reading of Marx's comment in 1858 that he had turned again to Hegel and found him useful was that Marx was actually surprised to have found anything useful in Hegel at all, given the way that he linked Hegelians with a feeble or febrile politics that he despised. Nonetheless there are early studies by Marx that address Hegel directly, putting the Hegelians to rights. There is one on Hegel's dialectic, and another on his *Philosophy of Right*, and in both Marx shows his own contemporaries how to do an immanent critique philosophically, and what the limitations of the Hegelian outlook amount to politically. Before Germany was anywhere near adopting representative institutions and modern economic doctrines, Marx exposed the hypocritical 'liberal' settlement, arguing that it divided 'free' citizen from 'economic' man, in his *On the Jewish Question* (1844). Hegel's bureaucratised constitutional monarchy in the *Philosophy of Right* never got even that far, and Marx trashed it without mercy in his critique. Obviously Marx wrote these early published works, and early works intended somehow for publication, with an audience of the 1840s in mind, assuming that they would know the literature. Approaching such questions from that perspective in the 1860s would have seemed distinctly odd, hence the need for Engels to 'frame' Marx with a suitable narrative.

As Marx was hardly a household name, Engels needed a peg to hang him on, and Hegel seemed an appropriately august figure, provided of course that he was properly contextualised and then bettered at his own game. While one may safely assume that Hegel was little read by then, he nonetheless had the reputation of filling the library shelves (his students having nearly finished a collected edition) and having ascended to a German Parnasus of nationalistic intellectual achievement. His encyclopaedic pretensions, his philosophical inscrutability, and his nationalist appeal were all to Engels' purpose. But Engels' move begs the question whether Marx had to be hitched to anyone else at all, or if so, whether it had to be Hegel? Why not just present Marx as a critic of economic science, a veteran communist of the 1840s, and an effective German stylist unbeholden to anyone in particular? Or indeed, as a polymath of astounding originality?

In looking at Engels' review of 1859, and his subsequent reworkings of this material in books and pamphlets of his own, and in his introductions and prefaces to Marx, I think we are dealing with Engels' own autodidactic agenda. There is an air here of Engels reliving the heady days of lectures at Berlin University, while he bunked off parade drill and gun-cleaning duty. It was Engels who broadened the focus beyond the critique of political economy (to include life, the universe and everything, i.e. laws of 'nature, history, and thought'); it was Engels who singled out Hegel, quite exclusively, without noting the importance of the scholastic tradition, whether Aristotelian or otherwise; and it was Engels who contradictorily attempted to make Marx easier by putting the world's most difficult philosopher between him and his audience.

This is not to say that the strategy was unsuccessful. As Tom Bottomore once forcefully reminded me, nineteenth-century didacticism was rife amongst the working classes, and study groups were readily formed. Indeed scientific system-building was something to which Engels was responding, as well as responsive, and eventually he produced his own (rather self-denying) reply, in the form of *Anti-Dühring* (1887–78), Eugen von Dühring being a system-builder and penny-populariser *par excellence*. In my view Engels' book was only politely noticed by Marx (Engels' somewhat enigmatic comments to the contrary), and the same with the excerpts *Socialism, Utopian and Scientific* (1880) – to which Marx wrote a brief introduction, signed 'Paul Lafargue' (see chapter eight above). Characteristically Marx's contributions on 'economics', posted to Engels at manuscript stage, were omitted by Engels from the first edition. My feeling is that Engels could never quite get the message that 'economics' was the message. His insertion of Marx's materials into subsequent editions of the text had more to do with Marx's bodily assumption to a pantheon of socialist intellectuals, than with the thrust and direction of Engels' own argument in *Anti-Dühring* itself. Unlike *Capital*, *Anti-Dühring* was very, very widely read indeed.[9]

In my view Marx himself is the best guide to the importance of Hegel in his work, as indeed he would be to the importance of Aristotle or Paracelsus. In his Postface (1873) to the second German edition of *Capital* (1872), Marx did say teasingly that he had coquetted with Hegelian terminology – but how seriously are we to take this? And he did say that he found 'Hegel's Logic' useful in considering profit and its conceptual relationship with value, money, and capital.[10] This hardly seems to justify the familiar grand narrative of Marx, portrayed as Jacob in a lifelong wrestling match with the angel Hegel. Worst of all, the Hegelian turn feeds the fantasies of commentators searching for exactly what Marx says isn't there: a 'historico-philosophic' key to history and to what he is saying about it.[11] Somehow, for most commentators, there has to be a simple secret to guide us through the twists and turns of Marx's argumentative prose. And on the assumption that there is, it then follows that he was the sort of mystical Grand Master who wrote that way. I actually sympathise with hermetic readings of Hegel – he asked for it! – as Hegel really used Rosicrucian imagery and alluded to mysterious entities and incarnations of truth.[12] But in my view Marx did not do these things, and it is worth reading each sentence of *Capital*, for example, right where it is, and seeing how it fits into an argument, however multi-layered and ironic. *Capital* is a text that is not without its difficulties, but the way to address these is hardly singular, hardly uncomplicated, and hardly Hegelian (see chapter two through chapter four above).

Before arguing that a strategy of 'minimising Hegel' would be a good one at present, even if only to get us away from the too familiar tram-lines of almost 150 years of commentary, I should like to offer an olive branch to tradition by following through one of Marx's own citations of Hegel – the one connected with the concept of profit in *Capital* – and developing a reading of an important turning point in his critique of political economy that depends explicitly on Hegel, and indeed on what is explicitly Hegelian. This then leaves me free to argue against the view, taken by rational-choice Marxists, that contemporary readings of Marx are best when they owe least to any ideas of 'darkly Hegelian origin'.[13]

Marx – and 'Hegel's Logic'

It is well known that Marx was interested in 'Hegel's Logic' and that on his own testimony he found it extremely helpful. But before this information can be of much assistance in understanding and evaluating Marx's methods and views, we must have a view as to what this work is, and what use Marx made of it. In this section I argue, with detailed examples, that the terminology of Hegelian logic is not as far removed from the English philosophical tradition as is generally believed; and I discuss the various versions of a 'Logic' prepared by Hegel and his editors, in order to show which texts Marx was actually using. Then I examine Marx's use of 'Hegel's Logic' while he was at work in 1858 on the *Grundrisse* manuscripts, so that the reasoning behind an essential part of his critical theory of capitalist society is laid bare. I conclude that, as a master key to Marx's work, 'Hegel's Logic' has been over-rated, but as a methodological sourcebook for Marx, it has been lamentably under-appreciated. It is also chronically under-rated as a precursor to social theory after the 'linguistic turn' (see chapter one and chapter two above).

Present-day English readers have more points of contact with Hegel's treatises on logic than is generally realised by commentators on Marx.[14] In his works Hegel presents a revision of logic as it was understood and taught by his contemporaries, including the logic derived from the Greeks and modified by the medieval scholastic tradition. That logic was until Hegel's time much the same in English and in German. Today it is an elementary form of logic, so some of the distinctions which were basic to it are still in use, although they are not of much interest to mathematically minded logicians: quality–quantity, analysis–synthesis, reality–appearance, essence–accident, subject–object are examples. Also there are terms in this elementary, traditional logic which have a special sense different from their modern everyday meaning.[15] Some of the now unfamiliar terminology in the works of Hegel and Marx is actually neither particularly Germanic nor peculiarly Hegelian. It is simply the technical terminology of the traditional logic derived from the Greeks and the medieval schools (see chapter four above). Definitions for these technical terms can be extracted from, among other sources, Grimms' *Deutsches Wörterbuch* and the *Oxford English Dictionary* (OED).

What is 'Hegel's Logic'?

It is no simple matter to turn to any of the three collected editions of Hegel's works and pick out his 'Logic'.[16] Moreover Hegel has not made it obvious which of the two versions of his 'Logic' represents his definitive views, nor does Marx usually make it plain which version he had in mind when he spoke of 'Hegel's Logic'. It is possible, however, to surmount these difficulties, so that the 'Logic' becomes for the reader an accessible work, and it is also possible to state with certainty which version of it Marx found most useful in drafting his *magnum opus*, the critique of political economy.

Hegel's *Wissenschaft der Logik* – his *Science of Logic* – appeared in three parts in 1812, 1813 and 1816.[17] A second edition of the first part was prepared by Hegel in 1831, the year of his death. An abbreviated version of the *Science of Logic* was incorporated by Hegel in his *Enzyklopädie der philosophischen Wissenschaften im Grundrisse* – The *Encyclopaedia of the Philosophical Sciences in Outline* – first published in 1817, only a year after the *Science of Logic* was completed. The latter work is sometimes known as the *Heidelberg Encyclopaedia*, and its opening section as the 'Shorter Logic'. The *Encyclopaedia* as a whole was published in two later editions (1827 and 1830) with Hegel's own revisions to the text. But in the Werke edition of 1840–45 the *Encyclopaedia*, including the 'Shorter Logic', became a much longer and substantially different work, since the editors of the collected works (students and associates of Hegel) added their own lecture notes and comments throughout the book.[18]

At points in the text where the same subjects are covered, there are significant differences between the 'Shorter Logic', as it appears in the *Encyclopaedia*, and the *Science of Logic* (sometimes known as the 'Greater Logic'), but it is unclear which version of his views Hegel finally preferred. The second (partial) edition of the *Science of Logic*, on which Hegel was working just before he died in 1831, reproduced certain points in the 1812 edition. These passages had been altered by Hegel for the 'Shorter Logic' and reproduced in its three editions: 1817, 1827, 1830. Hence it appears that Hegel endorsed what he had said in 1817 when he prepared the 1830 edition of the *Encyclopaedia*, and then reverted in 1831, while working once again on the *Science of Logic*, to what he had said in 1812. In his *Commentary*, James MacTaggart suggests that neither the 1830 *Encyclopaedia* nor the 1831 revisions to the *Science of Logic* represent a definitive text where the same subjects are covered. Marx used both the 'Shorter' and 'Greater' Logics; when he preferred the 'Shorter', he cannot be said to have used something elementary or inferior.[19]

In a letter of 10 November 1837 to his father, Marx mentioned that he 'got to know Hegel from beginning to end'.[20] During the rest of his career Marx occasionally referred to Hegel's works without giving precise references, but it is certain that when he was writing the *Economic and Philosophical Manuscripts* of 1844 he made use of the 'Shorter Logic' (as it appeared in the 1830 edition of the

Encyclopaedia).[21] The *Science of Logic* (in the Werke edition of 1841) was used by Marx as he and Engels were writing *The Holy Family*.[22] While he was working on the first volume of *Capital*, Marx used the 'Shorter Logic', though this time it was the expanded Werke version of 1840–45.[23] I have shown elsewhere that the 'Greater Logic' was very much in Marx's mind during his work on what was to become the final version of his critique of political economy.[24] It is the *Science of Logic* which I use below in analysing important arguments from the *Grundrisse*, and then relating that material to its final formulation in *Capital*.

English Hegelians

It is generally assumed that Hegel's philosophy, and, to be sure, Marx himself, were virtually unknown in English intellectual circles of the early 1850s. This was not quite the case. The first attempt at an English translation of 'Hegel's Logic' was a paraphrase entitled *The Subjective Logic of Hegel*, published in London in 1855 by John Chapman, who was friendly with various intellectuals interested in German philosophy, and, as it happens, an acquaintance of Marx. In a diary entry for 27 July 1851 Chapman wrote: 'Went with my brother to dine at Mrs Johnsons, met Freiligrath and a Herr Merks [*sic*], another exile'.[25] Chapman was also the publisher of English versions of Strauss's *Life of Jesus* (1846) and Feuerbach's *Essence of Christianity* (1854), both influential works in Hegelian circles and both, as it happens, translated into English by Marian Evans, better known as George Eliot. He also published English translations of J. G. Fichte's works, and brought out a version of Friedrich von Schelling's *The Philosophy of Art*, translated by Andrew Johnson, which appeared in 1845. Johnson was a friend of Marx's correspondent Ferdinand Freiligrath (who figures anecdotally in most accounts of Marx and his use of 'Hegel's Logic') and of Marx himself. On 28 October 1852 Marx wrote to Engels: 'If you have to write to me on important matters, do it under the address: A. Johnson, Esq., (Bullion Office, B[ank] of E[ngland]' – it seems that Marx wanted to use the Bank of England (of all places) as a postal drop.[26] Johnson was the author of works on the gold supply and the theory of cur-

rency published in 1852 and 1856, a period generally – and wrongly
– thought to be fallow for Marx's economic studies, whereas actually
he was at work on just those aspects of political economy.[27]

Marx's critique – and 'Hegel's Logic'

The exact connections between Marx's critique of political economy
and his use of Hegelian categories are still obscure. The *Grundrisse* has
been said to be a 'Hegelian' work, but what precisely does this mean?
Why, in such a work, did Marx turn to Hegel for help? And why in
the Afterword to the first volume of *Capital* (an essay which postdates
the *Grundrisse*, *Theories of Surplus Value*, the manuscripts for *Capital*, vol.
3, and nearly all of the manuscripts for vol. 2) did Marx announce that
he was *still* a pupil of Hegel?

Marx made considerable use of 'Hegel's Logic' in formulating the
fundamental arguments of his critique of political economy, the work
which functions as a foundation for his political and social thought.
The connections between Marx's arguments and Hegel's can be elu-
cidated from the texts, and Marx's arguments can only then be grasped
and analysed. The results may not impress present-day economists,
even of the Marxist schools, but useful or not, Marx's arguments in this
specific context will continue to generate little but confusion until
they are read in the first instance on his own terms. If Marx's work on
such a basic economic category as profit, for example, were 'de-
Hegelianised', even by a well-meaning interpreter, the result would
perhaps be more obviously 'economic', as the term is generally understood today (see chapter four above), but it would have little to do
with Marx, and the full import of his work would never emerge. But
by the same token, this does not licence a general 'Hegelianising' of
Marx.

The logic of profit

While Marx was working on the principal notebooks of the
Grundrisse, he wrote to Engels (on 16 January 1858) that he had found
'Hegel's Logic' useful in dealing with a particular economic category
– profit. Freiligrath had offered him Mikhail Bakunin's old copy, pre-

sumably an edition of the *Science of Logic*, in October 1857.[28]

The difficulty with profit for Marx, as for numerous orthodox political economists, was explaining where in the economic process it arises (see chapter four above). If it arises from the *exchange* of commodities, is it a surplus created by the exchange of one commodity for another of *greater* value? Or, could profit arise even on a 'fair exchange', in which one commodity is exchanged for another of *equal* value? Alternatively, if profit arises from the *production* process, is it a *joint* product of labourer and capitalist? Or is it simply a portion of what the labourer produces that is *deducted* for various purposes by the capitalist?

Marx's method for solving these problems was to analyse the basic concepts involved – what he called the 'simple determinations'. This was why he turned to 'Hegel's Logic', as Hegel's philosophical work was overtly occupied with conceptual analysis. What emerged from this encounter was immensely significant for his views on the structure and future of capitalist society. Once the economic 'law of motion' of capitalist society had been 'laid bare', other social phenomena would be seen to fall into place, and the eventual political development of capitalist society would become clear.[29]

The 'two-fold character of labour' and the theory of 'surplus value' together represent Marx's ultimate answer to the problems about profit posed above. But these theories presuppose a view of the fundamental 'motion' of capitalist society. According to Marx the capitalist system is not in equilibrium; rather he claims that it has an in-built tendency to collapse because of the necessity to produce ever-increasing profits.[30] But what exactly is this alleged necessity to produce ever-increasing profits? Why is the circulation of capital 'not a simple circle, but a spiral, an ever-expanding curve'? Marx set that very problem for himself in the *Grundrisse*:

> It is damned difficult for Messrs the [political] economists to progress theoretically from the self-preservation of value in capital to its expansion; that is to say, this [expansion] in its fundamental definition, not just as accident nor merely as result.[31]

If Marx could establish an 'expansion' in the fundamental definition of capital, it would follow that the production of ever-increasing profits was an essential, even a definitional part of the capitalist system, rather than something that capitalists might or might not generally choose to do. Marx undoubtedly recognised that individual capitalists might choose (somewhat eccentrically) not to employ their capital in a way that would increase their profits, though doubtless they would soon find themselves undercut and thrown out of business by others who had invested more wisely in the productive process. He also fully recognised that some capitalists might fail to employ their capital successfully because of bad luck or bad judgement. But at the end of the argument he concluded that capitalists could not, in general, decide not to employ their capital in order to increase their profits. That is, he decided that 'expansion' is no mere 'accident'[32] but is an essential part of the concept 'capital':

> Chit-chat that no one will employ his capital without drawing a profit on it either amounts to the absurdity that upstanding capitalists will remain capitalists even *without* employing their capital; or to saying in a very homely way that profit-yielding employment lies in the very concept of capital. Well. That would just have to be demonstrated.[33]

In the ensuing demonstration that 'profit-yielding employment lies in the very concept of capital', Marx finds a 'contradiction' in money used as capital – a contradiction between its *quality* as the representative of all forms of wealth to an infinite amount, and its limit as a specific *quantity* at any given time:

> The sole utility which an object can generally have for capital can only be to maintain or to increase it. We have already seen in the case of money, how value differentiated as such – or the general form of wealth – is capable of no other motion than quantitative; of increasing itself. According to its concept it is the epitome of all use-values; but as [it is] always but a specific quantity of money (here capital) its quantitative limitation is in contradiction with its quality.[34]

Marx draws our attention to two aspects of money as it is used in capitalist production: money stands for wealth in a way that is absolutely general and theoretically *limitless*; but it must always exist in limited amounts as coins, notes, money of account, that is, it must always be expressed as some numerical figure or other. From this contradiction Marx concludes: 'There lies in its [money's] nature a continual driving beyond its own limitation' (see chapter two and chapter three above).[35] In the *Grundrisse* Marx develops the implications of this conclusion by arguing that capital requires the production of ever-increasing profits:

> For value, which retains its character as value, an increase in amount coincides in consequence with its self-preservation, and it is preserved only in that it continually drives beyond its quantitative limitation, which contradicts its definitional form, its inner generality. Enrichment is thus the inner purpose. The end-determining activity of capital can only be that of enrichment, i.e., the amassing, the increasing of itself. A specific sum of money (and money always exists for its owner as but a specific quantity, [it] is always there as a specific sum of money) ... can fully satisfy only a specific consumption in which it has ceased to be money. But as representative of a limited wealth, it cannot do that. As a quantitatively specific sum, a limited sum, it is either only the limited representative of general wealth or the representative of a limited wealth, which goes precisely as far as its exchange-value; is exactly measured by it. Hence in no way does it have the capacity, which according to its general concept it ought to have, of buying all pleasures, all commodities, the totality of the material substance of wealth ... Retained as wealth, as the general form of wealth, as value which serves as value, it [money] is therefore the continual drive to go beyond its quantitative limit: an endless process. Its own life-quality consists in just this: it *preserves* itself as exchange-value performing its function distinct from use-value, only in that it is itself *continually* expanding ...[36]

In the above passage Marx has evidently done just what he set out to do: '... to progress theoretically from the self-preservation of value in capital to its expansion ... this [expansion] in its fundamental definition, not just as accident nor merely as result.'

Money – and 'Hegel's Logic'

However, in the course of Marx's analysis of money as capital, two crucial questions arise: Why were the qualitative and quantitative aspects of money as capital said to be 'in contradiction'? And why does it follow from this that money by its very nature entails 'a continual driving beyond its own limitations' and hence a 'continual drive to go beyond its quantitative limit' in functioning as capital? In setting out these views Marx's line of argument follows very closely Hegel's discussion of 'the finite', its negation as 'limitation', and the negation of this negation when it 'transcends its limitation'. These arguments are developed in the *Science of Logic*:

> Something with its immanent limit, posited as the contradiction of itself ... is the finite ... The finite is thus inwardly self-contradictory ... Something's own limit [is] thus posited by it as a negative ... The limitation of the finite is not something external to it; on the contrary, its own determination is also its limitation ... But now further, the finite as ought[37] transcends its limitation ... its limit is also not its limit [38] ...

Hegel concludes: 'It is the very nature of the finite to transcend itself, to negate its negation and to become infinite.'[39] Marx's development of the 'life-quality' of money in capitalist society is exactly parallel with the progression of Hegel's argument. Like 'the infinite', money is 'inwardly self-contradictory'; its 'quantitative limitation' is its 'own', not merely 'external'; it 'transcends its limitation' by 'continually expanding' – a 'continual driving beyond its own limitations'. For money, as for Hegel's 'finite', 'its limit is also not its limit'.

In general, capitalists do try to increase their profits, and if a capitalist were *not* to behave in this way, we would think it odd and seek some explanation, perhaps eccentricity or lassitude. Similarly, it would be difficult to imagine an economic system in which those with capital generally did *not* try to increase their profits; we would find it difficult to refer to such a system of behaviour as 'capitalism'. If it is to these generalisations about behaviour that Marx was referring when he argued from a 'contradiction' in the concept 'money' to the conclusion that 'profit-yielding employment lies in the very concept of capital', then his point is well taken. However, Marx's actual conclusion about a 'drive' within money functioning as capital does not follow *merely* from the arguments (derived from the *Science of Logic*) which he specifically adduces: the self-contradictory character of something finite (money), its negative relationship with a limitation (in this case, a quantitative one), and its drive to transcend this limitation by continually expanding. Do Marx's 'Hegelian' arguments in the *Grundrisse* have any bearing, then, on his work in *Capital*, where we might expect to see conceptual analysis and substantiated generalisations in close alignment?

Capital – and 'Hegel's Logic'

When Marx wrote that he had found 'Hegel's Logic' useful in investigating profit, he left us – as we have seen – a valuable clue to an otherwise puzzling exposition of views in the *Grundrisse*. On my reading, these are views behind those expressed in *Capital*, where the necessity for ever-increasing profits is simply assumed to be an immanent law of capitalist production. Marx pointed out in *Capital*, as he had done in the *Grundrisse*, that the reproduction of capital is not a circle, but a spiral.[40] Unlike the text of the *Grundrisse*, however, the argument in *Capital* proceeds without an analysis of the relevant 'simple determinations'. I think it likely that the Hegelian exposition in the *Grundrisse* confirmed Marx in his view that 'expansion' is inherent in the 'fundamental definition of capital'; and he might reasonably have considered that even a polished version of his work on the relevant 'simple determinations' in the *Grundrisse* was an unnecessary and possibly confusing step in putting his case to the reader of *Capital*.

Marx's theory of the 'contradictory character of money', whether or not it is plausible for the reasons he adduces in the *Grundrisse*, made it easy for him to argue the possibility of a new type of society, in which conventional behaviour would be very different from that in capitalist society. He drew the contrast in *Capital*:

> He [the capitalist] is fanatically intent on the valorization of value; consequently he ruthlessly forces the human race to produce for production's sake. In this way he spurs on the development of society's productive forces, and the creation of those material conditions of production which alone can form the real basis of a higher form of society, a society in which the full and free development of every individual forms the ruling principle.[41]

Once Marx had shown that 'profit-yielding employment' lay 'in the very concept of capital', he had located certain patterns of human motivation and behaviour within the historically specific conventions of a particular type of society. Had he located the profit motive in, for example, an apparently invariant 'human nature', as other theorists had done,[42] then it would have been difficult for him to argue that a qualitatively different society was a realistic possibility (see chapter four and chapter five above). But as I read him, Marx held the view that humans make – and re-make – their own nature and the societies in which they live through their productive activities, and that out of these activities come their ideas about themselves and their social possibilities.[43] Hence his thesis was that the abolition of money and of its attendant contradictions would follow a reorganisation of production along communist lines, and the resultant society would not be a slave to the continual 'expansion' inherent in capital.

Propositions from 'Hegel's Logic', whether cited behind the scenes in the *Grundrisse* or presupposed without specific reference in *Capital*, vol. 1, do not themselves prove for Marx, or for his readers, either that his account of the economic categories contains some necessary logic or that it reflects some immanent necessity in human behaviour. Rather the strength of Marx's account is that it sits precisely on the nexus between interlinked ideas and meaningful activities, without any presumption that scientific analysis must push factitiously to distinguish one from the other. With that in mind I turn in conclusion to Elster's attempt to 'make sense of Marx'.

Vicious/virtuous circles

Contrary to my lines of analysis, Elster tackles the Hegel–Marx nexus very much as Engels understood it, focusing on 'dialectics', which he quite mistakenly says that Marx invoked 'on numerous occasions'. Marx's actual references to 'dialectic' are notably few, whereas the importance that Engels ascribed to this concept was absolutely fundamental, the major link between the one great thinker – Hegel – and his superior successor – Marx.[44] As with most commentators, Engels' narrative inspires them to imagine that Marx must frequently have said what Engels says he believed, whereas I find it impossible to discover Marx saying even once what Engels claims is the foundation of 'the system' – the three 'laws of dialectics'.[45] Admittedly I take the view that one cannot simply read Engels back into Marx, but rather that for traditional commentary to be persuasive, Marx must be seen to be making the case about and for his own work just as Engels puts it, not simply using the same words in his own discussions. Indeed in the 1859 Preface to *A Contribution to the Critique of Political Economy*, the book Engels was reviewing when the 'grand narrative' about Hegel and Marx first emerged, Marx famously set down the 'guiding thread' for his studies. My view of those paragraphs is that they are themselves hasty and ill-written, and later barely noticed in a footnote to *Capital*, vol. 1, but leaving that evaluation aside, it still seems to me to be striking that the word 'dialectic' does not occur there at all.[46]

Elster boils the Hegel–Marx connection down to 'three strands': a 'quasi-deductive procedure' inspired by Hegel's *Logic* and used in the *Grundrisse* and *Capital* (exactly what I discuss above); Engels' 'three laws of dialectics', which in my view are Engels' and not Marx's; and finally a 'theory of social contradictions' derived from Hegel's *Phenomenology of Spirit*. Elster and I agree about the second category – Engels' 'laws of dialectics', that they are neither Marx's nor interesting. Contrarily I agree with Elster that the third category – a theory of 'social contradictions' – is both Marxian and interesting, though Elster seems rather over-anxious to me in reducing what is of interest here to an exemplification of the 'fallacy of composition' – the view that what is in everyone's best interest collectively is necessarily in the best interest of every individual. Unsurprisingly then, Elster and I disagree very clearly about the first 'strand', in that his methodologically individualist premises rule out a conceptual analysis of money, such as Marx attempted at length in *Capital*, and by which I am sufficiently intrigued to construct a reading (see chapter two through chapter four above). Elster legislates that those who are not methodologically individualist in his approved sense are methodological collectivists (surely a loaded term politically – they could be philosophical 'holists'). Moreover he also somewhat overloads his criticisms by characterising further Marx's presumed position as incoherent and confused.

My complaint is that Elster's binary reductions (and abuse) lead to him to inveigh against the very question that I think it is interesting to ask: 'whether the self-determination of capital is conceptual or behavioural – or whether we are meant to conclude that this very distinction is superseded' – a conclusion I take Elster to be rejecting superciliously.[47] There are moments in analysis when drawing a distinction is not a helpful thing to do in the first place, and this is one of them. This is because the conceptual–behavioural distinction, to which Elster is wedded (and I am not), is the very one that rules out just what social science in my view is there to investigate – the circularity that necessarily obtains between ideas, individuals, and action. This circularity is neither analytically vicious nor merely logical. It is life, and only a 'textualising' theory can make sense of it – and of Marx. In the next chapter I consider further topics and concepts that occur in contemporary Marx studies, namely women and gender, using narrative analysis. This method also applies just as much to commentators as it does to what they do – or fail to do – when they re-read Marx. While politics has altered considerably since Marx's time, I argue that he can be a productive partner in creating dialogue on the sexual politics of our day.

Notes

1 See Scott Meikle, *Essentialism in the Thought of Karl Marx* (London, Duckworth, 1984).
2 I make and support this claim in Terrell Carver, *Engels* (Oxford, Oxford University Press, 1981), ch. 5.
3 G. A. Cohen, *Karl Marx's Theory of History: A Defence* (Oxford, Oxford University Press, 1975), pp. 1–27.
4 For a detailed study of Marx's early career as a Young Hegelian see David McLellan, *The Young Hegelians and Karl Marx* (London, Macmillan, 1969 repr. 1980).
5 See William J. Brazill, *The Young Hegelians* (New Haven CO, Yale University Press, 1970), and Lawrence S. Stepelevich (ed.), *The Young Hegelians: An Anthology* (Cambridge, Cambridge University Press, 1983).
6 These points are amplified in Terrell Carver, *Friedrich Engels: His Life and Thought* (London, Macmillan, 1989), ch. 6.
7 Terrell Carver, *Marx and Engels: The Intellectual Relationship* (Brighton, Wheatsheaf, 1983), pp. 105–6.

8 Carver, *Engels*, p. 50.

9 Carver, *Marx and Engels*, ch. 5.

10 Karl Marx, *Capital*, vol. 1, trans. Ben Fowkes (Harmondsworth, Penguin, 1986), pp.102–3; Karl Marx and Frederick Engels, *Collected Works*, vol. 40 (London, Lawrence & Wishart, 1983), p. 249.

11 Marx to the Editorial Board of the 'Otechestvenniye Zapiski', November 1877, in Karl Marx and Frederick Engels, *Selected Correspondence*, 2nd edn, ed. S. Ryanzanskaya, trans. I. Lasker (Moscow, Progress Publishers, 1965), p. 313.

12 G. W. F. Hegel, *Philosophy of Right*, ed. and trans. T. M. Knox (Oxford, Oxford University Press, 1965), pp. 12, 303, n. 34.

13 Jon Elster, *Making Sense of Marx* (Cambridge, Cambridge University Press, 1985), p. 124.

14 See, for example, John Plamenatz, *Man and Society*, vol. 2 (London, Longmans, 1963, repr. 1968), *passim*; Bertel Ollman, *Alienation* (Cambridge, Cambridge University Press, 1971), pp. 3–42; István Mészáros, *Marx's Theory of Alienation* (London, Merlin, 1970), pp. 12–13.

15 See the notes on the following terms in Terrell Carver (ed. and trans.) *Karl Marx: Texts on Method* (Oxford, Basil Blackwell, 1975): determinate/determined (p. 47), determination(s) (pp. 50-1), subject/object (p. 48), ideal (p. 48), universal (p. 51), difference (p. 51), reflection (p. 55), moment (p. 53), mediate (p. 57), immediately (pp. 58–9), virtually (p. 60), transcending (pp. 63-4), intension/extension (p. 70), indifference (p. 77).

16 The three editions are the *Werke* (various editors) published 1832–87, the *Jubiläumsausgabe* (Jubilee Edition) edited by Glockner and published during the 1920s and 1930s, and the critical edition undertaken by Lasson, published 1905–40 (see n. 18 below).

17 A copy of the first edition in the British Library (C.43.a.13) contains annotations, often sarcastic, by Samuel Taylor Coleridge (see n. 26 below), for example in the first book of the first volume: 'This is the first sensible Remark I have met with. It occurs in Plato ...' (p. 89) 'My Stars! Now we *pop* upon it all at once. *The to self*-subsist[ing] determinate itself into The Self-subsisting, order zum Eins – &c&c!! – And so comes Repulsion, Attraction, and Quantity. What christian Heart could desire a clearer account – a more luminous elucidation?' (p. 91).

18 For his critical edition of the *Science of Logic* (vols 3-4 of Hegel's *Sämtliche Werke*) Lasson takes the first (1812–16) edition as copy-text, explaining that Hegel's revisions for a second edition of the first 'book' were difficult to read; as far as I can gather, this is a comment on the texts of 1833 and 1841 in the posthumously edited *Werke* edition, which allegedly took Hegel's revisions into account. Lasson seems unaware that the partial second edition was actually published. The date of publication for this volume is usually given as 1831, since Hegel's Preface is dated 7 November of that year, but the book itself (now very rare) is actually dated 1832 (loan from the University Library, Leipzig). Glockner gives the 1840–45 expanded text of Hegel's *Encyclopaedia* the title *System der Philosophie* (vols 8–10 of the Jubilee Edition) and reproduces the 1817 Heidelberg edition separately as vol. 6.

19 James M. E. MacTaggart, *A Commentary on Hegel's Logic* (Cambridge, 1910), pp. 2–3.

20 Karl Marx and Frederick Engels, *Collected Works*, vol. 1 (London, Lawrence & Wishart, 1975), p. 19.

21 Karl Marx and Frederick Engels, *Collected Works*, vol. 3 (London, Lawrence & Wishart, 1975), p. 330.

22 Karl Marx and Frederick Engels, *Collected Works*, vol. 4 (London, Lawrence & Wishart, 1975), p. 138.

23 Karl Marx, *Capital*, vol. 1, p. 285 n.

24 Carver, *Texts on Method*, pp. 43, 55, 77, 89, 112, 113, 115, 117, 119-20, 127, 130, 131, 132, 137, 139–40. The 'Greater Logic' is available in an English translation by A. V. Miller as *Hegel's Science of Logic* (London, Allen & Unwin, 1969); Miller has based his work on Lasson's text of 1923, rather than the corrected edition of 1932-34. The 'Shorter Logic', as it appeared in the expanded *Encyclopaedia* of 1840–45, has been translated into English by William Wallace as *The Logic of Hegel* (Oxford, Oxford University Press, 1874, 2nd edn 1892, 3rd edn 1975).

25 Gordon S. Haight, *George Eliot and John Chapman*, 2nd edn (Hamden CT, Archon, 1969), pp. 124, n. 195. Mrs Johnson was the wife of Andrew Johnson (see below). Ferdinand Freiligrath had worked with Marx on the *Neue Rheinische Zeitung* in Cologne during 1848–49, and like Marx, emigrated to London; he was the author of a biographical memoir of Coleridge, and the translator of numerous British and American poets into German, as well as a poet in his own right.

26 Karl Marx and Frederick Engels, *Collected Works*, vol. 39 (London, Lawrence & Wishart, 1983), p. 227.

27 Marx, *Texts on Method*, pp. 23–7.

28 This copy has evidently disappeared; another was reported missing by Marx in 1861 when he received a shipment of books which had been in store in Germany for ten years. Marx and Engels, *Collected Works*, vol. 40, p. 249. Manfred Häckel (ed.), *Freiligraths Briefwechsel mit Marx und Engels* (Berlin, Akademie Verlag, 1968), vol. 1, p. 96; Bruno Kaiser (ed.), *Ex Libris Karl Marx und Friedrich Engels* (Berlin, Dietz Verlag, 1967), pp. 9–11, and *passim*; also Karl Marx and Frederick Engels, *Collected Works*, vol. 41 (London, Lawrence & Wishart, 1985), p. 616, n. 244.

29 Karl Marx, *Grundrisse: Foundations of the Critique of Political Economy (Rough*

Draft), trans. Martin Nicolaus (Harmondsworth, Penguin/New Left Review, 1973), p. 266; Marx, *Capital*, vol. 1, p. 92.

30 Marx, *Capital*, vol. 1, pp. 739, 929.

31 Marx, *Grundrisse*, pp. 266, 270–1.

32 'A property or quality not essential to our conception of a substance; an attribute.' OED, *s.v.* Accident II.6. *Logic.*

33 Marx, *Grundrisse*, p. 270.

34 Marx, *Grundrisse*, p. 270.

35 Marx, *Grundrisse*, p. 270.

36 Marx, *Grundrisse*, p. 270.

37 'This *in-itself*, therefore, as the negative relation to its limit (which is also distinguished from it), to itself as limitation, is the ought.' *Hegel's Science of Logic*, p. 132.

38 *Hegel's Science of Logic*, pp. 129, 136, 132, 133.

39 *Hegel's Science of Logic*, pp. 831, 834, 837.

40 Marx, *Capital*, vol. 1, pp. 230–2, 252–5, 449–50, 726–8, 739.

41 Marx, *Capital*, vol. 1, p. 739.

42 See, for example, the opening chapters of three works criticised on this point by Marx: Adam Smith, *The Wealth of Nations* (first published 1776); David Ricardo, *On the Principles of Political Economy and Taxation* (2nd edn 1821); Thomas Robert Malthus, *An Essay on the Principle of Population* (first published 1798).

43 Marx, *Capital*, vol. 1, pp. 171–3, 283–4.

44 Carver, *Engels*, ch. 5; Carver, *Marx and Engels*, ch. 4.

45 Terrell Carver, 'Marx, Engels and dialectics', *Political Studies* 28:3 (1980), 353–63.

46 Terrell Carver, *Marx's Social Theory* (Oxford, Oxford University Press, 1982), passim.

47 Jon Elster, *Making Sense of Marx* (Cambridge, Cambridge University Press, 1985), pp. 37–48.

CHAPTER TEN

Women and gender: Marx's narratives

Decentring Marx

At present Marx's record on these issues – sex and gender – looks much the same as that of any other (dead, white, male) social theorist. Neither sex nor gender is an especially important analytical category in his scheme of things, in his theoretical works or in his political activities. Nor is there any really extended discussion – however marginal or ancillary – of the topics that are most usually pointers to interests cognate with the ones that are today grouped together under headings such as these: family life, childhood, dependency, reproduction, sensual pleasure, 'the body', sexualities, and so on. This is not to say that Marx never mentioned these things, nor that he failed to remark on various 'fundamentals' which generally include these ideas and practices. Indeed, as will become evident below, he did have things to say. Rather that with the best will in the world, and whether reading 'with the grain' or against it, there are considerable difficulties in either adjudicating on Marx as an authority worth reading in, say, feminist theory or gender studies, or in simply finding material to cite that would constitute any very impressive contribution, one way or another, to contemporary debates.

This 'lack' is in itself grounds for considerable criticism. These criticisms range from fairly generous excuses for his evident 'gender-blindness' on grounds that few, if any of his (male) contemporaries did any better, to harsh rejections of virtually all of his work on grounds that it is predicated on a 'masculinist point of view' that is always (or at least currently) unacceptable to women, and perhaps now (or eventually) also unacceptable to men (or at least to some of them). From the broader perspective of sexuality studies, it is further evident that a gay, or at least non-binary and non-heterosexist recovery of Marx would be even more difficult and problematic. Nonetheless there are moments in the feminist and gay literatures when Marx surfaces, and not necessarily as someone who 'got it wrong' or did not 'get it' at all with respect to sex, sexuality and gender. In so far as writers in those literatures concern themselves with commodification as a general phenomenon, and with the commodification of human beings as 'wage-labour' in particular, then Marx has a role to play in their discussions of the 'sex and gender' issues listed above. But it is, however, rather a walk-on part, and I doubt very much that Marx will ever figure as a star of this particular show.[1]

Given these difficulties, is there anything further to say? I think that there is, and I also think that considering Marx in relation to sex and gender can usefully function as an instance highlighting more general interpretive projects and difficulties. These projects can be highly productive, as interpretive issues show up best when they arise out of controversy, provided that the controversy is very coolly handled. Moreover the phenomena under consideration here – caught in the shorthand 'women and gender' – will also show up better when considered against an 'other' to currently accepted assertions. Interrogating Marx is one way of constructing this type of debate, though hardly the only one. At the end of this chapter I propose to explore very briefly two kinds of criticism of Marx mounted by two kinds of critics, but to do this I need to develop an over-arching account of 'sex and gender' that will help the reader to understand my use of these concepts, both in context here and, I hope, in other contexts unconnected with this book.

I emphasise that the following discussion of the concepts 'sex' and 'gender' makes no concession to what might be construed as an historical context appropriate to interpreting Marx. Rather my account is wholeheartedly related to issues that I believe are current and familiar to present readers. Historical contexts, as constructed for Marx, in any commentator's 'now', need to be clear about that commentator's understandings of the analytical concepts employed and of the commentator's ambitions for the discussion. Contexts for Marx, or for any writer similarly situated as a commentator's object, are not 'found' by viewing 'history'. What the commentator 'sees' in history, as contextual construction occurs, is always highly coloured by what the commentator understands about concepts and issues very generally. Concepts and issues as seen and understood by Marx, for example, cannot be encountered by an anyone's 'open mind' today. Thus I beg the reader's indulgence while I discuss 'sex' and 'gender' in ways that are avowedly anachronistic in relation to Marx; history will then be addressed in a suitably respectful manner below as the discussion moves along.

Sex and gender

In the last hundred years or so sex has become established as a biological category, supposedly derived from observation of the body. Gender is often (though not exclusively) regarded as a sociological category referring to the ways that sexual behaviour (as masculine or feminine) is manifested by individuals in social circumstances. Once it was noticed that, e.g. masculine behaviour is not always manifested by males, and can indeed by manifested by females (and that the same is true of feminine behaviour), then two strategies emerged: one was to create categories of deviancy (e.g. effeminate and/or homosexual men – on various assumptions), and the other was to slide the unit of analysis away from sex as a binary aspect of the body towards sexuality as a manifold realm of 'behaviours', or at least 'orientations'.[2]

In about the last fifty years feminist analysis and politics has raised the issue of gender in the context of the ways that women are oppressed or at the very least disadvantaged by men individually and collectively, and the ways that overarching presumptions about men and women, masculinity and femininity, work to structure and reproduce this behaviour. Thus in many contexts today a reference to gender is a reference to women, as if men, males and masculinities were still unproblematic in that regard, or indeed perhaps simply nothing to do with gender at all, though there are of course circumstances where gender is used to indicate both sides of a binary.[3] A usage of gender to designate women, whilst putting men to one side, can very readily become a way of making women problematic, once again, in a way that marginalises them as 'a problem'. This leaves men where they have always been, doing pretty much what they like, or more accurately, what some of them like. On the whole there have only been minimal concessions in power relations from men to women, and none at all in the basic construction of gendered, i.e. power-ridden identities derived rather incoherently from presumptions about sex and sexuality. These identities, or perhaps rather identity claims, are the real stuff of the asymmetrical social relationships that are culturally and politically transmitted across the generations. Few people, if any, really 'have' these identities with utter consistency and conviction. Rather they claim them as they are performed, and in doing this they establish the symbolic codes from which disciplinary and (re)productive practices emerge.[4]

In the common parlance of recent times, gender has also become a euphemism for sex, i.e. male or female, M or F, man or woman, as biologically, socially and legally defined. These definitions, though, are hardly unambiguous. In doctrines of family, parenthood and personal dignity (cited, for instance, with regard to trans-sexuality) considerations of individual preference and social functionality begin to cross-cut the commonplace stereotyping on which our elaborations of the two supposedly opposite yet seemingly co-requisite sexes are based. This synonymy of gender for sex seems to me to be a step backward, or at least it marks a kind of inertia. It constantly reinscribes the allegedly obvious and supposedly well-understood categories male and female, men and women, back into political ideas, just when these ideas are starting to be really problematic, politically interesting, and interestingly complex. Why map gender on to sex as one to one, just when the term was helping to make visible the ambiguities of sexuality, orientation, choice and change that have been undercover for centuries? Indeed modern technologies of the body, and modern methods of political mobilisation, have rendered these questions not just visible but very pressing within the media, the institutional apparatus of courts and legislatures, and all the professions in society.

A one-to-one mapping of gender on to a commonplace categorisation of sex as male/female is over-simple, even with respect to biology and medicine, as there are chromosomal variations and syndromes, not to mention morphological and behavioural ones, that create genuinely ambiguous individuals. Even supposing that 'normality' with respect to the M/F distinction (as medically and socially enforced) is good enough for most analytical purposes, why then limit gender to a restatement of that? Indeed the term was coined to do more than restate the (supposedly) obvious, by decoupling (simplified) biology from (stereotyped) behaviour. Discourses and practices of toleration and liberation have to some extent replaced the more sinister approaches and institutions – utilising concepts of normality and deviance – which historical and sociological work on the history of the human sciences have exposed as disciplinary or worse. There is yet more room in political life for discourses of variation or 'difference'. Indeed it seems to me that we simply do not know how many genders there are, as the answer must vary according to what is assumed about sex and sexuality before any particular concept of gender is then constructed.

For instance, if there are normal or characteristic ways of *being of the male or female sex*, called masculine and feminine, and if these are socially learnt rather than biologically determined, then there are four genders, rather than two, as masculine men, masculine women, feminine women and feminine men become logically possible and empirically observable. If gender is the way that *sexuality is expressed* between the sexes, then perhaps there are two genders, heterosexuality and homosexuality (or three, if celibacy is an option), on the assumption that these categories include both Ms and Fs, depending on whether sexuality is M to F and F to M (heterosexuality), or M to M and F to F (homosexuality). Alternatively perhaps there are four or six genders, as the lineup might then be heterosexual men, heterosexual women, homosexual women, homosexual men, celibate women, and celibate men. Perhaps historically there were three genders (heterosexual men, heterosexual women, celibates) or four (heterosexual men, heterosexual women, celibate women, celibate men), before homosexuality as a sexual identity was developed, at least as a sexual identity that we would recognise as homosexual, or that the social actors themselves would identify as such.[5] Adding bisexuality as either one further gender, or two 'sexually' differentiated genders, then runs the total up further. In terms of *object of desire* (a male or a female), then perhaps there are two genders, one encompassing heterosexual women and homosexual men (desiring men), and the other encompassing heterosexual men and homosexual women (desiring women). Arguments in some sex discrimination cases are going this way, i.e. sexuality is mapped back on to object choice: men and women should be equally free to choose a man as a sexual partner, and equally free from disadvantage for doing so. The former (heterosexual women and homosexual men) is actually a well-known combination as 'best friends', whereas the latter (homosexual women and heterosexual men) does not seem to have attained much social reality or visibility, that I know of. If bisexuals are added, then in terms of object of desire they are definitely one gender unto themselves, as the differentiation into 'women who desire women and men' and 'men who desire women and men' seems rather pointless, as genital identity seems transcended on both sides of the equation.

Once the mapping of gender has turned from bodily organs (which may or may not have anything much to do with reproduction, i.e. conception, pregnancy, parturition, lactation, etc.) to objects of desire, whether human or otherwise, or to performance and 'dressing up', then the variations and possibilities move swiftly towards infinity. How one defines the bounds of sexuality is by no means unambiguous. This is relevant, for example, even to an activity that is often presented as somehow asexual and only guiltily of the body, namely parenting. This then raises issues of power and politics. If gender is part of a political identity, a group basis for political coalitions, a field of individual interest where people find common cause in similarity, then perhaps 'parent' is itself a gender, transcending the bodily differences that are usually identified as not just sexual, but 'opposite'.

Considerations of *difference* can also be relevant here, as women in feminist politics were not the first to discover. But this immediately raises the question of *similarity* against which 'difference' is supposed to be pertinent. Class and 'race'/ethnicity amongst women were points of reference from which quite different notions of gender politics were constructed in terms of substantial demands and coalition strategies. The notion of gender politics as necessarily a politics of sexual polarisation has been made highly problematic: could it be that the gender politics of working-class women should be oriented away from issues of 'male domination' and towards solidarity with working-class men in an anti-imperialist struggle? Perhaps the masculine as a threat to feminist politics was correctly located in rich, white, capitalist societies, and not in 'men of colour' in any significant way?

If gender is tied to gender politics, rather than to individualised conceptions of sex and sexuality, then perhaps privileged white men, and poor exploited men, are in different genders as political subjects, as well as political objects? Gender politics amongst men is not a topic that often surfaces in political theory. It works to divide them as men, and when divided, to draw them together in ways that may be hierarchical or egalitarian, 'homosocial' or homoerotic, within the divisions that are created around sex and sexuality.[6] Gender politics amongst men is thus by no means always in opposition to women or to conceptions of women's interests. On the one hand naturalised or commonplace categories like sex, gender, class and 'race'/ethnicity are manipulated in politics to construct inclusions and exclusions with respect to groups, an inside and an outside with respect to a 'border' or boundary-line, and various maps of identity and difference such that allies and enemies, partners and opponents, powerful and powerless are produced as societies apparently 'function'. But on the other hand these constructions, despite all the disciplinary apparatuses employed, map poorly onto the varieties of experience that individuals can still manage to generate in living out their lives as human agents.[7]

My 'working definition' of gender is 'ways that sex and sexuality become political'. This is not supposed to legislate what gender is (always and already, as the phrase goes), but is rather intended to alert readers to the ways that the term is used. In my view using gender to mean M/F is an attempt to erase/silence the complexities of sexuality into some essentialist or reductionist idea of what is supposed to be right, culturally validated, natural, desirable or whatever. This is not only a matter of the complexity that marginalised sexualities add to 'the heterosexual matrix' – rather, as Judith Butler says, heterosexuality denies its own variousness, as well. Heterosexuality is under-theorised and under-investigated, and so are men generally, and 'straight' ones in particular.[8] Unsurprisingly this is all very true of Marx. However, my strategy is not to reveal the obvious but rather to engage the silences, hints and ambiguities of his texts in what I hope are illuminating ways, in as much as his own perspective – involving production, technology and class – must necessarily play a part in any contemporary understanding of sexual politics.

Men and women in *The German Ideology*

The reader will note that my conceptualisation of gender does not leave men on the side, and it most particularly does not consider gender a synonym for women, or a synonym for topics thought to be women's issues exclusively.[9] Thus the subtitle for this chapter is rather specially 'loaded': readers may well assume that women and gender signal each other – making practices problematic that were not so before, making women visible, making sexual oppression a public issue – and that men's issues, if there are any, should occupy other minds in other places. My strategy is different, against the grain both in Marx and in a good deal of current theorising. I take gender to involve the binaries of male/female sex and hetero/homo orientation, and not even exhausted there as a concept, though in this context I will not be pushing it any further. Thus my investigation of Marx's narratives will involve a narrative, or rather implied narrative about men, as well as about women.

There is certainly no space here to pretend to a comprehensive survey of Marx's record on gender issues, conceptualised in the way I have elaborated above. Nor is there probably much need. Rather I shall take a number of illustrative examples from Marx, and read them in what I hope is an interpretively imaginative and useful way. After that I will, as promised, address very briefly two sorts of critics, both of whom have considerable reservations about Marx, though from two quite different points of view, and employing two quite different critical strategies.

Probably the best place to start is in *The German Ideology*, jointly written with Engels. While there may be authorial issues of significance here (see chapter five above), I am going to leave them to one side, taking the published passages to be ones that Marx wrote, or at least generally agreed with. They certainly seem to me to chime well with, rather than to grate against, both his earlier and later writings in so far as he alludes to such 'basics' as sexual reproduction in human species-life. Given the scattered character of Marx's and Engels' thoughts as they appear physically on the manuscript sheets of *The German Ideology* – giving rise, I realise, to insoluble interpretive difficulties – I have constructed the following excerpt with free use of ellipses:

> Since we are dealing with the Germans ... we must begin by stating the first premise of all human existence and therefore, of all history ... namely, that men must be in a position to live in order to be able to 'make history'. But life involves before everything else eating and drinking, a habitation, clothing and many other things ... The second point is that the satisfaction of the first need ... leads to new needs; and this production of new needs is the first historical act ... The third circumstance which, from the very outset, enters into historical development, is that men, who daily remake their own life, begin to make other men, to propagate their kind: the relation between man and woman, parents and children, the *family*. The family, which to begin with is the only social relationship, becomes later, when increased needs create new social relations and the increased population new needs, a subordinate one ... and must then be treated and analysed according to the existing empirical data ... These three aspects of social activity are not of course to be taken as three different stages, but just as three aspects or ... three 'moments', which have existed simultaneously since the dawn of history and the first men, and which still assert themselves in history today.[10]

The first interpretive (and contextually constructive) point to make here is that *The German Ideology* was intended to be a satire on the 'German ideologists' Ludwig Feuerbach, Bruno Bauer, and Max Stirner, a triumvirate of Marx's own making. In that way much of Marx's discussion is then structured by views on what these three had got wrong. Hence the whole business of developing 'premises' for history is manifestly suspect to Marx in terms of the discussion that survives, though whether this kind of over-arching narrative – 'premises for history' – is wholly or merely partly suspect is unclear. I pursue this point below.

Although responding to others, but undaunted by their mistakes, Marx elaborates conceptual premises, not so much for the explication of historical stages as for an understanding – in aid of contemporary political campaigns, assuredly – of human society, any society perhaps, but most pertinently European industrialising society, and its recent history. The narrative outcome of *The German Ideology*, such as we have it, is a theory and demonstration of the class struggle in modern history and modern society. While it may seem odd that reproduction of the species only emerges as number three in the list that Marx constructs – albeit a list of historically and empirically simultaneous 'moments' or 'aspects' in an analytical structure – nonetheless there is some overall sense in this. Given that Marx was arguing against philosophical idealists whose account of history and society depended crucially on 'ideas' or 'concepts' (which had a supposed logic and attributed 'development'), it follows that he would think first of production for subsistence, second of further needs, and only then of social relationships, of which he considered the family – a presumed sexual and reproductive unit – the evident origin.

There are certainly similar ways of making a narrative out of what we know, or presume to know, about human history, pre-history and supposed 'basic requirements'. One famous example occurs in Rousseau's *Discourse on the Origin of Inequality* (1755). There are certainly other very different ways of doing this, such as Sigmund Freud's or Max Weber's, depending on what contrary positions are being addressed in debate. My point is that taking *The German Ideology* to express presumptions about human life that were effectively immovable for Marx is a dubious strategy for readers and commentators to follow. A good deal of Marx's narrative (which I have mostly omitted in the ellipses but have recounted above) pursues a serious debate on the nature of society, albeit in tandem with intense ridicule of a threesome who can do no right philosophically or politically.

Elsewhere in *The German Ideology* Marx's discussion of these matters takes on a form more akin to that of claim and evidence in the most general sense, in that relations between 'different nations' (presumably in recent history, or possibly including classical history) are stated to 'depend upon the extent to which each has developed its productive forces, the division of labour and internal intercourse (i.e. socio-economic relationships and activities)'. Moreover 'the whole internal structure of the nation itself depends on the stage of development reached by its production ...'[11] Presumably the alternative, against which Marx argues at length, was a view that cultural or racial differences, placed on a hierarchical and developmental scale, accounted for the differential development of individual nations compared with others, and indeed for the propensity of some to triumph over others as history 'develops' or 'ascends'. In persuading readers of his thesis – that inter-state and intra-state relations depend crucially on the level of development of productive forces – Marx delineates three forms of ownership (of productive resources and of resulting products), leading up to the development of modern private property and of industrialised production in a money economy.

The first of these is said to be 'tribal ownership', when 'a people lives by hunting and fishing, by the rearing of cattle or, in the highest stage, agriculture'. Following the analytical priority given to production, as previously claimed, Marx comments:

> The division of labour is at this stage still very elementary and is confined to a further extension of the natural division of labour existing in the family. The social structure is, therefore, limited to an extension of the family: patriarchal family chieftains, below them the members of the tribe, finally slaves. The slavery latent in the family only develops gradually with the increase of population, the growth of wants, and with the extension of external relations, both of war and of barter.[12]

This slavery inherent in the family is explained elsewhere in the text. In that discussion Marx's analytical purpose is evidently to draw out the notion of a division of labour and to explain that historically there has been an '*unequal* distribution, both quantitative and qualitative, of labour and its products, hence property'. The first instance of this ubiquitous social form and historical fact – slavery – is then located by Marx in 'the natural division of labour in the family and the separation of society into individual families opposed to one another'. However, this raises certain questions which he does not deal with, in *The German Ideology* or elsewhere. The first is the force of the term 'natural' in this kind of discussion, and the second is the depiction of women and children as victims of men.

While Marx describes this early form of slavery as 'crude', he does not hasten to ascribe this epithet to his own analysis. Given his evident anxiety to develop a social theory of human life as almost wholly developmental in terms of human ambition and intellect, and very little indebted to presumably immovable 'natural' limitations or barriers, his forays into naturalising discourse are notably rare. On the one hand he would probably have been offending very few people at the time by naturalising the family in this way and drawing it out of the realm of changing social relationships and variable cultural constructs. But on the other hand he (again with Engels) took care to promise, in the *Communist Manifesto*, that there would be a new relation between the sexes when communists had broken through the exploitation inherent in the 'bourgeois' economic system. Marx, however, simply did not say anything about what this new relationship was going to be like.

This narrative strategy is highly risk-averse and characteristic of what could be characterised today as masculinist attitudes. As attitudes today descend from those of the past, it does not cause me that much difficulty assigning them in some minimally meaningful way to Marx, even if the context of contemporary sexual politics would be largely (though not, I think wholly) foreign to his thoughts. My point is that read politically as the work of a conventionally gendered heterosexual male, the passage makes sense: a genuflection to the eternal character of reproduction, conveniently and restfully conceptualised as a 'family' relationship, combined with a nod to the sexist oppression of women, and exploitative practices towards children, as manifested by male heads of household (in whatever class). Indeed this was extensively documented in Marx's time, whether in factual reports or crusading novels. Given that sexual politics, and childcare concerns, were not Marx's specific analytical focus, it is perhaps surprising that these topics rate a mention at all. These things certainly were not a primary focus for the 'German ideologists' either, whose strategy in these matters was not all that different, no doubt for similar reasons.

Marx's main complaint about the German ideologists was that they organised a bogus history of humanity, purportedly derived from 'concepts'. These 'concepts', so Marx argued, merely tracked their conventional and confused predilections and thus fogged any possibility of a truly radical understanding of contemporary society. In pursuing this critique Marx necessarily had to offer alternative principles (contemporary, historical and general inferences concerning 'production'), and alternative factual illustrations (which in this text are really just sketches). Ultimately in *The German Ideology* he got down to sexual and reproductive basics in arguing that the 'production of life, both of one's own in labour and of fresh life in procreation ... appears as a double relationship: on the one hand as a natural, on the other as a social relationship'.[13] While the text develops a notion of the 'social' as a 'mode of cooperation', which necessarily varies with the specific stage of the 'mode of production', today's reader might reasonably wonder, once again, what exactly is intended when he uses the concept 'natural'? Marx concludes, *contra* the 'German ideologists', that the '"history of humanity" must always be studied ... in relation to the history of industry and exchange', and that in Germany 'it is impossible to write this sort of history, because the Germans lack "evidence of their senses"' owing to their preoccupation with what they deem 'consciousness'.[14]

Presumably the quotes that Marx placed around 'history of humanity' indicate a certain distance from that kind of conceptualisation, and indeed that sort of activity in the first place, and the ones around 'evidence of their senses' suggest that the German ideologists are so muddled by idealism that they do not see what is actually happening in their own and neighbouring societies. Nonetheless just as Marx needs to offer an alternative account of history in what he deems to be empirical terms, focusing on productive activities and relationships, so he also needs to offer an alternative account of 'consciousness' and its development – however little he was actually interested in this, and however ironic and distanced his delivery. This he does in an abbreviated recapitulation of his pre-historical sketch, and in doing so he digs a little deeper into sexuality and reproduction, conceived as 'natural' in some unspecified sense, and into consciousness and culture, conceived as specifically human and potentially developmental, though only when linked with production.

Here we learn that 'the division of labour ... was originally nothing but the division of labour in the sexual act', followed by 'the division of labour which develops spontaneously or "naturally" by virtue of natural predisposition (e.g., physical strength), needs, accidents, etc., etc.'[15] While Marx may have thought quite correctly that this type of empirical reference to reproduction, and his supposedly plausible supposition about pre-historic 'tribal' relationships, would anchor their account in a factuality that no one could reasonably question, this is no bar to re-opening these issues today, or indeed to conceptualising them as issues for debate rather than evidence for some proposition. What could possibly count as a basis for any inference about activities and relationships in pre-history is certainly the subject of controversy at present,[16] and what relevance such accounts have for any arguments or conclusions concerning contemporary social relationships is a further matter of debate. One wonders whether Marx would have dabbled in this area at all, had he not constructed his remarks in answer to a kind of history, and a pattern of historical enquiry, of which he clearly disapproved. *Capital*, for instance, is notably free of this type of speculation; where there are presumed eternal verities in question, such as the specifically human (rather than animal) character of labour-power, Marx in that text – not written in answer to the German ideologists – tends to offer ahistorical generalisations, rather than what are very nearly 'just so' stories. In *The German Ideology* these stories are then propped up with allusions to tribal societies as an imputed guide to the past (now a very suspect notion, too).

The presumed level of 'biological basics' as 'first historical acts' does not figure in *Capital*, either. While I have attributed much of the substantive discussion of *The German Ideology* to Marx's necessary interaction with the German ideologists' agenda and views – as the genre of critique would dictate – I nonetheless conclude that in that text Marx interrogates himself on the general themes of nature and culture, men and women, reproduction and the family, and that his views and values, and most importantly his silences and evasions, become manifest.

One huge silence is on the subject of men, deployed in a characteristic (but now suspect) generic manner, presuming an application to people of both sexes. As with other (male) authorities, this apparent gender neutrality, or more properly sex-blindness or androgeny, dissolves when 'wife' appears and when family-centred narratives of reproduction state or assume a child-rearing (rather than strictly child-bearing) role for women as 'mother'. Typically in these accounts, little if anything is noted about or prescribed to 'fathers' other than duties as head of household and economic provider which, by apparent implication, 'wife' and 'mother' do not or cannot fulfil, at least 'normally' or 'generally'. The 'division of labour' ascribed by Marx to 'the sexual act', from which by implication the class struggle – and indeed all important historical development and change – eventually proceeds, might rest ambiguously in a conspiracy of silence between authors (male) and readers (presumed male). It might be left there, were it not for the worrying (for men) discussion of the origin of inequality, placed not directly in the sexual act, but rather located in the 'family', in which 'wife and children are the slaves of the husband'. What male characteristics – eternal? malleable? – account for the motivation to create this slavery and the – general? inevitable? – 'success' of the institution, as *The German Ideology* tells the story?

Attributing this (im)balance of power to naturalised attributes of 'physical strength' is today unthinkingly careless but unsurprisingly near-universal; it is of course likely that further presumptions about maleness as opposed to femaleness, and about a fixed or changing boundary between immovable nature and malleable culture, are lurking behind the rather hasty gallop through pre-history that Marx has left us. This is to say that on the one hand Marx is not that much better at posing issues in sexual politics than most male social theorists are today. But on the other hand his drift away from naturalising limitations on human development and change – whether these limitations come from supposed biological and physical 'basics' such as 'race', or from supposed rationalities inherent in eternal or self-developing 'concepts' – and his espousal of an increasingly self-conscious developmental trajectory for important activities in human social life – are at least a possible point of departure for social constructionist, and political activist, theorisations of gender.

Men and women in *Capital*

As indicated above, *Capital* is a rather different kind of text from *The German Ideology*. It is basically the work of Marx, rather than something closer to a kind of collaboration with Engels, and while it is a critique, the object of attack was not the German ideologists but the 'political economists', most particularly David Ricardo and subsequent authorities of the British school (see chapter four above). More importantly it was a published text, seen through three German editions (and a French translation) by the author himself, and while not perfectly free of loose ends in textual terms, it is certainly a work that has been substantially polished. Again, as indicated above, the text has a rather different take on what might be termed 'bedrock' arguments, tending towards plausible but ahistorical generalisations, rather than the perhaps less plausible but more vivid 'just so' story about pre-history that figures in *The German Ideology*. The following passage gives the flavour of the ahistorical generalisation; insofar as this narrative does not issue in an account of 'family' life, or indeed the sexual act, as the originary moment in conceptualising human labour, the signifier 'man' could perhaps be genuinely androgenous for author and reader:

> Labour is, first of all, a process between man and nature, a process by which man, through his own actions, mediates, regulates and controls the metabolism between himself and nature. He confronts the materials of nature as a force of nature. He sets in motion the natural forces which belong to his own body, his arms, legs, head and hands, in order to appropriate the materials of nature in a form adapted to his own needs. Through this movement he acts upon external nature and changes it, and in this way he simultaneously changes his own nature. He develops the potentialities slumbering within nature, and subjects the play of its forces to his own sovereign power. We are not dealing here with those first instinctive forms of labour which remain on the animal level.[17]

Worryingly, and typically, we are not told what 'forms of labour' are 'on the animal level'. It might be tempting to ascribe reproductive and birth labour to this level, as consonant with the naturalising presumptions and discourse of *The German Ideology* detailed above, but then it is not at all clear in the discussion in *Capital* whether Marx is keeping to the 'dual-systems' view that *The German Ideology* makes explicit: labour is both labour outside the body on nature, and labour inside the body (as it were) in sexual and reproductive activities. On the one hand, this omission *might* save Marx from a charge that he unthinkingly focuses on a masculinist concept of labour, whilst leaving reproduction and childcare (and further 'family' dependencies) in a feminised realm; on the other hand, the fact that any significant discussion of procreation and inter-generational social life is omitted lends credence to the complaint that he really does see the world in masculinised terms.

While *Capital* develops a number of themes currently conceptualised under gender studies and sexual politics, and in particular considers these in industrialised societies dominated by commodified exchange relations (otherwise known as 'the capitalist mode of production'), it also contains passages in which Marx notably revisits the narratives of pre-history, as developed in *The German Ideology*. The treatment in *Capital* is much briefer: 'Within a family and, after further development, within a tribe, there springs up naturally a division of labour caused by differences of sex and age, and therefore based on a purely physiological foundation'.[18] Again, and typically, there is no discussion to tell us exactly what this 'purely physiological foundation' is, and what differences of 'sex and age' there (necessarily? generally?) are. And just as briefly, readers are catapulted out of a realm of naturalisation and stasis into a realm of mutability and development when Marx considers a transition from capitalist exploitation to a 'higher form' of social relations, conceptualised without attributing much significance at all to a public/private boundary:

It was not however the misuse of parental power that created the direct or indirect exploitation of immature labour-powers by capital, but rather the opposite, i.e. the capitalist mode of exploitation, by sweeping away the economic foundation which corresponded to parental power, made the use of parental power into its misuse. However terrible and disgusting the dissolution of the old family ties within the capitalist system may appear, large-scale industry, by assigning an important part in socially organized processes of production, outside the sphere of the domestic economy, to women, young persons and children of both sexes, does nevertheless create a new economic foundation for a higher form of the family and of relations between the sexes.[19]

While slavery within the family is attributed in the above passage to the exploitation that is foundational to the capitalist economic system, it is not clear how this relates to any primordial division of labour such that slavery was inherent in the 'first' family form. Nor is it clear what power relations are going to be attributed to and within the 'higher form of the family', other than some parental power over children. What is clear is that the discourse has moved away from 'the father', who figured in *The German Ideology* (against a significantly unmentioned mother). 'Husband' and 'wife' from *The German Ideology* seem also to have dropped away in the proposed new 'relations between the sexes'.

Once again, my point is not to hold Marx to a theoretical agenda that has been generated largely (though not wholly) since his time, but rather to note that his terminological swings and rather exceptional lack of curiosity are symptomatic of a strategy. The strategy was to gain support and not create enemies, and to have the argument both ways: an unspecified realm of naturalisation, and an open realm of possibility. The extent to which this strategy was fully conscious in Marx's mind is not really the issue; the issue for us today is reading Marx in dialogue with both an imputed audience, one whose presumptions may not have changed all that much since the publication of *Capital* in 1867, and also with a present-day theoretical and political agenda, one concerning sex and gender, which is certainly different.

In that light it is quite interesting to examine some of Marx's bolder passages in *Capital* concerning women. These are quite difficult to read nowadays for a rather different reason, namely that – as is almost a cliché – there are many feminisms. Read against one kind of mid- to late twentieth-century feminism, Marx's comments and

presumptions are patronisingly sexist; but read against another feminism of our day, Marx's views actually emerge as in some (limited)
sense a feminist of his time. The latter is a difficult argument to make,
and not one that could be pushed very far. In the biographical record,
as indeed in the texts examined above, Marx does not link his work
overtly to any feminism of his day, whether of a theoretical or a practical character, beyond his support of, and participation in, the workers' movement. In some senses, as we know from mid- to late twentieth-century feminist history, a link to feminism would have been possible; indeed by Marx's later years, and certainly in Engels', this kind of
move was virtually required within the socialist movement. However,
it is also known that Marx had many suspicions of campaigns and individuals supportive of women and issues they espoused in that frame.

Marx's immediate objections to feminism were the class character of
the activists (largely middle and upper class) and the class analysis of
their proposals, judged against his ever-ready conceptualisation of proletarian interests as the unified interests of a single class. Where the participants and proposals were acceptably proletarian, however, Marx
could evidently see little gain for the movement (in his conceptualisation, obviously) in separate agendas or organisations. These issues surfaced in conjunction with the International Working Men's
Association, and later with August Bebel's *Woman under Socialism*
(1883) and Engels' work in *The Origin of the Family, Private Property and
the State* (1883). In sum, it is quite difficult to make Marx out to be a
feminist in an activist sense. My argument here is that reading what he
says specifically about women in *Capital* is a fruitful exercise only
when done in conjunction with a generously nuanced view of the
nineteenth-century feminist scene. Here are a few examples:

> Before the labour of women and children under 10 years old was for-
> bidden in mines, the capitalists considered the employment of naked
> women and girls, often in company with men, so far sanctioned by
> their moral code, and especially by their ledgers, that it was only after
> the passing of the Act that they had recourse to machinery ... In
> England women are still occasionally used instead of horses for haul-
> ing barges, because the labour required to produce horses and
> machines is an accurately known quantity, while that required to

maintain the women of the surplus population is beneath all calculation.[20]

The above passage illustrates one of Marx's themes in *Capital*, which
is the way that an increasingly mechanised factory system absorbed
and exploited the labour of women and children. He treats them
together as persons of 'slight muscular strength, or whose bodily development is incomplete, but whose limbs are all the more supple', and
concludes that the 'labour of women and children was therefore the
first result of the capitalist application of machinery!'[21] This counters
an argument which Marx thought current: that machinery 'saves'
labour and promotes 'civilisation'. By quoting official sources extensively he was concerned to portray the horrors of the factory system
as intrinsic to the capitalist mode of production, bound to get worse,
and egregiously uncivilised by 'bourgeois' standard of gentility. Women
were conceptualised here in Marx's work in physiological terms as
generally less strong but more supple; this is controversial now but at
least has a kindly, caring air about it of protecting the vulnerable, albeit
from the economic system, not from 'men' as such.

That theme surfaces later in Marx's discussion where he quotes, with
evident approval, a public health report concerning the introduction
of an industrial system into agriculture, and its effects again on women
and children:

> 'Married women, who work in gangs along with boys and girls, are,
> for a stipulated sum of money, placed at the disposal of the farmer by
> a man called the "undertaker", who contracts for the whole gang.
> These gangs will sometimes travel many miles from their own village;
> they are to be met morning and evening on the roads, dressed in short
> petticoats, with suitable coats and boots, and sometimes trousers, look-
> ing wonderfully strong and healthy, but tainted with a customary
> immorality and heedless of the fatal results which their love of this
> busy and independent life is bringing on their unfortunate offspring
> who are pining at home.' All the phenomena of the factory districts
> are reproduced here [Marx comments], including a yet higher degree
> of disguised infanticide and stupefaction of children with opiates.[22]

In a footnote to this passage Marx adds: 'Infants that received opiates "shrank up into little old men", or "wizened like little monkeys". We see here how India and China have taken their revenge on England.'[23]

Interestingly these passages capture both female independence in the labour market as an upside, and female vulnerability (or is it moral weakness?) as a downside. Childcare in relation to adult employment also surfaces, but without much suggestion, other than the catch-all 'family' in Marx's texts. Or rather it surfaces in Dr. Hunter's words in his public health report, which Marx quotes: 'happy indeed will it be for the manufacturing districts of England, when every married woman having a family is prohibited from working in any textile works at all'. Marx seems to quote this approvingly, but says nothing further on the subject.[24] Men are intriguingly missing from this discussion, though Marx does give a general reference to Engels' *The Condition of the Working Class in England* (1844); Engels does not solve childcare issues in any very startling way either, though he does portray the distress felt by out-of-work males when their female partner is employed outside the home, and they (males) are left with the children.[25]

It cannot be claimed that the inter-relation between women, mothers, men, fathers, children and employment/unemployment in industrialised societies has been resolved to all that much satisfaction anywhere in the world, either theoretically or practically, though there are certainly notable gradations in benefits, attitudes, opportunities, and perceptions far too complex to go into here. My point in this discussion is that it is untrue to say that Marx never noticed these things, nor that his approach and conclusions can be captured in any very simple way. Moreover the silences of his texts (not unusually in this respect) do theorise men implicitly. In the above discussions men are, by implication, physically strong, sexually aggressive, and absent (or at least distant) fathers on the bread-winner-outside-the-home model. As a general conceptualisation this is hardly surprising and reflective of a contemporary image which was, no doubt, in an ambiguous relation to varied ways that individuals behaved; what is perhaps at least slightly surprising is the lack of curiosity in conceptualising this problem, which evidently grated on Marx quite considerably, especially considering his own anguish as a father, which we have from correspondence, and his own jovial role as *pater familias*, at least as this appears in surviving memoirs.[26]

Family slavery resurfaces in *Capital*, though in an economically determined context, not in one determined by 'nature' and the beginnings of culture, as in *The German Ideology*. Marx comments:

> Machinery also revolutionizes ... the agency through which the capital-relation is formally mediated ... our first assumption was the capitalist and the worker confronted each other as free persons ... But now the capitalist buys children and young persons. Previously the worker sold his own labour-power ... Now he sells wife and child. He has become a slave-dealer. Notices of demand for children's labour often resemble in form the inquiries for Negro slaves ...[27]

This, of course, portrays men as victims of the economic system, but also once again as slave-masters within the family, both as husband and as father. Male sexuality is never raised as a topic of discussion, in this (pre-capitalist or capitalist) world (as it were) or the next (socialist) one; Marx's strategy in *Capital* in considering both the primordial world of reproductive instincts and the socialist world of social rationality and absence-of-struggle is to portray reproductive sexuality as egalitarian in 'the act', and early childcare as women's work. Unsurprising as this is, re-reading Marx can help to re-raise issues like these in the contemporary context rather than to close them down in familiar ways. Perhaps unexpectedly, for instance, he ventures a developmental sketch on female sexuality. Though a quotation, again from a public health report, the context is explicitly approving:

> Each moulder [of bricks] ... supplies his subordinates with board and lodging in his cottage. Whether members of his family or not, the men, boys and girls all sleep in the cottage ... all on the ground floor, and badly ventilated. These people are so exhausted after the day's hard work, that neither the rules of health, of cleanliness, nor of decency are in the least observed ... The greatest evil of the system that employs young girls on this sort of work, consists in this, that, as a rule, it chains them fast from childhood for the whole of their after-life to the most abandoned rabble. They become rough, foulmouthed boys, before Nature has taught them that they are women. Clothed in a few dirty rags, the legs naked far above the knees, hair and face besmeared with

dirt, they learn to treat all feelings of decency and shame with contempt. During mealtimes they lie at full length in the fields, or watch the boys bathing in a neighbouring canal.[28]

And similarly:

In some branches of industry, the girls and women work through the night together with the male personnel ... 'young girls and women are employed on the pit banks and on the coke heaps, not only by day but also by night ... These females employed with the men, hardly distinguished from them in their dress ... are exposed to the deterioration of character, arising from their loss of self-respect, which can hardly fail to follow from their unfeminine occupation'.[29]

These passages raise questions about childhood/adulthood and heterosexuality, and particularly sexual difference, that are again unresolved in Marx, and still unresolved in contemporary society.[30] While it might seem that Marx's comments merely evoke Victorian values of fragile femininity and female purity, it is also a reasonable supposition that there were differing views on these matters in Marx's time, even though the overall framework for discussion – when there was discussion – was not that of present-day sexual politics. Giving some consideration to just this openness and variability of context is essential to a rich and productive reading of Marx. This issue takes me to two different kinds of criticism that have been mounted since the 1880s. I shall consider passages from Michèle Barrett and Jeff Hearn, not because they exhaust the field, but because the two represent very different critical strategies, and elicit from me two quite different reactions.

Two concepts of criticism

In a commemorative article, 'Marxist-Feminism and the Work of Karl Marx' (in a volume marking the centenary of Marx's death), Barrett berates Marx for his 'naturalism' in regard to the family (as detailed in the passages from *The German Ideology* quoted above), and sexism in regard to his general assumption that wage labourers are male. Barrett says that he devalues women wage workers as 'little other than a threat to the male worker', because factories replaced male labour with that of women and children (as detailed in the passages from *Capital* quoted above). Marx has 'unreflectively sexist presuppositions', according to Barrett, and therefore 'assumes as a baseline that there is a (pre-given) housewife engaged in domestic labour in the home'. Barrett concludes that this 'is hardly an unspeakable crime', but that 'it is not what we might expect from a mind that did not rest at appearances'.[31]

Given Barrett's assumptions, these conclusions are probably fair enough, but this is really to raise the question, what exactly are her assumptions? I sense that they are really rather different from mine, as a strategy for reading Marx. It seems to me, first of all, that Barrett is really trying to read Marx as an authorial mind, rather than to read his texts. While texts can hardly be read at all without some sense of who the author is, and why the text was written,[32] it certainly does not follow that texts have to be seen as a window on the author's views, and little else. Even if these texts were read as merely a window on 'what Marx thought', it seems to me that Barrett's reading promotes an interpretation of the authorial mind as singular and certain in having just one view. With a more exploratory reading, and with a strategy of filling in the silences with more than one possibility, it seems to me that a more complex and more interesting authorial Marx can be usefully constructed. In short, I think we are looking at selective quotation and ungenerous interpretation. This is curiously mirrored in Barrett's treatment of nineteenth-century feminism, in that she rightly does not accept that Marx can be exonerated for his 'feet of clay' on feminist issues by declaring that he lived in a 'pre-feminist' culture.[33] And she argues, also rightly, that the currency of feminist ideas in the nineteenth century should not be under-estimated. Unfortunately, however, her own deployment of feminism reflects neither any specifically nineteenth-century quality to these ideas, nor any diversity within this putative nineteenth-century context. While it is my intention to argue methodologically here, and not specifically to get Marx off any hook, least of all a feminist one, nonetheless it does seem to me that, viewed against a more complex and diverse 'take' on feminist ideas and movements of the nineteenth century, Marx begins to look slightly better.

As there are many feminisms today, so there were many in the nineteenth century. It is by no means agreed that the liberal feminist campaign to get equal opportunities for women in the labour market, nor the socialist feminist campaign to bring power to working-class women, nor the radical feminist campaigns to end oppression in a so-called private or domestic sphere – all of which are invoked by Barrett – were individually or severally the dominant doctrine and practice in Marx's time. All these issues were there, of course, but it is arguable that in practice, and in at least somewhat theoretical terms, a very significant feminism of the time assumed, somewhat contrarily, that women were inherently domestic, with responsibilities for child-bearing, child-rearing, home-making, and similar considerations that worked against waged employment outside the home – which was said to be a realm for men. Moreover this often took on an overtly moralistic character, with arguments that women had a special purity, quite unlike men's character, and indeed that women had responsibilities for keeping men's activities in check – particularly where alcohol was involved. Rather than see Marx as an author inexplicably in the grip of Victorian *sexual* values (given that he detested Victorian *social* values), it might be interesting to see him reflecting some version of Victorian *feminist* values, albeit ones that have largely faded from view today, or at least largely faded from the view of academic writers. Feminist history can be constructed in highly different ways, depending on the writer's purposes and politics; Barrett's purpose seems to have been to cut Marx loose from Engels on 'the woman question', and to pick over his work for 'howlers'.[34] While I do not share Barrett's view that Engels is all that much better,[35] I nonetheless welcome debate. However, I think that Barrett has impoverished Marx quite considerably, and deliberately, by narrowing the historical contextualisation down unduly in terms of feminist history, and by narrowing Marx down as an authorial consciousness to the point where he seems brain damaged.

It can be useful to prise texts loose from the authorial mind somewhat, and that is very largely what I have tried to do in my discussions above. On the one hand I have no problem with producing a more interesting authorial Marx as a matter of interpretive generosity (why focus on 'howlers'?) and exploratory contextualisation (bringing in an unfashionable feminism). On the other hand I have also tried to create dialogue between texts of the past and texts of the present by distancing the author and foregrounding the commentator, hence the critical strategy of lining my readings of Marx up with my readings of contemporary sexual politics. This is more like the strategy employed by Jeff Hearn in a highly critical yet productive reading of Marx's texts that he undertakes in *The Gender of Oppression*. Rather than taking Marx to task for failing to meet a contemporary agenda, Hearn explores the discursive strategies deployed by Marx in passages concerning reproduction and the family, on the one hand, and the material production of useful goods and services, on the other. My emphasis was on the former area – reproduction and the family – as a way of arguing that these texts are actually rather more interesting than they might at first appear, whereas Hearn's is on the latter – material production of useful goods and services – as a way of linking the two areas together. Rather than simply cast doubt on Marx's conceptualisations of reproduction and the family, which is easy enough to do, Hearn probes into Marx's characterisations of both reproduction and production, contrasting them with Mary O'Brien's 'focus on "reproductive labour" and [Catharine] MacKinnon's on "sexuality"'. Doing this, he argues, disrupts 'taken-for-granted conventions of production-based (male-dominated) marxisms'.[36] It is not that Marx 'said the wrong things about reproduction and domestic labour', as it were, but rather that he left the partriarchal character of the very definitions and value-hierarchies involved in these activities untroubled.

This is to say that Marx reads quite a lot directly off 'sexual difference' when he (briefly) remarks on reproduction, childcare and domestic labour, but that he is also reading quite a lot off sexual difference, albeit covertly, when he makes 'productive' activities crucial in historical change and political progress. These activities are not merely reflective of sexual difference, in that they are commonly coded male or masculine, but rather they are constitutive of sexual difference in countless ways, not least in the child-rearing and educational presuppositions and practices that produce men and women as identifiably and consistently different. That there is a conceptual separation at all is, in Hearn's view, a patriarchal strategy. He concludes that '[e]ither the notion of labour needs to be enlarged to incorporate *all* such aspects of material being, or it needs to be complemented by a firmer notion of material being that is beyond and outside narrow "works".' This opens issues up (by making both gender and labour problematic), rather than closing them down (by taking them both for granted as unrelated). This is the kind of thing I have tried to do in this chapter, and indeed in this book, in reading the 'postmodern Marx'. Further to this theme I present the reader with a brief Epilogue, explaining that the 'postmodern Marx' is necessarily multiple or 'multi-vocal'.

Notes

1 For two recent examples where Marx 'surfaces' in important ways, see David T. Evans, *Sexual Citizenship* (London: Routledge, 1993); and Judith Grant, *Fundamental Feminism* (London: Routledge, 1993).

2 R. W. Connell, *Gender and Power: Society, the Person and Sexual Politics* (Cambridge: Polity Press, 1987).

3 Terrell Carver, *Gender is Not a Synonym for Women* (Boulder CO: Lynne Rienner Publishing, Inc, 1996), pp. 4–5.

4 Judith Butler, *Gender Trouble: Feminism and the Subversion of Identity* (London: Routledge, 1990).

5 Jeffrey Weeks, *Sexuality and its Discontents: Meanings, Myths and Modern Sexualities* (London: Routledge & Kegan Paul, 1985).

6 Jeff Hearn and David Collinson, 'Unities and Differences between Men and between Masculinities', in Harry Brod and Michael Kaufmann (eds) *Theorizing Masculinities* (Newbury Park CA: Sage, 1994), pp. 97–118.

7 See Tim Edwards, *Erotics and Politics: Gay Male Sexuality, Masculinity and Feminism* (London: Routledge, 1994).

8 See R. W. Connell, *Masculinities* (Cambridge: Polity Press, 1995).

9 This point is argued through in Carver, *Gender is Not a Synonym for Women*, pp. 32–4.

10 Karl Marx and Frederick Engels, *Feuerbach: Opposition of the Materialist and Idealist Outlooks* (Part 1 of *The German Ideology*) (London, Lawrence & Wishart, 1973), pp. 31–2.

11 Marx and Engels, *Feuerbach* (*German Ideology*), pp.19–20.

12 Marx and Engels, *Feuerbach* (*German Ideology*), p. 20.

13 Marx and Engels, *Feuerbach* (*German Ideology*), p. 33.

14 Marx and Engels, *Feuerbach* (*German Ideology*), p. 33.

15 Marx and Engels, *Feuerbach* (*German Ideology*), pp. 34-5.

16 See, for example, Michael Shanks and Christopher Tilley, *Social Theory and Archaeology* (Cambridge: Polity, 1987).

17 Karl Marx, *Capital*, vol. 1, trans. Ben Fowkes (Harmondsworth: Penguin, 1986), p. 285.

18 Marx, *Capital*, vol. 1, p. 471.

19 Marx, *Capital*, vol. 1, pp. 620–1.

20 Marx, *Capital*, vol. 1, p. 517.

21 Marx, *Capital*, vol. 1, p. 517.

22 Marx, *Capital*, vol. 1, p. 522.

23 Marx, *Capital*, vol. 1, p. 522, n. 51.

24 Marx, *Capital*, vol. 1, p. 522.

25 Frederick Engels, *The Condition of the Working Class in England*, ed. Victor Kiernan (Harmondsworth, Penguin, 1987), p. 168.

26 See David McLellan, *Karl Marx: His Life and Thought* (London: Macmillan, 1973), pp. 274–5, 330.

27 Marx, *Capital*, vol. 1, p. 519.

28 Marx, *Capital*, vol. 1, pp. 593–4.

29 Marx, *Capital*, vol. 1, p. 368 and 368, n. 61.

30 For a discussion of 'age of consent' legislation in analytical and historical terms relating to both sexes and varied sexualities, see Matthew Waites, 'Sexual citizens: legislating the age of consent in Britain', in Terrell Carver and Véronique Mottier (eds), *The Politics of Sexuality: Identity, Gender, Citizenship* (London, Routledge, 1998).

31 Michèle Barrett, 'Marxist-Feminism and the Work of Karl Marx', in Betty Matthews (ed.) *Marx: 100 Years On* (London: Lawrence & Wishart, 1983), pp. 210–14.

32 I discuss the relationship between biography as a genre and the historical contextualisation of authors in the political theory canon in *Gender is not a Synonym for Women*, pp. 2–3; see also my 'Methodological issues in writing a political biography', *The Journal of Political Science*, 20 (1992), 3–13.

33 Barrett, 'Marxist-Feminism', pp. 199, 216–17.

34 Barrett, 'Marxist-Feminism', pp. 214–15.

35 I have critiqued Engels' *Origin of the Family* from two perspectives. See 'Engels's feminism', *History of Political Thought*, 6:3 (1985), 479–89, and 'Theorizing men in Engels's *Origin of the Family*', *masculinities*, 2:1 (1994), 67–77.

36 Jeff Hearn, *The Gender of Oppression: Men, Masculinity and the Critique of Marxism* (Brighton: Wheatsheaf, 1987), pp. 98–9.

37 Hearn, *The Gender of Oppression*, p. 100.

Multiple Marxes

There have always been multiple Marxes, and each one is a product of a reading strategy. A reading strategy involves a choice of texts in a biographical frame, philosophical presuppositions about language and meaning, and political purpose – whether acknowledged or not. As there were multiple Marxes, so there were multiple debates. By now these have long sedimented into further layers of text and tradition that readers must address. While Marx may have thought that he could scorn the issue by saying that he was 'not a Marxist', he nonetheless left behind a vast legacy of works and writings of very different sorts, advising against any 'master-key' to history, yet jotting down an enigmatic 'guide for my studies'.[1] This has set the stage for a modern patristics concerned with orthodoxy and revisionism, Leninism and Social Democracy, the Frankfurt School, Gramsci and Althusser, rational-choice and analytical Marxists, 'the return of the political' in discourse theory and the 'society of the spectacle' in late capitalism. This list is of course just a selection. Rather than recount these familiar themes and add yet more variations, I have tried to do something rather different. This has entailed looking carefully at what these famous debates actually are – what narrative structure is invoked in this debating process – and offering an alternative to readers who think they might be interested in Marx. That is what is signalled in the title *The Postmodern Marx*.

Generally such debates have been conducted from positions of assumed authority and had a trajectory towards closure and exclusion, or to put it simply, 'We're right and you're wrong'. While it is difficult to escape from the traditional partisanship of scholarly discourse – and I am sure that there are places in my text where this shines through – I have nonetheless made an effort to pull back from 'Marx' as a point of truth, where alternatives are excluded and 'proof' closes in on the reader, in order to let a self-consciously constructed 'Marx' raise issues and provoke controversy. Paradoxically I also contend that one way of constructing a Marx that will do this effectively is to pay more rigorous attention to the methods and protocols of historical and textual scholarship – the way that words get on to the page, and the way that dates and chronologies get fixed – than many previous commentators have been able to do. No doubt there are shortcomings and imperfections in what I have achieved, but my purpose has been to generate both clarity in detail and complexity in analysis.

The 'other' to this methodology is reductionism, credulity and tendentiousness. In my view there is really no paradox in turning facticity back on itself, by employing techniques formerly used to 'discover' a supposedly singular truth, and redeploying them as discursive tools to 'produce' a political debate. Rather the paradox was in the way that scholars traditionally talked past each other, precisely because the narrative structure of debate was so binarised and constricting. Rather than looking productively at themselves as narrators-in-a-context, they focused instead on Marx as a supposed object in himself. Assuming him to be 'one', they often mapped this same assumption back on to themselves as scholars, supposedly united in purpose and set on a similar goal, that of finding the 'real' or the 'relevant' Marx. In denying their own plurality, they denied Marx his in relation to us – Marx is plural for us because our problems are plural. In reassessing Marx I have tried to turn attention to the following issues:

- Which concepts are the important ones in constructing the world in which we live? To what extent and through what processes are these variable and malleable?
- To what extent do these concepts have a structure which human activity realises? Can such a structure be specified, and what difference would it make to specify it?
- Is there any developmental trajectory to human society? Are there, or could there be, any mechanisms for choosing and producing change?

- Given that there have been pre-commodity societies, can there be a post-commodity form of life? How and why do sex and gender interact on, or form part of, larger systems of labour and production?
- To what extent is the liberal tradition of democratic politics predicated on the economic tradition of possessive individualism? Is there any point now in revisiting socialist and communist views and visionaries?
- How has Marx been voiced and translated as an authority on these and numerous other issues? What reading strategies have stimulated an audience for his work, and with what results?

Neither the Marx I have constructed nor my authorial persona has the answer to these questions, nor does any answer belong to a person rather than to a culture or 'form of life'.[2] I am merely hopeful that my postmodern Marx has put issues like these to readers, and that readers will find it interesting and useful to pursue them.

Notes

1 Engels to Conrad Schmidt, 5 August 1890, in Karl Marx and Frederick Engels, *Selected Correspondence*, 2nd edn ed. S. Ryanzanskaya, trans. I. Lasker (Moscow, Progress, 1965), p. 415; Marx to the Editorial Board of the Otechestvenniye Zapiski, November 1877, in *Selected Correspondence*, p. 313; Karl Marx, Preface to *A Contribution to the Critique of Political Economy*, in *Later Political Writings*, ed. and trans. Terrell Carver (Cambridge, Cambridge University Press, 1996), p. 159.
2 Ludwig Wittgenstein, *Philosophical Investigations*, trans. G. E. M. Anscombe (Oxford, Basil Blackwell, 1958).

Select bibliography

Arthur, Christopher J. (ed.), *Engels Today: A Centenary Appreciation*, London, Macmillan; New York, St. Martin's Press, 1996.

Avineri, Shlomo, *The Social and Political Thought of Karl Marx*, Cambridge, Cambridge University Press, 1968.

Buchanan, Allen E., *Marx and Justice*, Totowa NJ, Rowman & Littlefield, 1982.

Callinicos, Alex, *The Revolutionary Ideas of Marx*, London, Bookmarks, 1983.

Callinicos, Alex, *The Revenge of History: Marxism and the East European Revolutions*, Cambridge, Polity Press, 1991.

Callinicos, Alex, *Theories and Narratives: Reflections on the Philosophy of History*, Cambridge, Polity Press, 1995.

Carver, Terrell (ed.), *Karl Marx: Texts on Method*, Oxford, Basil Blackwell, 1975.

Carver, Terrell, *Engels*, Oxford, Oxford University Press, 1981.

Carver, Terrell, *Marx's Social Theory*, Oxford, Oxford University Press, 1982.

Carver, Terrell, *Marx and Engels: The Intellectual Relationship*, Brighton, Harvester/Wheatsheaf, 1983.

Carver, Terrell, *Friedrich Engels: His Life and Thought*, London, Macmillan, 1989.

Carver, Terrell, and Thomas, Paul (eds), *Rational Choice Marxism*, London, Macmillan, 1995.

Cohen, G. A., *Karl Marx's Theory of History: A Defence*, Oxford, Oxford University Press, 1978.

Derrida, Jacques, *Specters of Marx*, trans. Peggy Kamuf, New York and London, Routledge, 1994.

Draper Hal, (ed.), *The Adventures of the Communist Manifesto*, Berkeley CA, Center for Socialist History, 1994.

Elster, Jon, *Making Sense of Marx*, Cambridge, Cambridge University Press, 1985.

Elster, Jon, *An Introduction to Karl Marx*, Cambridge, Cambridge University Press, 1986.

Engels, Frederick, *The Condition of the Working Class in England*, ed. Victor Kiernan, Harmondsworth, Penguin, 1987.

Forbes, Ian, *Marx and the New Individual*, London, Unwin Hyman, 1990.

Gilbert, Alan, *Marx's Politics: Communists and Citizens*, Oxford, Martin Robertson, 1981.

Hearn, Jeff, *The Gender of Oppression: Men, Masculinity, and the Critique of Marxism*, Brighton, Wheatsheaf Books, 1987.

Hunt, Richard N., *The Political Ideas of Marx and Engels, vol. 1: Marxism and Totalitarian Democracy 1818–1850*, London, Macmillan, 1975.

La Capra, Dominick, *Rethinking Intellectual History: Texts, Contexts, Language*, Ithaca NY and London, Cornell University Press, 1983.

Levine, Norman, *Dialogue within the Dialectic*, London, George Allen & Unwin, 1984.

Lukes, Steven, *Marxism and Morality*, Oxford, Oxford University Press, 1987.

McLellan, David, *The Young Hegelians and Karl Marx*, London, Macmillan, 1969, repr. 1980

McLellan, David, *Karl Marx: His Life and Thought*, London, Macmillan, 1973.

McLellan, David, *The Thought of Karl Marx: An Introduction*, 2nd edn, London, Macmillan, 1980.

Marx, Karl, *Grundrisse: Foundations of the Critique of Political Economy (Rough Draft)*, trans. Martin Nicolaus, Harmondsworth, Penguin/New Left Review, 1974.

Marx, Karl, *Capital* (3 volumes) trans. Ben Fowkes, Harmondsworth, Penguin, 1976, 1978, 1981.

Marx, Karl, *The Communist Manifesto*, ed. Frederick L. Bender, New York, W. W. Norton, 1988.

Marx, Karl, *Later Political Writings*, ed. and trans. Terrell Carver, Cambridge, Cambridge University Press, 1996.

Marx, Karl, and Engels, Frederick, *Selected Correspondence*, 2nd edn, ed. S. Ryanzanskaya, trans. I. Lasker, Moscow, Progress, 1965.

Marx, Karl, and Engels, Frederick, *Feuerbach: Opposition of the Materialist and Idealist Outlooks* (Part 1 of *The German Ideology*), London, Lawrence & Wishart, 1973.

Marx Karl, and Engels, Friedrich, *Die deutsche Ideologie: Kritik der neuesten deutschen Philosophie in ihren Repräsentanten, Feuerbach, B. Bauer und Stirner, und des deutschen Sozialismus in seinen verschiedenen Propheten. 1. Band. 1 Abschnitt*, ed. W. Hiromatsu, Tokyo, Kawadashobo-Shinsha,1974.

Marx, Karl, and Engels, Frederick, *Collected Works*, London, Lawrence & Wishart, 1975 – series incomplete.

Marx, Karl, and Engels, Friedrich, *Das Kommunistische Manifest*, ed. Thomas Kuczynski, Trier, Karl-Marx-Haus, 1995.

Meikle, Scott, *Essentialism in the Thought of Karl Marx*, London, Duckworth, 1984.

Mészáros, István, *Marx's Theory of Alienation*, London, Merlin, 1970.

Miller, Richard W., *Analyzing Marx*, Princeton NJ, Princeton University Press, 1984.

Moseley, Fred (ed.), *Marx's Method in Capital: A Reexamination*, Atlantic Highlands NJ, Humanities Press, 1993.

Ollman, Bertel, *Alienation*, Cambridge, Cambridge University Press, 1971.

Peffer, R. G., *Marxism, Morality and Social Justice*, Princeton, Princeton University Press, 1990.

Roemer, John (ed.), *Analytical Marxism*, Cambridge, Cambridge University Press, 1986.

Rorty, Richard, *Contingency, Irony, and Solidarity*, Cambridge, Cambridge University Press, 1995.

Steger, Manfred, and Carver, Terrell (eds), *Engels after Marx*, University Park PA, Pennsylvania State University Press, forthcoming 1999.

Tucker, D. F. B., *Marxism and Individualism*, Oxford, Basil Blackwell, 1980.

Tully, James (ed.), *Meaning and Context: Quentin Skinner and his Critics*, Cambridge, Polity Press, 1988.

Warren, Mark, 'Marx and methodological individualism', *Philosophy of Social Science*, 18 (1988), 451–4.

White, Hayden, *The Content of the Form: Narrative Discourse and Historical Representation*, Baltimore MD, Johns Hopkins University Press, 1987.

Index

Note: works solely or jointly authored by Marx are included in this index under title.